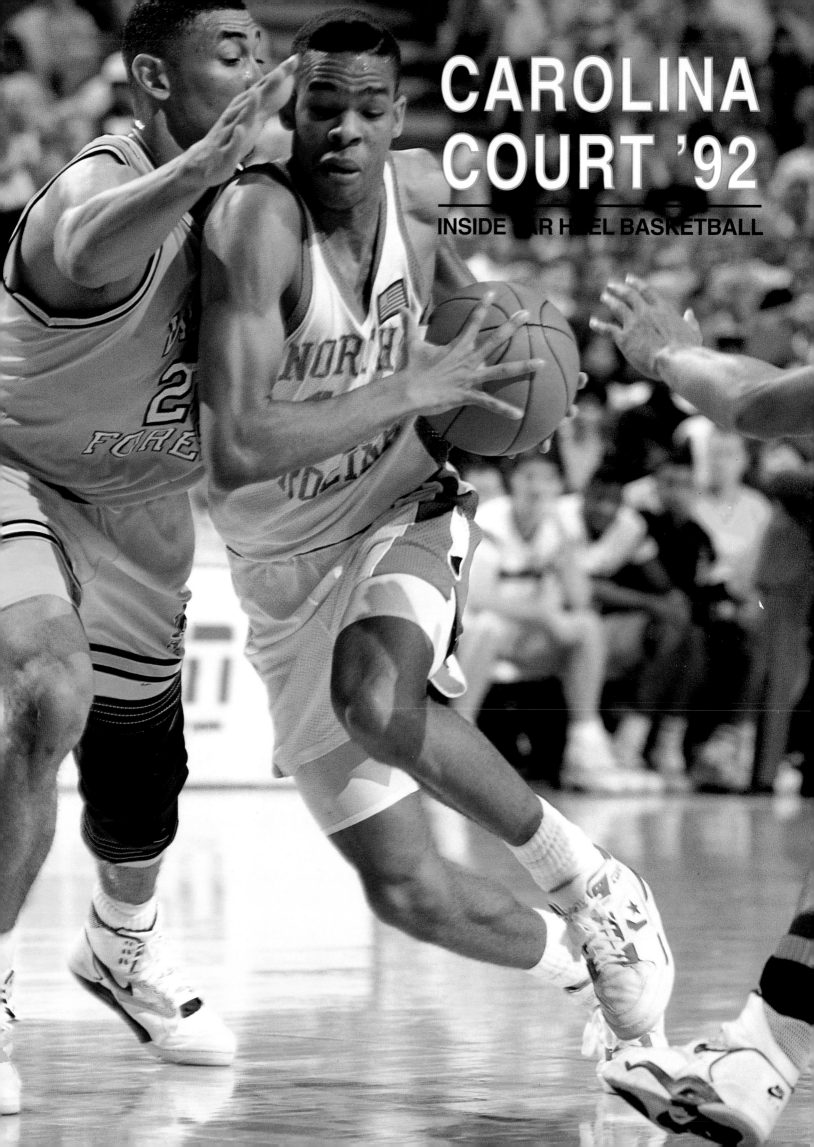

CAROLINA COURT '92

INSIDE TAR HEEL BASKETBALL

CONTENTS

 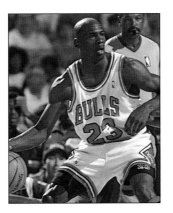

ON THE COVERS
Dean Smith is all smiles during the Tar Heels' 96-74 defeat of Duke in the 1991 Atlantic Coast Conference championship game; on the back cover, senior Hubert Davis and his teammates signal another 3-pointer has just fallen.

PHOTOS BY BOB DONNAN
AND SCOTT HOFFMAN, *GREENSBORO NEWS & RECORD.*

Not Wooden, Nor Rupp, Nor Knight on Dean's List.

Let's try to put what Dean Smith has done into perspective.

Smith has won conference championships and taken teams to the Final Four of the NCAA Basketball Tournament in four different decades. No other basketball coach has ever done that.

John Wooden won 10 NCAA titles, all in the 1960s and '70s. He didn't take a team to the Final Four in the '50s, and he retired midway through the '70s.

Adolph Rupp, who coached for 41 years and won the most college games in history (875), was a regular at the Final Four in the 1940s, '50s and '60s, winning four national titles. Rupp coached only three years into the '70s and never got back to the big dance.

Bob Knight has already won three NCAA Tournaments, one in the '70s and two in the '80s. Would you bet on Knight returning to the Final Four at least once in the '90s? How about again after the year 2000?

Mike Krzyzewski has had success in his first 11 years to match Smith's — five Final Four teams. In order for Coach K, who is 44, to equal his rival's longevity record, he would have to coach into the second decade of the next century, have one Final Four team between the years 2000 and 2009 and one more after that. If he were to do it in the very first year of his fourth decade, Krzyzewski would be 63.

And it's not like Dean Smith "sneaked" into this four-decade thing by beginning his career in, say, 1968 or '69. He started in 1961. Now, he's into the '90s without showing a single sign of slowing down.

This special anniversary edition honors all of those years behind the Dean of Carolina basketball and all of those apparently still ahead of him. We look back on Smith's NCAA Championship 10 years after and find out the five starters haven't wandered very far from our consciousness.

The nation watched Jordan, Perkins and Worthy play for the NBA title last spring; Matt Doherty is coaching at nearby Davidson, and Jimmy Black is at Notre Dame, which is on Carolina's schedule this season.

Even our tribute to the 1957 national champs — 35 years later — is related to Smith, because head coach Frank McGuire was smart enough to recommend his young assistant when he resigned in the summer of '61.

No, Smith wasn't on McGuire's staff when the Tar Heels went 32-0 (he joined two years later). But imagine had he been.

That would have meant coaching in Final Fours in *five* different decades!

CAROLINA COURT 1992: Inside Tar Heel Basketball © 1992 Village Sports Publishing, A Proud Part of The Village Companies. P.O. Box 3300, Chapel Hill, NC 27515. (919) 968-4801.
All rights reserved. Reproduction in whole or in part without consent of publisher is prohibited.
Publisher: Art Chansky. Editor: Dave Glenn. Associate Editors: Leslie Kovach, Jim Wilson. Editorial Assistance: Doug Hoogervorst.
Advertising Manager: Sharon Gupton. Advertising Sales: Karen Cates, Kimberly Hancock, Brooks Johnson. Retail Manager: Beth Collawn.
Special thanks to the UNC Basketball Office and Sports Information Office. Printed by The Hickory Printing Group, Inc.
ISBN 1-880123-01-0

THE 1991-92 TAR HEELS

No.	NAME	HT.	WT.	CL.	HOMETOWN
00	Eric Montross	7-0	258	So.	Indianapolis, Ind.
3	Pat Sullivan	6-7	215	So.	Bogota, N.J.
5	Henrik Rodl	6-7	196	Jr.	Heusenstamm, Germany
11	Scott Cherry	6-4	175	Jr.	Ballston Spa, N.Y.
14	Derrick Phelps	6-3	184	So.	Pleasantville, N.Y.
21	Donald Williams	6-3	183	Fr.	Garner, N.C.
31	Brian Reese	6-5	214	So.	Bronx, N.Y.
33	Kevin Salvadori	7-0	220	So.	Pittsburgh, Pa.
34	George Lynch	6-7	218	Jr.	Roanoke, Va.
40	Hubert Davis	6-4	183	Sr.	Burke, Va.
55	Matt Wenstrom	7-1	250	Jr.	Katy, Texas

Head coach: Dean Smith
Assistants: Bill Guthridge, Phil Ford, Dave Hanners, Randy Wiel.

1991-92 SCHEDULE

Sat.	Nov. 9	Blue/White	Chapel Hill	4:00 p.m.	
Fri.	Nov. 15	High Five America	Chapel Hill	7:00 p.m.	
Sun.	Nov. 17	Soviet Nat. Team	Chapel Hill	2:00 p.m.	
Sun.	Nov. 24	The Citadel	Chapel Hill	2:00 p.m.	
Wed.	Nov. 27	Houston	Houston, Texas	7:30 CST	
Sat.	Nov. 30	Towson State	Chapel Hill	2:00 p.m.	
Sun.	Dec. 1	Cornell	Chapel Hill	2:00 p.m.	
Wed.	Dec. 4	Seton Hall	E. Rutherford, N.J.	9:00 p.m.	ESPN
Sat.	Dec. 7	Central Florida	Chapel Hill	2:00 p.m.	
Sun.	Dec. 15	Florida State	Chapel Hill	2:00 p.m.	
Tues.	Dec. 17	Jacksonville	Jacksonville, Fla.	7:30 p.m.	
Sat.-Sun.	Dec. 21-29	European Trip	Canary Islands & Germany	TBA	
Thu.	Jan. 2	Purdue	Chapel Hill	9:00 p.m.	ESPN
Sat.	Jan. 4	Colorado	Chapel Hill	1:00 p.m.	
Thu.	Jan. 9	Clemson	Chapel Hill	8:00 p.m.	R/JP
Sat.	Jan. 11	Notre Dame	New York, N.Y.	1:30 p.m.	NBC
Mon.	Jan. 13	Maryland	Chapel Hill	7:30 p.m.	
Thu.	Jan. 16	Wake Forest	Winston-Salem	7:30 p.m.	ESPN
Sun.	Jan. 19	Villanova	Chapel Hill	2:45 p.m.	CBS
Wed.	Jan. 22	N.C. State	Raleigh	9:00 p.m.	ESPN & R/JP
Sat.	Jan. 25	Virginia	Chapel Hill	4:00 p.m.	NBC
Sun.	Feb. 2	Georgia Tech	Atlanta, Ga.	1:30 p.m.	ABC
Thu.	Feb. 6	Duke	Chapel Hill	9:00 p.m.	ESPN & R/JP
Sat.	Feb. 8	Wake Forest	Chapel Hill	Noon	R/JP
Sat.	Feb. 15	Clemson	Clemson, S.C.	12:30 p.m.	R/JP
Wed.	Feb. 19	Virginia	Charlottesville, Va.	9:00 p.m.	ESPN
Sat.	Feb. 22	N.C. State	Chapel Hill	3:00 p.m.	R/JP
Thu.	Feb. 27	Florida State	Tallahassee, Fla.	7:30 p.m.	ESPN
Sun.	Mar. 1	Maryland	College Park, Md.	1:00 p.m.	ESPN & R/JP
Wed.	Mar. 4	Georgia Tech	Chapel Hill	9:00 p.m.	ESPN & R/JP
Sun.	Mar. 8	Duke	Durham	1:30 p.m.	ABC

ACC Tournament — Charlotte, N.C. — ESPN & R/JP

Thu.	Mar. 12	First Round	7:00
Fri.	Mar. 13	Quarterfinals	12:00, 2:00, 7:00 & 9:00 p.m.
Sat.	Mar. 14	Semifinals	1:30 & 3:30 p.m.
Sun.	Mar. 15	Final	TBA

1990-91 RESULTS

W	San Diego State	99-63
W	Jacksonville	104-61
L	*South Carolina	74-76
W	*Iowa State	118-93
W	#Connecticut	79-64
W	Kentucky	84-81
W	Alabama	95-79
W	at Purdue	86-74
W	**DePaul	90-75
W	**Stanford	71-60
W	at Cornell	108-64
W	Notre Dame	82-47
W	Maryland	105-73
W	at Virginia (2 OT)	89-86
L	at Duke	60-74
W	at Wake Forest	91-81
L	Georgia Tech	86-88
W	at Clemson	90-77
L	at N.C. State	91-97
W	N.C. State	92-70
W	Virginia	77-58
W	Wake Forest	85-70
W	at Maryland	87-75
W	The Citadel	118-50
W	Clemson	73-57
W	at Georgia Tech	91-74
L	Duke	77-83
W	##Clemson	67-59
W	##Virginia	76-71
W	##Duke	96-74
W	'Northeastern	101-66
W	•Villanova	84-69
W	•Eastern Michigan	93-67
W	•Temple	75-72
L	•Kansas	73-79

*Tournament of Champions
#ACC/Big East Challenge
**Citrus-Red Lobster Classic
##ACC Tournament
•NCAA Tournament

CAROLINA GENTLEMEN

The 1991-92 Tar Heels gather at the statue of Silent Sam on campus. From left to right:

DONALD WILLIAMS

DERRICK PHELPS

KEVIN SALVADORI

HUBERT DAVIS

MATT WENSTROM

SCOTT CHERRY

SILENT SAM

ERIC MONTROSS

BRIAN REESE

GEORGE LYNCH

HENRIK RÖDL

PAT SULLIVAN

TEAM PORTRAIT BY
HUGH MORTON.

Sometimes I can't help laughing. These big guys all think they own the paint. Then here I come driving the lane. Six foot, one. And they yell, get that little Kevin Johnson out of here. Only they don't call me Kevin Johnson. They call me, well, I can't tell you what they call me. See, they like to think basketball is still a big man's game. But it's not. Not anymore. Now it's a speed game. A guard's game. I don't mean to say it's enough just to be fast. Speed may be a god-given thing. But it's no guarantee that you're going to make it. There are a million fast guys out there. A million guys with lots of natural ability who don't make it. Because to play at this level it takes heart. It also takes dedication and hard work. I learned that from

my granfather. He was a sheet metal worker. And he understood that hard work you better at what you did. A better person, too. That wasn't a lesson he preached. It was a lesson he lived. If you wanted to be the next Dr. J when you were a kid, that meant practicing every split. Back then, the all your friends wanted their basketball shoes to have were Converse Chuck Taylors. If you had Chuck Taylors at least it looked like you knew what you were doing. But this new Accelerator™! Have you worn them? I played a game last week and I said to someone, it's really wild. I didn't realize how fast I was.

The Shoe Of The Tar Heels   For The Last 30 Years.

It was a Carolina Blue weekend in Charlotte, as the Tar Heels celebrate and pose for a team picture; seniors Chilcutt, King Rice and Rick Fox hoist trophy; Hubert Davis and teammates salute fans and Fox shows off Everett Case Award as Outstanding Player.

PHOTOS BY BOB DONNAN

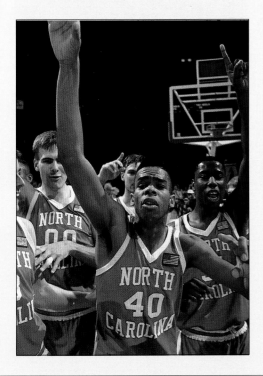

Why Settle For 80% Of Your Home Value When We Can Let You Access 100%?

Other banks' home equity lines might shortchange you. But at Southern National, we'll give you the credit you deserve. To find out more, stop in and ask us about our Tax Advantage Loans. (For a limited time, you can save up to $100 in closing costs.)

SOUTHERN NATIONAL
Tax Advantage Loans

the final buzzer sounds on victory No. 694 of Dean Smith's 30-year head coaching career. The magical No. 700 is less than a month away as tomorrow's news flashes on the Smith Center scoreboard — UNC 95, Alabama 79 — but the coach's work is just beginning. First, he extends the traditional smiles and handshakes to yet another set of defeated opponents. After a brief meeting with his players and assistants, and another with the media, Smith retires to an office upstairs in the building that bears his name.

Alone with his thoughts in the middle of December, Smith is surrounded by the shade of blue he has helped make famous. Another day's deeds are almost done. But first, away from the microphones and the headlines below, he pauses to reflect on the seven-game-old 1990-91 season. For the first time, he sees the potential for something big. Very big.

"That Alabama game is the one where we first said, 'Hey, we have a chance to be a very good basketball team,'" Smith says. "From that point on, I think we continued to improve."

Of course, it's tough to improve on a 6-1 record, which is where the Tar Heels' tally stood after that fateful matchup with the Crimson Tide. But Smith, even in December, saw all the elements of success that eventually would take his Tar Heels to yet another Final Four.

DEAN SMITH:

"That Alabama game was the one where we first said, 'Hey, we have a chance to be a very good basketball team.' From then on, I think we continued to improve."

The seniors, Smith's traditional bedrocks, were playing well. Rick Fox, who would go on to become the Tar Heels' leading scorer, was becoming a leader with the kind of two-way play that turned him into an NBA first-round draft pick at season's end. Pete Chilcutt, another eventual first-rounder, blossomed as a dependable force on the boards and in the scoring column. And King Rice, Smith's iron-man point guard from October through March, led the team with undying effort and effective play from baseline to baseline. With the keystones in place, the only question became what to do with the rest of the talent assembled on the Tar Heels' bustling 15-man roster.

"After Alabama, we finally got into a playing rotation," Smith says. "I think everybody knew his role down the line."

Indeed, as the Tar Heels stretched their impressive start to a 13-1 mark in mid-January, the roles in the winning script were well-defined.

In support of the senior trio, sophomores George Lynch and Henrik Rödl and junior Hubert Davis stepped up and helped turn a good North Carolina team into a great one. Lynch, who would lead the squad in rebounds, ran the floor and hit the boards with authority. Rödl, a defensive ace and passing whiz, seemed to come through with an important assist, a clutch bucket or a key steal night after

night. Davis, a blossoming star, improved his deadly three-point marksmanship while showcasing an array of impressive moves and emotional play at both ends of the floor. And then, of course, there were the rookies.

"We finally got over all the hubbub about the freshmen," Smith says. "That was very important."

Yes, it took a few months for the publicity surrounding the Fabulous Five (Eric Montross, Derrick Phelps, Brian Reese, Clifford Rozier and Pat Sullivan) to take a back seat to the successes of Fox, Chilcutt, Rice and Co. But the true transition started way back in October, while ever-fickle recruiting analysts were still crowning the Tar Heels' new crew "the best recruiting class in the history of college basketball." Familiar with hype, the upperclassmen yawned and went about the business at hand. They were among the few who knew the big secret of the time: The freshmen were learning their humility lessons long before the rest of the college basketball world got a chance to see them in blue and white.

It only took a few early five-on-five practice sessions in October — "They absolutely killed us," Sullivan says — for the newcomers to realize they had a lot to learn. Still, they eventually had a lot to offer. Montross, a center of attention in more ways than one, established himself early as a force in the paint. Phelps and Reese watched and learned from mentors Rice and Fox — "Rick really showed me the game," Reese says — and earned valuable playing time in relief while Rozier and Sullivan filled in effectively wherever and whenever needed. As the season wore on, it was often the heralded freshmen who found themselves in the unfamiliar role of the unsung hero.

"So many times, what is overlooked is the role players and the factor they play in a team's success," Smith says. "I don't think they get near the credit they deserve.

"I could go on and on with examples, but they all come down to one thing: In college rules, you can always stop somebody. I don't care who they are. Sometimes a game comes down to this guy over here who's not used to shooting. Now the question is, 'Will he knock down the open 15-footers when he has to?' or 'Will he do what he's supposed to do defensively?' That can often be the difference between winning and losing."

In many regards, the 1990-91 UNC season was like any other in the past 30 years. It was colorful, with the (DePaul) Blue Demons, The (Stanford) Cardinal, the (Cornell) Big Red and the Crimson Tide joining the schedule along with the rival (Duke) Blue Devils and (Georgia Tech) Yellow Jackets. The Tar Heels were personable, taking on the Aztecs (San Diego State), the Hurons (Eastern Michigan), the Boilermakers (Purdue), the Cavaliers (Virginia) and the Fighting Irish (Notre Dame). They were even kind to animals, playing with the Dolphins (Jacksonville), the Gamecocks (South Carolina), the Huskies (Connecticut, Northeastern), the Wildcats (Kentucky, Villanova), the Bulldogs (The Citadel), the Owls (Temple) and the Jayhawks (Kansas) — along with the familiar Tigers (Clemson) and Terrapins (Maryland). Sure enough, it was a jungle out there.

❊•❖•❊•••

There were the inevitable highlights and lowlights of a schedule in which 21 of the 35 games were against NCAA Tournament teams. The 13-1 streak to open the season quickly became yesterday's news when the Tar Heels encountered a difficult 2-3 stretch in late January and early February as the hotly contested ACC race came to a boil.

"Sometimes it's good to have a stretch like that," says Fox. "You never want to lose, but looking back, that may be what it takes to wake you up."

The alarmed Tar Heels proceeded to win 14 of their next 15 games, including a convincing sweep of Clemson, Virginia and Duke to claim their first ACC title of the '90s. The sly Fox, tricky in victory, sneaked away with Most Valuable Player honors.

That one wild weekend in Charlotte, coupled with the amazing successes that followed in the heart-stopping race for the Final Four, gave the 1990-91 Tar Heels a kind of title that can never be taken away: They're winners. And they're inheritors of a throne of success — from the '70s through the '80s and now the '90s — that began at a time when they were more familiar with a kind of dribbling that had nothing at all to do with basketball.

So who is the best?

It's certainly far too early to designate a Team of the '90s, but how about over the long haul? And how do you decide? What are the criteria? Certainly, the debate brings about more questions than answers.

"When you're talking about what constitutes the best, it's hard," Smith says. "That is an interesting question.

"Are you going to take the national champions? Do you have to win the national championship to say you have a great program? I don't know. N.C. State won it in '83, and they weren't the best team. Villanova won in '85. There are always so many teams that lost their last game that had great years.

"How about the Final 16? That's where we could say we're the best, because I imagine we probably have that record. Maybe Kentucky, but not consecutively. Now is that the hardest thing? You also have to be lucky to do that. It's whom you draw, how healthy you are.

"This year, we were lucky not to play Oklahoma State or Mississippi State, although I thought Temple was awfully good. You don't know what's coming next, and that's one of the things that makes the tournament so interesting."

Similarly, one of the things that makes the "Who's best?" argument so interesting is that it's practically impossible to examine all of the conceivable indicators of winning and

The Tar Heels' season ended with a loss to an old friend, Roy Williams.

formulate them into a cohesive standard of success.

Nevertheless, despite the constant flurry of unanswered questions, the argument for two teams can be made pretty easily — whatever the measure of success. North Carolina, of the ACC, and Indiana, of the Big Ten Conference, have been the most consistently and extraordinarily successful college basketball programs in the nation through the '70s, '80s and into the '90s.

UNC's model of consistency is best displayed by a laundry list of streaks that most schools could only dream about. The first four are NCAA records:

• 11 consecutive trips to the Final 16.
• 17 straight appearances in the NCAA Tournament.
• 18 seasons of 25 wins or more, tops in history.
• 21 consecutive seasons of 20 wins or more.
• 10 Final Four appearances, second only to UCLA's 14.
• 25 trips to the NCAA Tournament, trailing only Kentucky (33) and UCLA (27).
• 27 straight seasons among the top three teams in the

Jack Nicklaus. Cliff Drysdale. Pete Dye. And Landfall.
What a foursome!

Terrific golf in the form of two championship courses, one by Jack Nicklaus, the other by Pete Dye. Smashing tennis at Cliff Drysdale's magnificent Sports Center. And spectacular living at Landfall, an exclusive 2,200-acre recreational-residential community of custom homes, patio homes and villas along the Intracoastal Waterway near Wilmington, North Carolina, just minutes from Wrightsville Beach and Interstate 40. Residences priced from $225,000 to more than $1 million. Homesites from $75,000 to $650,000.

Nicklaus. Drysdale. Dye. And Landfall.

What a foursome!

Landfall

1801 Eastwood Road
Wilmington, N.C. 28405
Telephone (919) 256-6111
Toll-Free (800) 227-8208
In N.C. (800) 634-7857

The Tar Heels began the new decade by knocking off No. 1-ranked and top-seeded Oklahoma in the 1990 NCAA Tournament.

ACC. The Tar Heels have finished first or second in 24 of those 27 seasons.

Others have had their day in the limelight, but only the Tar Heels, under Smith, and the Hoosiers, in the 20-year rein of coach Bob Knight, have managed to compile the victories, conference championships and NCAA triumphs on what can now be called a regular basis. Even the most widely recognized success meter, the Associated Press poll, will attest to that.

"If you've been one of the best teams in the country, the polls—most of the time—will reflect that," says Smith. "If your program has been consistently in the top five, top 10, your school should feel pretty good. That means you've been consistently good that particular year."

Louisville, under Denny Crum, may be the closest to the Big Two. The Cardinals have won two NCAA titles since 1970, but they have only appeared in the AP Top 10 a total of six times in those 22 years. UNC has finished among the top 10 15 times during the same period, Indiana 10.

Consistency is also the difference with Georgetown, Duke, Kansas and Kentucky, other programs with valid claims to fame. The Hoyas, certainly one of the most dominant teams of the '80s, were nonentities during the '70s. Same with the Blue Devils, who went eight consecutive years ('70-77) without finishing in the Top 20 once. The Jayhawks, on the rise again in the '90s under former North Carolina assistant Roy Williams, had a similar spell in the early '80s. Even the Wildcats, the second-most winning program in college basketball history behind UNC, have hit tough times recently, missing the Top 20 in five of the last seven seasons.

But North Carolina and Indiana have withstood the tests of time.

The Tar Heels' record since 1970 is impeccable: 19 years in the Top 20, 15 in the top 10, seven in the top five, nine ACC championships, five Final Fours, and a national championship. The Hoosiers' slate is similarly impressive. And there is no end in sight.

"For the last three years, we've been playing our best late," Smith says. "That's what we want to do every year."

There's the president of the major contracting firm who believes that every job site should be cleaned up at the end of the day. Even if he has to do it himself.

There's the account supervisor who lives and breathes the very sport his largest client dominates, and has the inside track on players' attitudes and opinions even before his client does.

There's the printer who invests large amounts of his own time trying to find ways to reduce the cost of job quotes we've already approved.

There's the media director who typically spends much of her vacation talking to tourists about the magazines and TV shows they like.

And there's the owner of the dry cleaning chain who finds a way to collect and distribute over 25,000 coats each year to kids who might otherwise face a very cold winter.

We are very fortunate. Because these are our clients, our suppliers, our employees. They represent the many people we deal with who believe that a business *relationship* is more than just business, and that an attitude of trust, support, and involvement is the highest value that can be added to any product or service.

If this is an attitude you share, we invite you to call Mark Burris at 919-884-4249 to see how effectively it can be applied to the business of advertising.

THE BURRIS AGENCY

GREAT RELATIONSHIPS MAKE GREAT ADVERTISING.

The Burris Agency Inc. 1208 Eastchester Drive Suite 130   High Point NC 27265

Huuuu...

bert!

Carolina Blue Background Gave Davis His Chance.

By Dave Glenn

Sixteen-year-old Hubert Davis, Jr. wears a blank stare as he gazes out the front window of his family's white-faced suburban home, tucked away in a serene residential neighborhood in northern Virginia.

It is September, 1986. On most afternoons during the past several years, Davis has been launching basketballs at the aging basket on the blacktop driveway out front, nailing jumper after jumper from near and afar under the watchful eye of his best friend and father, Hubert, Sr.

But on this day, Davis is inside, alone with his thoughts. He's waiting for his mother to come home from work, just as he's done for what seems like every day for the past 16 years. A tear comes to his eye. He feels as if he's waited this wait and thought these thoughts 100 times in the past month.

Bobbie Davis, who had become half of Hubert's soul during his young life, never came home that day. She died of cancer in August of '86, in a tragedy her only son refused to accept for a long, long time. For a teenager, this was one big reason to be mad at life. For the next several years, Hubert, Jr., felt confused and cheated—hateful toward the expanding world around him. But mainly, and most painfully, he felt as if he had lost one of his two best friends.

If only she could see him now . . .

◆ ◆ ◆

At 21 years old, Hubert Davis, Jr. is everything his mother and father had hoped he would be. In the past five years, he has turned a Carolina Blue upbringing into an amazing college basketball career that looks like something right out of Storybook Land. More importantly, he has weathered the celebrity spotlights and remained the kind of soft-spoken, self-effacing young man his mother and father taught him to be.

It didn't take long for Hubert to find out how things worked in the Davis household. When it came to Hubert, Jr., dad was the "ruthless dictator" and mom was the softy. "If I wanted something, I'd go to my mom," Hubert says. "She'd give me everything." When it came to sister Keisha (KEE-sha), six years his junior, the roles were reversed. In the long run, he says, it couldn't have worked out better.

"My family was perfect," Davis says, rising above his usual reserved tone with a smile. "I'm not kidding. I feel so lucky to have had what I've had. We were like the Brady Bunch.

"The respect I have for my mom and dad is just unbelievable. I love the two of them so much it's incredible. Anybody would. I could talk about them forever. They're the two kindest people I know . . . To me, they're perfect."

Everything he's done, he says, he owes to his parents. In conversation, he refers to them often, in a fun, candid way that can easily slip notice. But almost every answer to every question has a reference to mom — often still in present tense — or dad. When he speaks of them, it is with complete respect, almost reverence. It is, to him, the story of his life.

Born May 17, 1970 in Winston-Salem, Davis entered the world with basketball in his blood, which, looking back, was probably blue. His father, a 6-4 forward who passed on his height and toughness to his namesake, was three years removed from an excellent hoops career at Johnson C. Smith College in Charlotte. It was there that Hubert, Sr. impressed a man named Dean Smith with the kind of emotional and competitive play that would become his son's trademark, under Smith, at North Carolina 20 years later.

Then there was Hubert, Sr.'s younger brother, a 17-year-old kid from Pineville, N.C., who was doing things with a basketball that most youngsters just don't do. Walter Davis caught Smith's eye, too, early enough for Smith to offer him a scholarship to UNC. Little did Hubert, Jr. know at the time, but Uncle Walter's stellar career with the Tar Heels, and his father's growing relationship with Smith, would slowly bring about an amazing turn of events that added a Carolina Blue flavor to just about everything baby Hubert came into contact with over the first 21 years of his life.

A look back proves one thing certain: If ever the Carolina fight song applies, if ever there has been a person truly "Tar Heel born and Tar Heel bred," that person is Hubert Davis, Jr.

Hubert doesn't even remember it all. It was 1973 when he first came into direct contact with the Carolina basket-

Davis led ACC in three-point accuracy last season with 48.9 shooting percentage from 21 feet.

BOB DONNAN

CONOVER

Conover proudly presents the finest collection of upholstered furniture available. You will find a wide variety of rich sophisticated styles to appeal to any mood or occasion. Our extensive fabric line offers a complete selection of colors, textures, patterns and fine leathers. Master cutters, sewers and upholsterers hand tailor each piece to ensure that every item of furniture meets our exceptional quality standards.

You can select Conover with confidence, because superior quality is reflected in everything we do.

Tarheel Traditions: Carolina, Dean Smith and Conover Chair.
Three Proven Winners.
CONGRATULATIONS DEAN FOR 30 GREAT YEARS!

Fred Sherrill '56
President

For a dealer nearest you contact:
Conover Chair Company • Post Office Box 759 • Conover, North Carolina 28613 • 704-464-0251

ball program. Uncle Walter, attending prep school in Delaware just a few hours away from the Davis' old home in Washington, D.C., often came to visit on weekends. It was there, with Hubert, Jr. bouncing around in the background, that Tar Heel assistant Bill Guthridge made his official visit to Walter. After arriving back in Chapel Hill, Guthridge sent a letter to Hubert, Sr. and Bobbie, thanking them for their hospitality. Then, he added this playful-but-prophetic declaration:

"At this time, we want to officially begin the recruitment of Hubert, Jr." The Kid was only three years old.

The plot innocently thickened three years later when Uncle Walter invited the rest of the Davis clan to Montreal for the 1976 Summer Olympics. Walter was there representing the North Carolina, er, United States team, which included Smith, the head coach; Guthridge, his eternal assistant; and Tar Heel playing stars Phil Ford, Mitch Kupchak and Tommy LaGarde. The Davises made the long journey to Canada in their old Mercury Marquis — "a real boat," says Hubert — leaving newborn Keisha with Bobbie's parents in Winston-Salem.

While the stay in Montreal remains mostly a blur to Hubert, the little kid in him remembers one thing for sure: The red, white and blue team won it all. "It was an incredible thrill," Hubert says, thinking back to his days as a ripened 6-year-old. "That really was the first time I started thinking about going to North Carolina to play basketball."

While the trip to the Great White North marked the sketchy beginnings of Hubert's early fascination with Carolina basketball, it turns out there wasn't much juice to the now-famous tale about young Hubert's 13-hour ride back from the Olympics. In fact, Olympic gold medalists or not, it was all pretty simple: mom and dad up front, Walter and Phil in the back, and Hubert in the middle. "We slept the whole way," Hubert says. Well, almost.

"For a little while, Hubert was jumping around in between Walter and Phil in the back seat," says Hubert, Sr., a sharp-minded wit who understandably has a better recollection of these early days. "The expression on his face was amazing. We stopped in Rocky Mount (Ford's hometown) and Chapel Hill before we came back home. Walter and Phil were great. For three days, everywhere they went, Hubert was right there with them."

Back at the Davis' home in Alexandria, Hubert started mounting blue things on the walls of his bedroom. Carolina fever was spreading rapidly. First, it was just a few pennants. Then a picture of Walter, a picture of Phil. Finally, he says, he even got a photo of Smith "just sitting there coaching." Later, he painted his bedroom (what else?) Carolina Blue. He even got his own picture taken, with Walter's Olympic gold dangling heavily from his skinny neck and wearing an ear-to-ear smile. Nowhere in his innocent eyes could he have seen 15 years down his fairy-tale road, when he would earn a gold medal of his own as the leading scorer for the U.S. team in the World University Games. Not in his wildest dreams. Never in a million years. Not yet, anyway.

Hubert was soaking up the atmosphere, all right. He

was surrounded by basketball. Hanging in his crib, probably. At 3 and 4, he tagged along with dad to youth league centers, where Hubert, Sr. coached 10- to 12-year-olds. At 7, there were a few trips to see Walter in UNC's Carmichael Auditorium, where he got to hang around in the locker room with the Tar Heel players after the game.

"It was around then that he started saying, 'Dad, that's where I wanna go. Dad, that's where I wanna go,'" says Hubert, Sr., who fed the growing desire by allowing Junior to attend the Carolina basketball camp. And soon after, there were a few years' worth of trips to the Capital Centre in Washington to see Kupchak, a good friend of the family, in his professional playing days with the Bullets.

"One time, I went to see the All-Star game there," Hubert says. "I was in the locker room with Kareem Abdul-Jabbar, Dr. J, Larry Bird, Earvin Johnson. It was just incredible."

Starry eyes aside, it didn't take long for Hubert, Jr. to

HUBERT DAVIS

Yr.	G	FG-FGA-Pct.	FT-FTA-Pct.	Reb-Ave	A	TO	S	PF-D	Pts	Ave
Fr.	35	44-86-51.2	24-31-77.4	27-0.8	9	12	3	10-0	116	3.3
So.	34	111-249-44.6	59-74-79.4	60-1.8	52	31	33	42-0	325	9.6
Jr.	35	161-309-52.1	81-97-83.5	85-2.4	66	37	30	35-0	467	13.3

learn that basketball ability is not a birthright, no matter what the family name. Watching is learning, he discovered, but the only way to become a great basketball player was to play an awful lot of basketball. So he did.

With one goal in mind, the same blue and white dream thousands of little boys have every year, Hubert, Jr. learned the game of basketball on the blacktop and hardcourt of northern Virginia. From the slanted driveway out front to the spacious arena at nearby Lake Braddock High School, he wondered of UNC, "Are they watching? Will I get my chance?" Up until the very end, he wasn't sure. All the while, Hubert, Sr. watched and helped his son grow, on and off the court. A few words of encouragement here, a little piece of advice there. In the process, his boy became a man. Somewhere in between, a

✼•❖•✼•••

basic philosophy of basketball was handed down from generation to generation. And these rules don't bend.

Rule No. 1: *Play hard and study harder.*

Hubert was extremely active as a youngster. At his mom's urging, he developed a fascination for the cello and played from third grade through 10th. He also played tennis, baseball and football. But he never strayed from his educational goals, not even for the hardcourt. "I didn't let Hubert go to a lot of the basketball camps," says Hubert, Sr. "I used to tell him you can have the basketball skills, but if you haven't applied yourself academically, the skills won't help you at all."

Rule No. 2: *Never give up and always do your best.*

Hubert, Jr. was eventually allowed to go to the prestigious Five-Star camp after his junior year. After one day against prep superstars Billy Owens, Alonzo Mourning and Malik Sealy — "one of the first times I played against anyone over about 6-4," Hubert says today — the shy guy from Burke, Va. desperately wanted to come home. In cases like this, Hubert, Sr. says he relies on one rule of thumb when it comes to his distant son's well-being: When the phone doesn't ring, everything is OK. On this occasion, of course, the Davis' phone was ringing off the hook for two days in a row: "Dad, these guys are all better than I am. I'm playing terrible. I shouldn't even be here." Senior's response: "Don't worry about it. Who cares? Everybody has bad days. Just go out there and do your best." For the next five days, the phones were silent in the Davis household. And when dad drove to Five-Star to pick up his son on Sunday, he found before him a newly crowned member of the camp All-Star team.

Rule No. 3: *Basketball is a physical game, get used to it.*

Hubert, Sr. played inside in college, and he didn't mind a little contact under the boards. After all, God gives elbows, knees, hips and shoulders for a reason, right? "When I was growing up, he was much stronger than I was," says Hubert, Jr., who found himself plastered across the Davis' driveway on more than a few occasions. "He'd bump me, foul me, knock me down. I mean he was just like Bill Laimbeer. He used to kill me. I remember I used to get so mad at him sometimes I wouldn't talk to him for a couple of days." Too bad, kid, because . . .

Rule No. 4: *Between the lines, basketball is all business.*

Father and son alike have no friends on the basketball court, including each other. "There is no friendship out there," says dad, who looks as if he could throw a pretty mean scowl. "You throw all that away when you're out there competing." Hubert, Jr., a quiet, affable sort in conversation, also takes on a new persona when the topic is competition. "When I'm on the court, I don't know why, but something changes in me," he says. "I'll get so competitive that I'll talk to you while I'm playing you. I'll be mean to you. I don't like you. I'm not scared of anything. There's something about playing basketball that makes me feel like I can do anything."

Rule No. 5: *Don't worry, be happy.*

This has been a big change for Hubert, Jr., a guy who says he's still shy and uncomfortable around people he doesn't know very well. "It's been a real key for me," he says. "My first two years were so stressful, I didn't have fun. My dad's right. Have fun out there. Smile if you want to smile. Yell if you want to yell. If you're 10 for 10, you're having fun. But if you're 0 for 10, you should still be having fun, too. If you feel like jumping up and down, do it. If you feel like waving a fist in someone's face, do that. If it gets you going, go for it."

Armed with the rules of sport, Davis excelled on the hardcourt and the gridiron at Lake Braddock. The latter fact has since become a famous "Did You Know?" among Carolina sports fans, the one about Davis catching passes from current Tar Heel quarterback Todd Burnett. But there's more.

In football, the Burnett-Davis combo led its squad to the first seven-win season in the 15-year history of a school that's packed with about 5,000 students in any given year. Davis not-so-quietly caught a school-record 58 passes for 666 yards and nine touchdowns while earning all-state honors. And it gets better.

On the hardcourt, Davis was well on his way to finishing his career as the school's all-time leader in scoring (1,604 points in 70 games), field goal shooting (62 percent) and foul shooting (87 percent). During his senior year, the team went 24-2. Davis had 15 games of 30 or more points, more than all of the players (combined) in the history of the school.

Yet, at this point in his blossoming two-sport career, Davis was still more famous for the six-pointer from the 50-yard line than the three-pointer from the 21-foot line. Strange but true: Davis, unwilling and unprepared to change his game for the experimental three-point rule, attempted only four treys during his entire senior season. Stranger but true: He only made one.

Maybe that shocking revelation helps explain the bizarre turn of events that followed. Dreams don't always come true, and Hubert Davis' heartfelt desires to play basketball at UNC weren't necessarily enough for this story to have a happy ending. Even with all of his high school accolades, his family connections, seven summers of Carolina basketball camp, and his most sincere hopes, Davis wasn't a sure bet to become a Tar Heel.

For one, Dean Smith wasn't sure he was good enough. And that's a very big one.

So it was on a Friday afternoon in September of 1987, as Hubert, Sr. and Smith sat down in the Davis' living room and talked about the future while the lad in question scurried about, preparing for another football game as the next four years of his life hung in the balance.

Smith, as is his wont, talked straight with his old friend. He called Hubert, Jr. "a fine gentleman" and related a story about John Crotty, a Tar Heel reserve from 30 years before whose son John had recently signed with the Virginia Cavaliers. He compared the situations, saying he thought Hubert could be a good player at a mid-Division I program, just as he thought the elder Crotty could have been in similar circumstances. He said he could make no promises, that he would feel bad if Hubert went to Carolina and

'Brady Bunch'
Hubert, Jr. and Keisha
with Mom in 1978 and
Dad last summer.

had to sit on the bench for four years. In the end, he could say no more.

"I told coach not to worry about that," says Hubert, Sr. "I told him, Hubert has a goal. A dream of going to North Carolina. It appears that he has done what he needs to do to be put into consideration. You're here and you're considering him.

"All I ask and all Hubert asks is that he be given a chance. If he's given a chance, then whatever falls out of that chance falls out. You don't have to make any promises to me."

Hubert Sr. never told his son about that conversation. It was Hubert's sophomore year at UNC, two years later, when he finally learned of the meeting of the minds.

"It was funny because I kept seeing all those articles about Coach Smith telling my dad I shouldn't play at North Carolina," Hubert says, still a bit amused by the whole scam. "My dad never, ever told me that. Now I know, but my dad never told me. I would always ask him, Dad, do you really think Coach Smith wants me? And he would say yes. Every time.

HUBERT DAVIS:

"I would always ask him, Dad, do you really think Coach Smith wants me? And he would say yes. Every time."

"He would say, yes, Hubert, I really think you can play at Carolina," Hubert says, laughing while trying to mimic what must have been his dad's deep, serious tone. "Yes, Hubert, he really wants you. Yes, Hubert, he really wants you. Who was he trying to kid?"

Hubert Davis did a lot of growing up during his first three years at UNC. On the court, he quickly impressed the coaching staff with quickness, athleticism and shooting ability unattributed him in previous evaluations. And, as his playing time increased steadily over the next three years, so did his scoring totals, from 3.3 to 9.6 to 13.3 points per game. "It shows what I know," Smith likes to say, assessing one of his few poor judgments with infallible hindsight as his guide.

In Chapel Hill, the Hubert Davis story became one of a self-made basketball player, a Horatio Alger in sneakers. There was plenty of hard work, the same rigorous routines every Carolina player goes through. And then there was that little bit extra. The Smith Center workouts before classes, between classes, after classes. The 500 three-pointers a day during the offseason. The thousands and thousands of free throws.

Davis has certainly shown a liking to this crazy three-point thing, adapting quickly as a freshman and gradually developing into one of the top three-point shooters in the nation. In the process, he's also joined an exclusive group of athletes (Hubie Brooks, Michael Cooper, Warren Moon and Lou Piniella, to name a few) who sound as if they're getting booed by the home crowd every time they do something well. "Huuuuuuubert," yell the Smith Center faithful, every time Davis uncoils to throw in yet another

lightning bolt from afar.

Last year, he led the ACC and ranked with the nation's best by hitting a school-record 48.9 percent from beyond the arc. Ironically, Davis' accuracy mark broke the record previously held by former Tar Heel Jeff Lebo, the guy Davis credits most with his own three-point success. "He taught me how to spot up and shoot quickly without having to look down at my feet," Hubert says. "He spent a lot of time practicing with me, helping me get a feel for where I was on the floor."

As a junior, Davis finished second among the Tar Heels in scoring (to good buddy Rick Fox) and really warmed up down the stretch. In the last 15 games of the season, including the pressure-packed run to the Final Four, Davis led the Tar Heels in scoring eight times, shooting 58 percent from the field and averaging a hefty 16 points per game.

More importantly, Hubert says, he's found a new attitude — one that will be able to help him long after he gives the arms-up, three-point signal for the last time. Last year, he became a Christian. He says it's helped him put basketball, and life, in a new perspective.

"My freshman and sophomore years, I was hurting real bad," he says. "I wasn't getting much playing time. I was away from home. I was homesick, and I was wondering where my mom was. I would take basketball too seriously. If I had a bad game, it would affect my school, affect my attitude.

"Now, I've become more relaxed and I've learned to be able to have fun again. Basketball means a lot to me, but it's not everything. It's just a game. If I have a bad game, I feel bad but then I'm done with it and I can go on with other things.

"That's the way life is sometimes. Like with my mom. I still don't completely understand it, but I just thank God for giving me the best mom in the world for 16 years, because I think anyone in the world would love to have had a mom like mine."

Hubert Davis thinks back to his sophomore year in high school, about 15 months before this 15-year-old would see his mother for the last time. He was playing for Lake Braddock in the basketball district championship game. As always, his mom was in the stands.

"We won the game, and I got MVP or something, so I was the last one cutting down the net," Hubert says. "I remember looking for her in the crowd. Finally, we kind of locked eyes on each other.

"I will never forget the picture of her face. She was so proud of me. She didn't even have to say anything, I could just tell. I almost started crying right there with the net in my hands.

"Now, every time I think of her, I picture her with that same look on her face, like she's saying, Hubert, you're doing OK. And I hope she's still looking down at me saying that same thing today."

GEORGE LYNCH

Another Year In The Paint Leaves Him Hungry For More.

George Lynch is a better basketball player than he was a year ago. In the fall of 1991, No. 34 is seeing the floor better, he's more confident in his perimeter game, and — now a junior — he's ready and willing to carry a bigger share of the load.

"Everybody knows what it takes to be a winner," says Lynch, pausing between workouts on the hardcourt and in the weight room on a warm September afternoon. "This year, we have a young team. It's going to be a part of my job, on and off the court, to make sure we all keep in mind what it takes to be a winner.

"Hubert Davis is our senior leader, but we all have to do our part. I worked hard this summer, and I'm prepared to work even harder in practice to show my leadership in that way."

Keep in mind that Lynch wasn't exactly a slouch last year. This is the same player who, as a sophomore, led the Tar Heels in rebounds (7.4 per game) and finished second in steals (49) and third in scoring (12.5). For an encore, he went on — along with Davis — to play a starring role for the victorious United States squad in the World University Games.

"That was a great experience," Lynch says. "Not only did I get to represent my country but I also got to play against some great competition, in practice as much as the games themselves.

"This summer showed me how far I have come along and how far I still need to go."

Yes, there is always more work to be done. More lifting, more running, more shooting, more everything. Lynch found the time this summer to do a little bit of everything. He says he wants to be prepared for anything, whether it's staying primarily at the power forward slot or finally getting the chance to move his offensive game more to the perimeter. He knows that the relative likelihood of these possibilities is out of his control. So he spends his time thinking about, and working on, those things that are within his control. If he stays on the inside, he's done it before and he'll do it again— only better this time. But just in case he goes outside, he's ready for that, too.

"I've worked on my jumper, playing on the perimeter and being more comfortable with the ball in the open floor," Lynch says. "I'm looking forward to getting an opportunity to play more on the perimeter, but whatever the team needs from me, I'll do."

There is one thing Lynch won't do, however, and that's show his frustration. Happiness, yes. Anger, no. Not about playing time or his position; he's never done that. But not about cheap shots or bad calls or anything else, either. Watch him sometime. On the basketball court, Lynch never stops smiling — particularly at those times when a bad call has most Carolina fans ranting and raving at their television sets. But not George.

"When I was younger, I used to pout all the time," Lynch says. "But then I had a coach who, every time I pouted, would take me out of the game right away. So I started smiling all the time, and he couldn't figure out when I was just smiling or when I was really mad, so he would just leave me in the game.

"So now, if there's a bad call against me, I won't show a bad expression. And maybe next time the call will go my way. What it comes down to is, every time I smile, I send a good message to someone."

Last season, more often than not it was UNC

> **GEORGE LYNCH:**
>
> ## "I've worked on my jumper, playing on the perimeter and being more comfortable with the ball in the open floor."

opponents who got Lynch's message. One method of delivery was the double-double, a statistical creation based on double-figure point and rebound totals that normally carries with it college basketball's unofficial seal of excellence. Amazingly, Lynch turned the trick six times, beginning with a 19-point, 10-rebound extravaganza against Jacksonville and continuing through Connecticut (12-14), Maryland (18-11), Georgia Tech (16-13 and 17-12) and finally NCAA Tournament foe Villanova (19-10).

For now, however, double-doubles and the benefits of smiling are the last things on Lynch's mind. He's says he's more concerned with things like winning games and ACC titles and national championships.

"We accomplished a lot in the last two years, but now we have to start all over," Lynch says. "We have a lot of young guys and, to be successful, every one of us is going to have to play a lot harder than we did last year."

Yr.	G	FG-FGA-Pct.	FT-FTA-Pct.	Reb-Ave	A	TO	S	PF-D	Pts	Ave
Fr.	34	112-215-52.1	67-101-66.3	183-5.4	34	66	37	105-6	292	8.6
So.	35	172-329-52.3	85-135-63.0	258-7.4	41	86	49	92-2	436	12.5

Lynch's power moves in the lane will again be a vital part of the UNC attack.

BOB DONNAN

HENRIK RÖDL

Heels' Versatile Swingman Finds New Role Off The Court.

In many respects, the summer months of 1991 were the same for Henrik Rödl as they were for his teammates on the Tar Heel basketball team.

He spent as much time as possible at the Smith Center. He played a lot of basketball. He hit the weight room. He worked on his strength, his quickness and his shot.

But, in another sense, this was an extra-special offseason for the Tar Heels' elder statesman, who turned the ripe old age of 22 last March.

On July 27, 1991, Rödl married his Chapel Hill High School sweetheart, former North Carolina volleyball player Susan Andrews, in a ceremony in Chapel Hill.

If that day seemed particularly shady to any outdoorsmen, it may have been due to the shadows cast by what must have been one of the largest wedding parties in Orange County history. Next to the man of the hour, who checks in at 6-foot-7, stood three guys who have shared the past two years with him: Carolina groomsmen Scott Cherry (6-4), George Lynch (6-7) and Matt Wenstrom (7-1).

The wedding also presented the perfect opportunity for a reunion of sorts for Rödl and the rest of his teammates, who are often scattered throughout the country and the world during the busy summer months. All summer long, of course, this special occasion was the talk of the town.

"I'm sure everybody is excited and anxious to see what is going to happen," Rödl says. "I think a lot of people my age don't really think of getting married, so it is a little bit of a different situation."

Still, nobody was even remotely surprised at this latest turn of events; Rödl and his new wife had been dating for almost five years and were engaged last year. In the past two seasons, if a teammate saw Rödl away from the basketball court, he was most surprised if the new Mrs. Rödl was *not* somewhere in the vicinity.

"We have always spent as much time together as we could," Rödl says. "We have been together through high school and now college.

"Susan was also an athlete at Carolina, so she really understands what I'm going through. She has always helped bring out the best in me — as a person, as a student and as an athlete. And I've tried to do the same for her."

Rödl showed glimpses of his best basketball last year as a sophomore, when he started 14 times and played quality minutes in all 35 games. One of his best scoring lines of the year (prior to "I do") came in the Tar Heels' 92-70 shellacking of N.C. State: five of five from the field, 12 points, four assists and one rebound. Rödl's proudest accomplishment of the night, however, was his constant harassment of Wolfpack shooting star Rodney Monroe, who was just seven of 20 from the field after scorching UNC for 37 points the previous night.

"My focus is on defense when I go in to play," Rödl says. "I like to go into a game against a player like Rodney Monroe or Dennis Scott and try to contain him."

In high school, Rödl himself was one of those players opposing defenses were worried about containing. As a senior, Rödl became North Carolina's Mr. Basketball by averaging 23.3 points and six rebounds a game, handing out 101 assists and shooting 65 percent from the floor. His dazzling performance led Chapel Hill High to a 30-1 record and the state 4-A basketball championship.

"Obviously, I haven't scored as much as I did in high school," Rödl says. "But I think I am able to adjust well to any kind of role in college.

HENRIK RÖDL:

> "Susan has always helped bring out the best in me — as a person, as a student and as an athlete."

"I think one of my strengths is that I can come into a game as either a role player or a scorer. If the team needed me to score more, I would be able to fill that role. Still, I'll never be a scorer like a Rodney Monroe or a Rick Fox. My strengths are in passing and defense and making the open shot."

This year, Rödl is looking forward to putting his new and improved talents on display in front of his countrymen. He gets his traditional Tar Heel "home games" when UNC travels to Germany for a Christmas tournament.

"Basketball is still a minor sport in Germany," Rödl says. "Everything is still tennis and soccer. Therefore, not many people over there know much about what I'm doing over here — except for my family and close friends.

"It should be fun. But I still think I could do just about anything over there, and I'd still be better known at Chapel Hill High than I am in my own hometown in Germany."

Yr.	G	FG-FGA-Pct.	FT-FTA-Pct.	Reb-Ave	A	TO	S	PF-D	Pts	Ave
Fr.	34	27-55-49.1	12-24-50.0	24-0.7	21	28	13	24-0	79	2.3
So.	35	46-81-56.8	23-37-62.2	53-1.5	62	36	13	39-0	127	3.6

Rödl likes to take it to the hole when he's not bombing away with his deadly three-pointers.

BOB DONNAN

SCOTT CHERRY

Practice Sessions Make Junior Point Guard Ford-Tough.

Early entry for the best trivia question of the 1991-92 basketball season: Who led the Tar Heels in field goal percentage and three-point field goal percentage last year and finished second on the team in assist-turnover ratio?

Without a hint, such as "His picture is about two inches above this question," that challenge could get the best of even the most attentive Carolina alumnus. So beware.

Scott Cherry made the most out of his second year on Carolina's Blue team, the squad whose ever-important job is to push the White team — the starting unit — until it can be pushed no longer. In a season-long montage of crowd-pleasing minutes, Cherry knocked down 10 of his 14 field goal attempts, buried his only three-point attempt and compiled 11 assists to only five turnovers.

Also in his storybook sophomore season, Cherry got the call to start a game against Cornell in Ithaca, N.Y., in front of a large crowd of familiar faces.

"That was a lot of fun," says Cherry, who hails from Ballston Spa, N.Y. "I was really happy to be able to start and play in front of my family and friends. It's something you can tell your kids about when you get older. 'I started for Carolina.' It worked out well because I thought I played pretty well and we won the game."

Not bad, huh? Wait, this story gets better.

Beginning with a five-point (2-2 FG) effort against San Diego State in the Tar Heels' season opener on Nov. 24, Cherry turned into UNC's version of Mr. Perfect. Come game day, every shot he took went in. Days passed and no one seemed to notice. Weeks passed and teammates began ribbing him about his perfect slate. Months, yes months, passed and even the secretaries in the basketball office started to get into the act.

"They started bringing it up about halfway through the season," says Cherry, who still seems underwhelmed by the whole thing. "They were asking me if I was ever going to miss."

He did miss, eventually, but not before carrying his streak of perfection into February. His line, when pieced together over parts of four months, was a masterpiece: 33 minutes, seven of seven from the field, 17 points, four assists and three rebounds.

While those kinds of numbers are enough to get any crowd on its feet, Cherry's rapport with the home crowd began well before his magnificent run. Sometimes, just the slightest movement of Dean Smith's hand in Cherry's general direction is enough to get the Smith Center stirring.

"Obviously, it makes me feel good when the fans start getting into it," Cherry says. "But I'd like to see them cheer the same for everyone else. It feels kind of strange when those guys work their tails off all game and I come in for a few minutes and everybody gets excited."

Cherry says there is one thing that matters to him much more than fanatical statistics or statistical fanatics: practice time. That is where he knows, and where he lets his coaches and teammates know, that he can do the job.

Not that practice is always fun, or ever easy.

Each day, one of Cherry's ballhandling drills involved taking the ball up the length of the court against another point guard — UNC assistant coach Phil Ford, a man who happens to be one of the greatest players in the history of Carolina basketball. While that in itself sounds tough enough, it gets worse. Much worse. The drill is designed for the defender to use any means necessary to put the ballhandler off-balance —

that includes, but is not necessarily limited to, hand checks, arm checks, hip checks and whatever else Ford has in his bag of tricks.

"He makes it fun," Cherry says. "He really gets into it. He bumps you and he pushes you and he makes you work.

"The idea is to work on keeping your balance while someone is guarding you closely. I think I improved in that area last year. I didn't turn the ball over as much in practice, and I felt much more confident as the year went along.

"The most important thing for me is that I saw a big improvement in my game over the year before. I improved my ballhandling and I got a better understanding of the fundamentals and what we were trying to do on defense.

"Every day, my teammates helped me. Hopefully, I was pushing them to become better players, too. That's what my job is all about."

Yr.	G	FG-FGA-Pct.	FT-FTA-Pct.	Reb-Ave	A	TO	S	PF-D	Pts	Ave
Fr.	8	1-7-14.3	0-3-00.0	1-0.1	2	1	1	1-0	2	0.3
So.	20	10-14-71.4	9-13-69.2	8-0.4	11	5	5	2-0	30	1.5

Ballhandling drills with UNC
assistant coach Phil Ford
have helped develop Cherry
into one tough customer at
the point guard position.

The difficult transition from high school to college has been a valuable learning experience for Wenstrom.

BOB DONNAN

MATT WENSTROM

Tall Tales Behind Him, Junior Looks To Contribute.

A college campus is often a haven, if not close to heaven, for an intellectually curious 17- to 22-year-old student.

A typical college student shares everything from class notes to groceries to cars to clothes with his roommates and friends. In the end, it makes everything a lot easier.

Matt Wenstrom is not your typical college student. He stands 7-foot-1, has trouble finding a comfortable seat in airplanes, couldn't dream of driving a typical sports car, and has never found one person with whom he could share clothes.

Until last year, that is. While some college basketball *conferences* don't have three seven-footers, the Tar Heel basketball team is blessed with three: Wenstrom and sophomores Eric Montross (7-0) and Kevin Salvadori (7-0).

"Eric was the first person ever in my life that I've shared clothes with," Wenstrom says. "A lot of tall guys are really skinny, and their pants are always too small in the legs. But Eric's built pretty well and he has some nice clothes, too. He and I can wear the same coats and jackets and stuff like that. I raided his closet all the time last year."

Not that Wenstrom has even the slightest complaint about his size. He wouldn't trade his height for anything, he says, but wouldn't mind leaving the accompanying expectations for someone else. That, in fact, was an issue with Dean Smith two years ago, when the freshman from Texas became the first player in UNC history to be listed at the magical seven-foot mark.

"Coach Smith has always believed that the title 'seven-footer' puts undue pressure on players, and he may be right," Wenstrom says. "But height, I think, does not have the same significance now that it had in college basketball in the past. It's still an advantage, certainly, but there's not as much emphasis on seven-footers in the game today. There are so many more incredible athletes today, it's

impossible to dominate a game just because of your height."

In high school, the likelihood of Wenstrom dominating a game was more possible, and more probable, than just about anything. But the game's a lot different in Atlanta and Chapel Hill and College Park than it is in Katy, Texas.

"The transition was a very big step for me," Wenstrom says. "In high school, when you're as tall as I was, it's pretty easy. Being 6-10 in high school is a much bigger advantage than being 7-1 in college, and it's taken me a little longer than expected to make that transition.

"But I'm very happy with where I am now. I would have liked to have gone a little faster, but if not, I just have to take a good look at where I am and work with that. I worked hard over the summer, and I think things look really good for this year."

Wenstrom also faces another difficult adjustment to the college game that has nothing to do with being a seven-footer. It's a change that almost every high school superstar has to face: playing time. Instead of touching the ball on every possession and playing 35 or 40 minutes a game, most freshmen and sophomores find themselves having to squeeze as much productivity as possible into precious few minutes of what the players like to call "PT."

"It helps when you can get into the game and get the feel for the game a little bit," Wenstrom says. "It's hard to jump in for just a two-minute spurt. You're in for two or three transitions and then you're out. You can get into any game by watching and

MATT WENSTROM:

> "Height, I think, does not have the same significance now that it had in college basketball in the past."

cheering from the sidelines, but it's so much different from actually experiencing it."

Wenstrom did get some valuable playing time this past offseason when he toured Europe with a group of Atlantic Coast Conference All-Stars. The team, coached by Wake Forest's Dave Odom, competed in Belgium, France and Italy during the month of August.

With lofty goals still within reach and a summer's worth of experience under his belt, Wenstrom says he's hoping to start building on some of the great moments he's already experienced in a Tar Heel uniform.

"It's kind of scary that my college career is already half over," Wenstrom says. "People say time flies in college, and it's hard to believe during the year because it seems to go slowly sometimes. But when you look back, it doesn't seem like such a long time at all."

Yr.	G	FG-FGA-Pct.	FT-FTA-Pct.	Reb-Ave	A	TO	S	PF-D	Pts	Ave
Fr.	32	10-19-52.6	9-14-64.3	20-0.6	2	7	1	17-0	29	0.9
So.	24	5-15-33.3	7-12-58.3	21-0.9	0	6	1	6-0	17	0-7

While he can leave a defender
hung out to dry on occasion,
Salvadori's main strengths
are his soft jumpshot and
shotblocking ability.

BOB DONNAN

KEVIN SALVADORI

Sizeable Development Provides Food For Thought.

Another offseason for Kevin Salvadori meant another summer of the same old things: a little basketball, a lot of eating and lifting, a little more basketball, a lot more eating and lifting, a little more basketball . . . you get the picture.

One might think he's getting tired of this routine by now. After all, he redshirted during his first year at UNC in order to — surprise — add some pounds and strength to his 6-foot-10 high school frame. Then, last summer, it was more of the same and the results were obvious. Salvadori grew an inch and put on 10 more pounds of muscle to check in at the 215 mark.

Still, it wasn't enough. This season, the trends continued.

"This summer, I primarily worked on weightlifting and trying to put on weight," Salvadori says. "My brother Craig helped me out a lot with that. He's really into it, and he pushed me hard. Very hard. He makes me take that extra step in the weight room."

Those extra steps are helping. With another year of eating enough for three people under his widening belt, Salvadori tips the scales at a solid 225. And whatever it is he's eating must be pretty nutritious. He's getting taller, too. As he enters his second year of eligibility, Salvadori joins teammates Matt Wenstrom (7-1) and Eric Montross (7-0) in the exclusive seven-foot club.

At first look, Salvadori's unique and intense eating and lifting regimen seems to be almost counterproductive to two other basketball-related goals: the improvement of his jumpshot and his quickness. Normally, players who want a soft touch don't immediately head for the weight room. "I had to be careful about that," Salvadori says. "So I made sure I worked on my jumpshot as often as possible."

Likewise, players seeking some extra quickness don't usually head for the dinner table umpteen times a day. But this year, believe it or not, the Kevin Salvadori meals-per-

day ratio has topped 1990's all-time record of six.

"These days, I'm eating about seven times a day, plus three weight-gaining drinks per day," Salvadori says.

And does he ever get tired of eating?

"No. One of my favorite things to do is eat, and I'm always hungry so I end up eating all the time."

Keep in mind that the number seven doesn't even take into consideration any munch-on-some-potato-chips-in-front-of-the-TV extravaganzas. And for the real meals, it's safe to assume carrots and celery aren't the main course.

"A night's dinner might be four or five chicken breasts, a couple of baked potatoes, and half a head of lettuce for a salad," Salvadori says. "Other times, I'll have a pound and a half of ground beef in one sitting. Or I'll have hot dogs, lunchmeat, you name it. The list goes on and on.

"It gets pretty expensive, too. When I was in Chapel Hill for first summer session, about a month, I spent more than $350 just on groceries for myself."

The '91-92 season will add an interesting twist to the Salvadori saga, as the big man takes his big appetite off campus for the first time. Along with new roommate Hubert Davis, he'll get to put his gourmet talents to the ultimate test.

"It's going to be interesting because I'll be cooking for myself a lot more often now," Salvadori says. "Hubert's going to have to keep an eye on me."

On the court this fall, Salvadori will focus on earning a spot in a UNC lineup that finds itself stacked with a trio of big men. Fortunately for the Tar Heels, Salvadori has spent most of

KEVIN SALVADORI:

> "A night's dinner might be four or five chicken breasts, a couple of baked potatoes and half a head of lettuce."

his time in the No. 4 slot, also known as power forward.

"I played mostly No. 4 last year and that's where I'm most comfortable," Salvadori says. "I think I'm quicker with my jumpshot than a lot of big guys and, on defense, I give us another big man to play alongside Matt or Eric."

The potential of this twin-tower lineup, in which Salvadori is matched with Montross or Wenstrom, could be enough to create some of the more interesting shot selections seen in the Atlantic Coast Conference for some time. Consider it the Tar Heels' version of a S.W.A.T. team.

"Shotblocking is probably my biggest asset right now," says Salvadori, who batted away eight shots last year in limited playing time. "I'm a quick jumper and I've always had pretty good timing."

Believe it or not, Salvadori actually *averaged* 10 blocks per game in high school. Come to think of it, can 10 meals a day be far behind?

Yr.	G	FG-FGA-Pct.	FT-FTA-Pct.	Reb-Ave	A	TO	S	PF-D	Pts	Ave
Fr.	31	18-35-51.4	12-19-63.2	27-0.9	0	5	1	13-0	48	1.5

It doesn't always take a knock over the head to get Montross pumped up about basketball.

ERIC MONTROSS

Pan American Selection Enters A Brand New World.

Yes, that was Eric Montross, high school basketball star from Indiana, being photographed at a Tar Heels' game in the Smith Center more than a year ago.

That was him again in the NCAA Tournament in March, a freshman helping UNC to an East Regional semifinal victory over Eastern Michigan with a sensational 17-point, six-rebound, three-block performance that led to what may have been one of the best quotes of the year. In the game, after absorbing a particularly flagrant elbow from one of the Eastern Michigan players, Montross further cemented his reputation as a mix-it-up, hard-nosed player by physically and emotionally sparking the Tar Heels to a convincing 93-67 victory. "Maybe he plays better after he gets hit on the head," said Dean Smith.

That was Montross quite a few more times in May and June, standing tall in your very own living room, making a pitch for the United Way and reaching out to all of the young people who look up to the seven-foot kid with the funny number as if he were from another world.

And, yes, that was him once more in July and August, representing the Tar Heels and the United States of America in the Pan American Games in Cuba — hooping it up in a way he had never quite experienced before and visiting a world most people have never quite understood.

The basketball was a great experience, Montross says, and he was extremely proud to represent his country. But his tone indicates there was much more to his latest venture than being a star or winning a game or doing a commercial.

"I was able to talk with the Cuban people," Montross says. "I didn't need an interpreter, so it was a little easier to get a sense of what is going on down there.

"The Cubans were very warm, cordial people. They were willing to do anything they could to help us out, and

they expected nothing in return. They acted as if it were important to them, personally, to be good hosts for their country. It's not like painting the buildings just for the Pan Am games to make everything look better than it really is.

"The people there make the country. They may have a terrible economy and their houses are bad, but they're proud of who they are and they try to make the best of what they have."

It was only after returning home in August, and having had more of a chance to reflect on his cultural experience, that Montross fully grasped the true scope of the harsh realities he saw with his very own eyes.

"It's sad when you see the way that country has been almost destroyed by socialism," Montross says. "I mean, you walk around and you see signs that say, 'Socialism Or Die.' What are you going to do?

"In the United States, you would be hard-pressed to find people you see every day who are in a worse situation than all of those people — with a few exceptions for Cubans in government and other high places.

"But when you see their way of life and their pride, when you see how clean they keep their houses that we would consider shacks, you see how immaterial material things should be. And you see how they do their best to live a life that's happy even though they lack an awful lot of things."

These impressions are lasting ones for a 19-year-old who's been asked about nothing but hoops for the past several years. Montross says when it comes to basketball, he tries to avoid all the talk. He'd rather think about what he needs to do to

> ### ERIC MONTROSS:
> "When you you have a game like (Eastern Michigan) at the end of the season, you know you've made progress."

become a good player and what the team needs to do to become a good team. And the levelheaded young man with the double zero emblazoned across his chest says he avoids the hype for one reason: He's afraid he might start believing it.

At the same time, he's dead serious about the sport. Any opposing player who happened to drift onto the big guy's turf last year could tell you that. Montross is always looking to improve, always willing to smash his seven-foot, 258-pound body into someone, and last year's game against Eastern Michigan was one dazzling example.

"When you have a game like that at the end of a season, you know you've made progress," Montross says. "It's not just that game that's important. I don't think it always takes a knock on the nose to get me to play above a normal level.

"It's more of a general feeling that I have matured as a player and that I'm capable of scoring and expanding my offensive game."

Yr.	G	FG-FGA-Pct.	FT-FTA-Pct.	Reb-Ave	A	TO	S	PF-D	Pts	Ave
Fr.	35	81-138-58.7	41-67-61.2	148-4.2	11	32	6	79-0	203	5.8

Phelps has a knack for finding the open man, even when nobody else can see him.

BOB DONNAN

DERRICK PHELPS

Seasoned Sophomore Finally Gets The Point.

The scene came dozens of times last season, just as it has come hundreds of times in the past 30 years of North Carolina basketball.

In practice, Derrick Phelps is running the Blue team against King Rice and the rest of the starting White unit. As the Blue squad's offensive set unfolds, someone — it doesn't matter who — is in the wrong offensive position on the floor. Dean Smith, who has been watching this kind of thing for three decades at UNC, isn't happy. He decides it's time to deliver a few brief messages, one to the mistaken player and one to . . . Derrick Phelps.

Phelps, a freshman at the time, is a little confused. He's not at all sure why he's catching the flak for his teammate's error. It just doesn't make sense to him.

King Rice, a senior, is well within earshot of Smith's instructive voice. He's seen it all before. He's lived through it, learned from it. After practice, Rice volunteers a few suggestions to his fellow point guard. From then on, Phelps says, it all started to make sense.

"King told me that even if it seems like it has nothing to do with me, it's still my job to know," Phelps says. "He told me the same message that Coach Smith was trying to get across. The point guard has to run the show. He has to be in control at all times."

The 1991-92 season is Phelps' chance to run the show. After averaging about 10 minutes a game last year, he has a chance to see that number increase at least threefold. It's up to him and fellow point man Scott Cherry to fill the void created by Rice's graduation.

Phelps knows the situation at hand. He knows what's expected of a UNC point guard. But he says he's not nervous about his opportunity or doubtful of his ability. In many ways he sounds like a senior already, confident in his ability but realistic about the challenge before him.

"I'm just going to take it as it comes," Phelps says. "I'm going to go out there and play my game and try not to worry about what everyone expects of me.

"If I do it any other way, I'm putting unnecessary pressure on myself. So I'm not worried about what other people want me to do out there. I'm more worried about what I'm trying to do and, in the end, what Coach Smith wants me to do."

If the above words don't sound like those of an ordinary sophomore, that's just the way the Tar Heels want it. In the North Carolina basketball world, if you're a point guard, being timid is not an option. Phelps, like UNC point guards Jimmy Black, Kenny Smith and Rice before him, is from the Big Apple. And, as everyone knows, New York and timid don't usually mix.

"If you're a point guard, you just have to be a leader," says Phelps, who hails from Pleasantville, N.Y. "It doesn't matter if you're a freshman or a senior, you're going to be a leader out there. When the time comes for that person, that leader, you have to go out there and just do it.

"You can't worry about being a sophomore or whether or not people are going to listen to you. You're the point guard, you're calling the plays. They're going to have to listen. If they don't, they're going to be sitting down."

Phelps has the point. The offense starts with the point guard's ability to bring the ball upcourt, create an opening and find the open man. The defense starts with the point guard's ability to prevent his opponent from doing the same. As a freshman, Phelps proved his ability to guard the ball. He also proved that, while many players think of defense as work and offense as play, he holds a different perspective.

DERRICK PHELPS:

> "If you're a point guard, you just have to be a leader. It doesn't matter if you're a freshman or a senior."

"I think defense makes offense," Phelps says. "If you put pressure on the ball, work hard to get the turnover and get an easy basket out of it, you can take a lot out of the other team. I think when you play good, tough defense, the offense comes naturally."

Phelps' offensive contributions last year could be best described as lost in the shuffle. In his last 18 games, after coming back from a midseason knee injury, he compiled 43 assists to only 19 turnovers. And in an NCAA Tournament game against Eastern Michigan, he had four points, four assists and a steal in just 13 minutes.

"I can score," Phelps says, "if that's what the team needs me to do for us to win."

Spoken like a true North Carolina point guard. And not even Black or Smith or Rice could've said it any better himself.

Yr.	G	FG-FGA-Pct.	FT-FTA-Pct.	Reb-Ave	A	TO	S	PF-D	Pts	Ave
Fr.	30	25-51-49.0	16-21=76.2	33-1.1	58	40	27	30-0	68	2.3

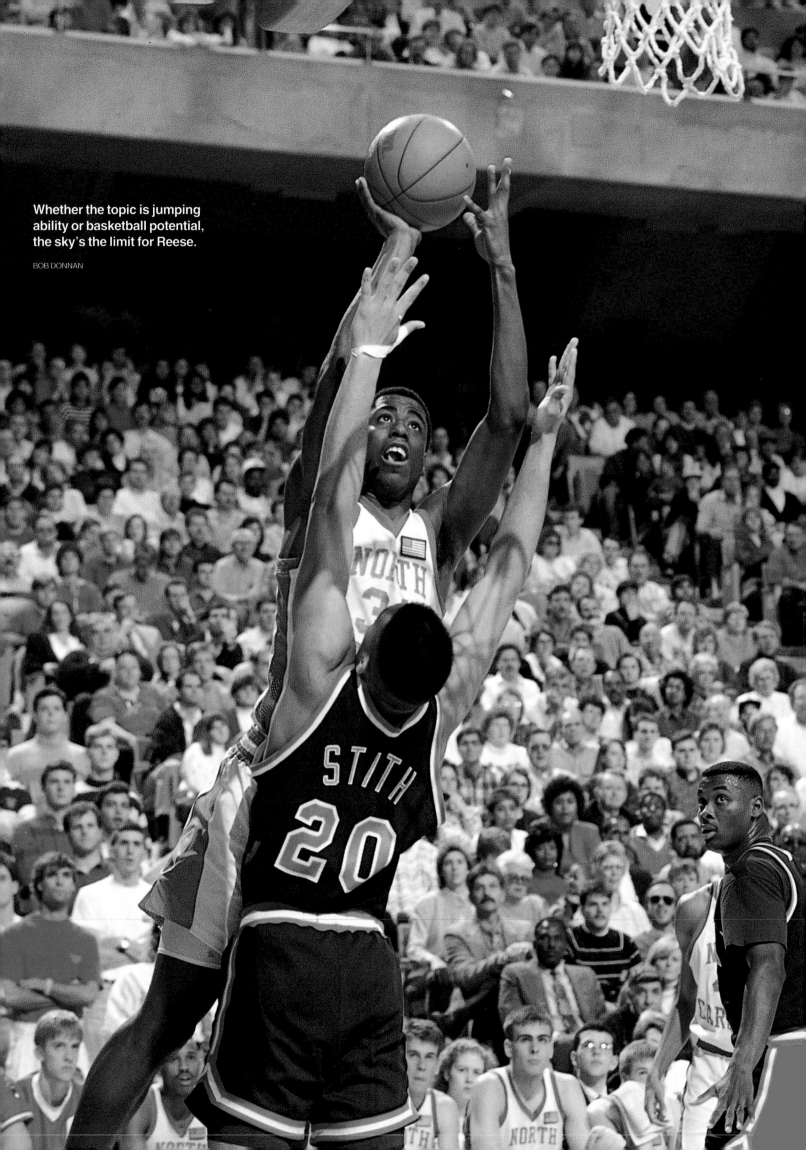

Whether the topic is jumping ability or basketball potential, the sky's the limit for Reese.

BRIAN REESE

Year Of Experience Gives Him New Outlook.

Not many basketball players would save the first dunk of their life for a real game. Then again, not many basketball players are like Brian Reese.

It was about eight years ago, while kids and adults in playgrounds and driveways all across the country were working countless hours for that one extra inch, that Reese surprised himself and all of the other 12-year-olds on the court that day by flying high above the magical 10-foot mark and throwing down the first dunk of his young but blossoming career. Eight years later, of course, most of those other 12-year-olds are probably still trying — while Reese enters his second season in Carolina blue.

"I remember it well," Reese says. "It was in a real game in an organized league. I didn't really think that much about it at first. I mean, it's not as difficult when you're the only one in the game who can dunk."

Reese has come a long way since that memorable day in 1983. He still likes to dunk, but his attitude toward slams and jams — and even about the game of basketball in general — has taken a significant turn in the past year. Since his arrival in Chapel Hill a year ago, Reese has literally had to relearn, from the ground up, the sport that turned him into a star.

"When I came here last year, I was expecting to play a lot more than I did," Reese says. "But I eventually realized that I had a job to do and I could help the team in a smaller role. Midway through the season, I think I really started to understand the system and I started to do the things Coach Smith wanted me to do."

For Reese, the reconstruction process involved living and learning some of the intricacies of the college game: playing team defense, setting screens, running the floor, finding the right man in the right spot at the right time. It's not that any of these hoops necessities were completely foreign to Reese. They weren't. But now he had to learn that there is a right way and a wrong way to set a screen, a right spot and a wrong spot, a good time and a bad time. It took a while, he says, before it all started to make sense.

"Freshman year was a big adjustment for me," Reese says. "I had to change my whole frame of mind about the game. It was difficult, but Coach Smith is a great teacher. He shows you why the game is much more than putting the ball in the hoop and dribbling it up and down the floor."

Playing exclusively at small forward as a freshman, Reese had an opportunity to work behind and play against a NBA first-round draft pick and the multi-talented Rick Fox. He says he tried to mimic Fox's work ethic, his attitude. Now, the revised depth chart indicates that it may be Reese who steps into Fox's old spot in the starting lineup. But No. 31 will not be an exact replica of No. 44.

"I'm more of a driver," Reese says. "I can hit the outside shot, but I think my greatest strength right now is my quick first step and my athleticism. I'm also built kind of low to the ground for someone my height, so I try to use that to my advantage, too.

"Our styles weren't the same, but I learned a lot from Rick. He really showed me the game. He taught me to work hard at moving without the ball and doing other things that don't always come naturally."

Reese took what he learned and began to produce, particularly as his playing time increased late in the year. If last year's stats are a sign of things to come, look out. In just 12 minutes of play vs. Iowa State, Reese had 12 points, three rebounds, two assists and two blocks. In only five minutes against N.C. State, he notched four points and four rebounds. And how about this line against the Citadel: 11 points, four assists, two rebounds, a block and a steal.

> ### BRIAN REESE:
> "Freshman year was a big adjustment for me. I had to change my whole frame of mind about the game."

"Last year, I settled into a role, especially in the NCAA Tournament, where I knew I could help the team if I played my game," Reese says. "Whether I'm starting this year or coming off the bench, that's not going to change. Whatever your role is, you can't try to do too much.

"You can't go out there looking for your shot too much or worrying about how many points you have that night. I just ask myself, 'What can I do to help the team win?' And then I try to go out there and do it.

"I'm not going to go into this year thinking, 'I have to do this or I have to do that.' My only goals are to work hard and to try to fit into the team in whatever way will give us the best chance to win."

Yr.	G	FG-FGA-Pct.	FT-FTA-Pct.	Reb-Ave	A	TO	S	PF-D	Pts	Ave
Fr.	33	56-105-53.3	18-33-54.5	54-1.6	17	20	9	14-0	133	4.0

Sullivan seems to like Chapel Hill and the Smith Center so much that there have been whispers about whether or not he ever actually leaves.

BOB DONNAN

PAT SULLIVAN

Hard-Working Sophomore Finds Home Away From Home.

The bowels of the Smith Center are curiously empty on a hot and steamy August afternoon. Every room is vacant, every hallway silent. The thick scent of wet paint lurks in the air, and several hand-written signs hang prominently on the wooden barriers at each entrance to the hardwood floor:

NOTICE: Floor closed for yearly maintenance program. PLEASE: For one year show your maintenance staff you will cooperate and stay off the floor! This will be greatly appreciated! THANKS.

Pat Sullivan, the Smith Center's resident gym rat and the only sign of life in the building's basement, rushes to the phone to call teammate George Lynch.

"G, we can't play at the Smith Center today. Grab Derrick and Brian and whoever else you can find and meet me over at Carmichael in an hour. We'll play there."

After going through his usual one-hour weight training routine, a lonely one this time, Sullivan races over to Carmichael Auditorium for a few hours of live action. Finally, someone has figured out a way to get Sullivan away from the Smith Center.

Later that day, a passerby asks Rick Fox if he's seen Sullivan. "Well, he's always around here somewhere," Fox says, breaking into a smile. "Either that or he's at Coach Smith's house. I think he's moved in over there."

Even though that last part isn't true, it is safe to say that Sullivan has found a new home in Chapel Hill. He calls it the "SAC," short for Student Activities Center, better known everywhere else as the Smith Center.

"The guys are always trying to get on me about that," Sullivan says. "But I think I'm just like any other player on the team. I guess it's just because I'm always down here working out or working on my game. Even when I'm not in the gym, I'm usually in the basketball office doing something."

So, while several of his teammates toured the basketball world or returned home this past summer, Sullivan was more than happy to be working out, doing his drills and playing games in the SAC, his new home away from home.

"Depending on how long guys want to play pickup games, I've been putting in three- or four-hour days," he says.

Sullivan's top priority last summer was to work on the three areas of his game suggested to him by the UNC coaching staff at the end of last year: three-point shooting, strength and guarding the ball.

Sullivan's superb work ethic paid off last year, when he appeared in 34 of the Tar Heels' 35 games as a freshman and made several important contributions in key games.

In the NCAA Tournament's East Regional final, the Tar Heels led Temple 73-72 with 8.6 seconds to play and had to get the ball inbounds under the Owls' basket. With the pressure mounting by the moment, UNC called timeout. In the ensuing Tar Heel huddle, the call went out for No. 3.

"Before that, I was only in the game for two minutes of the first half," Sullivan says. "During the timeout, Coach Smith said, 'Pat, you're going to take the ball out.' So he drew up a play where I had to bounce the ball to King."

With the entire nation watching and a Temple defender ready to jump down his throat, Sullivan inbounded to Rice, who was fouled. Eight seconds later, the Tar Heels were on their way to the Final Four, and the kid from Jersey was about to embark on the last leg of what had become a long, strange trip through the college basketball world.

> ### PAT SULLIVAN:
> "Depending on how long guys want to play pickup games, I've been putting in three- or four-hour days."

Several years before, as a prep star at Bogota High School in New Jersey, Sullivan outlined his college choices: Duke, Indiana, Notre Dame and North Carolina. In an ironic twist, his freshman season at UNC followed the recruiting trail almost to the letter: three games against the Blue Devils, a start against the Fighting Irish and a trip to Indianapolis for the Final Four.

"It's crazy that it's worked out that way," Sullivan says. "That's wild. I hadn't thought about the Indiana thing.

"It's so strange how things happen sometimes. I can even remember sitting down in a little classroom back in the ninth grade, telling my friends about the four places I wanted to go to school. And here I am.

"Now, I can't even like Duke. It's from being around Chapel Hill so much, I guess. Back in high school, I followed Duke and Carolina and I liked them both. Down here, I've learned you're not allowed to do that."

Yr.	G	FG-FGA-Pct.	FT-FTA-Pct.	Reb-Ave	A	TO	S	PF-D	Pts	Ave
Fr.	34	10-23-43.5	13-20-65.0	22-0.6	18	10	6	18-0	34	1.0

Williams, who will wear No. 21 for the Tar Heels, set state records for points and points per game last year as a senior at Garner High School.

BERNARD THOMAS
DURHAM HERALD-SUN

DONALD WILLIAMS

Sharpshooting Freshman Proves To Be Quite A Story.

Eddie Gray remembers the game as if it were yesterday. He recalls the names and numbers with ease. And he says he'll never forget the time Donald Williams brought the Garner High School basketball team back from the dead.

"We were playing Raleigh Milbrook, which has become a big rival of ours," says Gray, who coached Williams during his junior and senior seasons. "We were down by nine points with 2:44 to go, and things weren't looking too good. So I went into the huddle and said, 'Donald, start shooting the three.' "

Donald listened. Donald shot. Donald scored. Twice.

Finally, the Milbrook coach started to tell his players to foul Williams before he could shoot the ball. The idea, of course, was to try to limit the Trojans' ace scorer to "only" two points per possession. Note: In high school basketball, strategy of this sort goes well beyond respect, almost to the point of paying homage.

It didn't work.

"Donald realizes what's going on, so he starts taking shots before they could foul him," says Gray, seemingly still in a state of shock about the whole thing. "Instead of shooting the 19-foot three-pointer, he starts pulling up for the shot a couple of dribbles past halfcourt — and he's making them!"

Before anyone within sight of this one-man fireworks display knew what hit him, Williams had accounted for a season-high 55 points and Garner — which averaged more than 90 points a game for the year — was sneaking away with another in a long line of heart-stopping, come-from-behind victories.

Meanwhile, befuddled eyewitnesses were calling for a tape measure to figure out exactly what area code the Garner kid's lightning-bolt jumpers were coming from.

"People everywhere are still talking about that game and that performance," Gray says. "The time, the pressure, the range. It was unbelievable."

Although Williams' one-night performance may seem other-worldly to the casual observer, it was only one page in a yearbook's worth of memories for Garner basketball.

"I have never seen one player single-handedly win a game from the perimeter the way Donald can," Gray says. "When he gets into that zone, he's unreal."

North Carolina fans will be happy to note that Williams is, in fact, real and will be showing up wearing No. 21 for the blue and white this fall as the Tar Heels' lone freshman. Along with his immediate crowd-pleasing status as UNC's only in-state player, Williams brings a truckload of impressive credentials.

As a senior, he led Garner to a 19-8 record and the CAP-5 regular-season and tournament championships. In the process, the 6-foot-3, 183-pound boy wonder put up some mind-numbing numbers: 961 points (a state record) and awesome averages of 35.6 points (another state record), 7.2 rebounds, 2.4 assists and 2.2 steals per game. Throw in percentages of 50 percent from the field and 82 percent from the line and one must wonder:

After a season like that, could Williams have possibly left anything for an encore?

The answer is a hearty yes.

After the season, Williams was selected to play against the best players in the state and nation in two prominent high school All-Star games. In both games, he rose to the occasion time after time.

EDDIE GRAY:

"I've never seen one player single-handedly win a game on the perimeter the way Donald can. He's unreal."

In the North Carolina East-West game, Williams poured in 29 points and was named most valuable player. Then, in perhaps the most high-profile high school matchup of the season, he came oh-so-close to turning McDonald's game into Donald's game. Playing for the East squad in the star-studded McDonald's All-America game, Williams scored 20 points on 7-of-11 shooting. As if that weren't enough, when forced to handle the wing position defensively, he held Alan Henderson, a 6-9 Indiana signee, to just four points on 2-of-9 shooting.

Of course, all that changes now. As a freshman at UNC, Williams gets the last seat on the bus and the worst seat on the plane. He's the first to carry the bags and the last to get a water break during practice. And he'd be the first to tell you he has a lot to learn.

But Williams knows he'll always have those high school glory days. And just in case he ever forgets, one phone call to Eddie Gray will be more than enough to jog his memory.

"Red Auerbach once said, 'The best stat a coach can give about a particular player is what he sees with his eyes,' " Gray says. "In Donald's case, I've seen it all."

ONE SIMPLE IDEA CAN HAVE A POWERFUL EFFECT.

A single drop of water. It can effect change in a mass millions of times its size. In the same way, we believe our efforts should be far reaching. That's why we are dedicated to improving the quality of life through our medicines. And through our commitment to the community. To see the best ideas make waves.

A Pharmaceutical Research Company

Dean Smith in the fall of 1985 before the completion of UNC's Student Activities Center. Photo by Hugh Morton.

'We're Teaching

By Barry Jacobs

By now the years, the teams, the accomplishments have merged and blurred, like mountains of excellence enshrouded in fog. Groping for definition, an observer inevitably turns to statistics, measuring the achievements of Dean Smith's three decades at North Carolina with a familiar litany of consecutive this and record that, the cascade of numbers seemingly stretching to the very horizon of possibility:

• Seven hundred and seventeen wins in 926 games, most victories by an active coach and sixth all-time in Division I competition.

• A .774 winning percentage, fifth-best ever.

• A national title in 1982.

• An NIT title in 1971.

• An Olympic gold medal as the United States coach in 1976.

• Eight trips to the Final Four, including last season, second only to John Wooden's 12 at UCLA.

• Seventeen consecutive trips to the NCAA Tournament, a record.

• Eleven straight times to the regional semifinals or beyond.

• Forty-eight NCAA Tournament victories, tied for tops all-time.

• An unmatched 11 Atlantic Coast Conference titles, including one last season.

• Twenty-seven straight first-division finishes in the ACC.

• Twenty-one seasons in a row with 20 or more victories — another NCAA record.

Ask Smith how he'd like to be remembered, though, and he offers a far simpler measure. "I think I'm a teacher," says the 60-year-old. "I think we're teaching and coaching. We've thought up a couple of ideas and helped our teams."

To say the least.

Smith's ledger blurs into a cascade of stastistics and numbers of consecutive this and record that. . .

and Coaching.'

"What he's done is amazing, and that's why he's in the Hall of Fame, and that's why it's not called Jones Center, it's called Smith Center," says Mike Krzyzewski, the Duke coach. The "it" to which Krzyzewski refers is the Dean E. Smith Student Activities Center, at $33.8 million and 300,000 square feet perhaps the nation's most impressive public monument to honor a living private citizen.

Surely interest in basketball was strong at the University of North Carolina prior to the arrival of Dean Edwards Smith, the son of Emporia, Kan., teachers Vesta and Alfred Smith. After all, in 1957 the Tar Heels went undefeated and won the national title under Frank McGuire. UNC also is tops all-time in victories through the efforts of 15 coaches and 81 teams.

Besides, like Kentucky and Indiana, North Carolina, the nation's 10th most populous state, is enamored with men's college basketball.

But while other programs have fluctuated in prowess, under Smith basketball at UNC has enjoyed unremitting success and popularity for a generation. And the building that bears Smith's name — its rafters festooned with an armada of commemorative banners and 13 retired player jerseys, its sky blue vastness unmarred by commercial logos or clocks marking time in the world beyond — is the apotheosis of that popularity.

"They said I'm the common denominator of all the players," Smith says of his reluctant acceptance of the honor. "The way they said it — you're representing all the players — I couldn't say no."

This modesty and regard for his players are no pose, as a quick glance around Smith's classroom-sized office attests. Most members of the coaching profession adorn the walls of their inner sanctum with awards (if any), laudatory letters, framed articles, and photos of themselves in moments of triumph. Not Smith. The only photographs interrupting the wood paneling of his Smith Center office are views of Chapel Hill and framed composites featuring headshots of UNC players past and present.

Among those faces are some of the greatest

players of the modern game, including nearly 80 former Tar Heels who've played pro basketball here and abroad.

None has been more acclaimed, of course, than Michael Jordan, the most charismatic player in the game today. Other notable past performers include Larry Brown, Larry Miller, Billy Cunningham, Charlie Scott, Bob McAdoo, Mitch Kupchak, Bobby Jones, Phil Ford and Walter Davis. Then there are current National Basketball Association starters James Worthy, Sam Perkins, Kenny Smith, Brad Daugherty and J.R. Reid, and 1991 first-round draft choices Rick Fox and Pete Chilcutt.

But also included in Smith's picture gallery are numerous walk-ons who were happy, if not

❋•❖•❋••••

Four Corners was the most famous idea Smith's staff "thought up to help our teams."

HUGH MORTON

The junk bond blues. It isn't easy listening anymore. Used to be the prospects asked about the simple stuff like benefits and premium rates. But the hits keep coming. And now they want to hear about capital ratios, quality of assets, financial stability, and the company's exposure in the junk bond market. What can I say? Why do you think they call them 'junk bonds' anyway? What they really want to know is if we'll be around down the road when they need us.

Better Call JP

With a capital ratio more than three times the average of all life insurance companies in the U.S., JP is setting the standard for stability in the insurance industry. And for over 85 years we've provided our clients with a full range of dependable insurance products and innovative financial services. Which is why now, more than ever, your local JP agent is the one to call. Jefferson-Pilot Life Insurance Company, Greensboro, NC 27420.

Jefferson Pilot

INSURANCE / FINANCIAL SERVICES

Jefferson-Pilot Salutes
Tar Heel Basketball
For 30 Years Of Excellence!

content, to ride the bench, and virtual walk-ons who rose to starter's status, like Mike Pepper and current senior Hubert Davis.

Nowadays most players know what to expect upon entering Smith's exacting tutelage. "Certain guys won't go to play for Bob Knight, or certain people won't come to play here," says Smith, referring to the Indiana University coach known as an abrasive and occasionally violent disciplinarian. "Whether it's a perception that Bob's too tough, or we're too team-oriented, I don't know."

Smith, a mathematics major at Kansas, considers every possible factor that might affect him or his program, decides how best to approach the matter and codifies his preferences into an order that pervades UNC basketball. "I wish I could do as good a job organizing my desk as I do practice," he admits wistfully.

A prime factor in Smith's formulation is the desire to include on his squads only players willing to blend with others, subjugating their egos for the team's greater good, a trait uncommon among spoiled schoolboy hotshots. "It's a game where you need to be unselfish," says Smith. (He also calls basketball a "beautiful" game, and finds its nuances a source of perpetual fascination.)

Smith's interest in prospects only intensifies once they enroll at Chapel Hill, where attention to classwork and exemplary conduct on and off the court are stressed. Unlike at some schools, North Carolina players cannot participate in games if their grades dip below a level defined by Smith.

Not surprisingly given this setup, virtually every player or manager to participate in North Carolina basketball during Smith's years has graduated. Typical was Fox, who said last season, "I'm really grateful to be here, and as much as I hated it at first, I'm glad they care about us enough to make us go to class."

Smith goes to similar lengths to bring order to the fast-flowing chaos of the basketball court. His teams are notable for their painstaking execution of fundamental basketball, from opportunistic but solid defense to a passing game that perpetually seeks high-percentage shots. Tar Heel players say they never face a game situation they haven't already practiced.

This belief in order as a unifying principle is reflected in one of Smith's favorite sayings, that "the only free person in society is a disciplined

BOB DONNAN

person."

Smith gives his team similar aphorisms to memorize daily, along with basketball points of emphasis. Then the coach randomly picks a player to quiz prior to UNC's precisely timed and very private practice sessions. If the chosen player can't recall the day's words of wisdom, the entire squad must run laps.

The seeming regimentation of his program has brought Smith criticism from time to time. Those who know him best say the critics don't understand, especially when they use the word "system" to describe Smith's coaching regime.

"When you say a system, that gives a connotation that you're inhibiting somebody," says Roy Williams, the Kansas coach and former Smith assistant who defeated his mentor in the 1991 Final Four. "He's very disciplined with the players, but his whole goal is for you to be self-disciplined."

Though the limits are at times difficult for youngsters to accept, they also are welcomed, as evidenced by the steady stream of top players who choose to play for Smith and the ongoing loyalty of those who already have passed through the program. Many former players still speak regularly with Smith, who'll interrupt most any meeting to take their calls.

"It's a family," explains Eddie Fogler, a 1970

Jordan tops ex-players Smith sent on to pros and still sees in the off-season.

❁•❁•❁•••

We Salute The Tar Heels!

UNC grad and former Smith player and assistant now serving as head coach at Vanderbilt University. "I mean, outsiders just don't believe it, but it's true. People say it can't be that good. It's true."

Those who won't take Fogler's word for it cannot find out for themselves, however — the inner world of Tar Heel basketball is emphatically closed to outsiders. Smith prefers it that way, just as he prefers to deflect prying eyes that seek to plumb the depths of his private life.

Writers wishing to profile Smith find he has asked family members and friends to reject interview requests. He likewise balks at discussing himself or his life with second wife Linnea, a psychiatrist, and two pre-teen daughters. "He's very sensitive to personalized publicity," says Bob Spear, who gave Smith his first coaching job at the U.S. Air Force Academy in 1956. "That's just his nature. He'd rather give everybody else the credit and stay in the background."

That preference is in keeping with Smith's philosophy that satisfactions are most valuable when inwardly derived.

When discussing coaching, Smith frequently likens basketball to golf, his second athletic love, noting that a golfer must focus on beating par, an absolute standard based upon the difficulty of the course, rather than on defeating a particular opponent. Thus Smith rarely has his teams review film of the opposition before meeting them in action, and routinely dismisses mention of his victory totals and other achievements.

"I don't think we should get into coaching records," says Smith, who has hinted he'd rather retire than surpass Kentucky's Adolph Rupp as the coach with the most victories ever (875). "I think that's just American society."

Yet the fiercely competitive Smith acknowledges a continued preference for victory while playing poorly over losing while playing well. "That's my problem to deal with," he says. "As a coach, you should go by playing the course."

It's difficult to remember now, but the course hasn't always been smooth for Smith, an unknown and unproven coach when he replaced the flamboyant McGuire prior to the 1961-62 season. "Taking over when I did was not an ideal time," recalls Smith, who inherited a program on probation, its schedule and scholarships reduced. "My friends told me, 'Don't do it. There's no way.'"

That advice seemed sage at first. Smith's initial squad posted a losing record, the only one of his career. Even as his Tar Heels struggled, ACC rivals Duke and Wake made a combined four visits in five seasons to the Final Four.

Angry UNC fans responded by twice hanging Smith in effigy on campus. Things quieted down noticeably after Smith shepherded his sixth flock to the national semifinals in 1967.

Then, when the Heels made repeat Final Four visits in 1968, 1969, 1972, 1977 and 1981 and came away without capturing a title, critics labeled Smith a "choker." But that knock, too, dropped away after UNC won the 1982 NCAA crown by defeating Georgetown.

More recently, naysayers questioned Smith's ability to recruit top players, and took note of North Carolina's failure to win an ACC title or return to the Final Four since its title-winning season. Last year's freshman class and trip to the Final Four settled most of those

Bill Guthridge, Fogler and Williams lead long line of coaches and players who look up to Smith.

HUGH MORTON

❋•❖•❋•••

DECADES

Through the 1960s, '70s, '80s and into the '90s, Bill Guthridge has been the man behind Smith on the Carolina bench—whether in the heat of the battle, the calm before the storm or somewhere in between.

PHOTOS BY HUGH MORTON.

Among Smith's biggest victories were the 1982 NCAA Championship, when Carolina beat Georgetown and close friend John Thompson, and the 1976 Olympic Games, when Smith led the U.S. team to a gold medal.

Tar Heel Sports Network's Woody Durham and Mick Mixon.

SEE IT ALL ON YOUR RADIO

WRCS-AM 970 Ahoskie • **WZKY-AM 1580** Albemarle • **WKXR-AM 1260** Asheboro • **WSKY-AM 1230** Asheville **WYNX-AM 1550** Atlanta • **WPNF-AM 1240** Brevard • **WBAG-AM 1150** Burlington • **WIOO-AM 1000** Carlisle, PA **WCHL-AM 1360** Chapel Hill • **WOKE-AM 1340** Charleston, SC • **WBT-AM 1110** Charlotte • **WCSL-AM 1590** Cherryville **WGAI-AM 560** Elizabeth City • **WGQR-FM 105.7** Elizabethtown • **WGHB-AM 1250** Farmville • **WFNC-AM 640** Fayetteville **WAGY-AM 1320** Forest City • **WGNC-AM 1450** Gastonia • **WGBR-AM 1150** Goldsboro **WMAG-FM 99.5** Greensboro/High Point/Winston-Salem • **WIZS-AM 1450** Henderson **WHKP-AM 1450** Hendersonville • **WIRC-AM 630** Hickory • **WMFR-AM 1230** High Point **WHAP-AM 1340** Hopewell, VA • **WJNC-AM 1240** Jacksonville • **WKGK-FM 102.9** Kinston **WLNC-AM 1300** Laurinburg • **WJRI-AM 1340** Lenoir • **WLXN-AM 1440** Lexington • **WHLQ-FM 102.5** Louisburg **WAGR-AM 1340** Lumberton • **WBRM-AM 1250** Marion • **WKZQ-AM 1520** Myrtle Beach, SC **WCVP-AM 600** Murphy • **WKQT-FM 103.3** Newport • **WKBC-FM 97.3** North Wilkesboro **WZZU-FM 93.9** Raleigh • **WCBT-AM 1230** Roanoke Rapids • **WCVP-FM 95.5** Robbinsville **WSAY-FM 98.5** Rocky Mount • **WKRX-FM 96.7** Roxboro • **WSAT-AM 1280** Salisbury **WFJA-FM 105.5** Sanford • **WADA-AM 1390** Shelby • **WKHO-AM 550** Southern Pines **WCOK-AM 1060** Sparta • **WTOE-AM 1470** Spruce Pine • **WSIC-AM 1400** Statesville • **WJRM-AM 1390** Troy **WTYN-AM 1160** Tryon • **WSVM-AM 1490** Valdese • **WGH-AM 1310** Virginia Beach, VA **WADE-AM 1340** Wadesboro • **WKSK-AM 580** West Jefferson • **WYNA-FM 104.9** Whiteville **WWQQ-FM 101.3** Wilmington • **WVOT-AM 1420** Wilson

A Proud Part of The Village Companies

If you live outside of the Tar Heel Sports Network's coverage area and would enjoy hearing the Carolina basketball games, the live play-by-play is now available anywhere in the United States by calling **1-800-225-5551**. The cost of hearing the games is billed to your VISA or MasterCard .

questions, while UNC's 1991 ACC title was its second in the past three years.

Perhaps the only question remaining these days is when, and if, Smith will retire.

"That's so far off," Smith says of retirement, ignoring the fact he started the talk several years ago with statements he wouldn't surpass Rupp. "You find me something as meaningful to do, that's what I want to do. I love golf, but I can't play golf all the time."

Ironically, Smith and Rupp come from the same illustrious basketball family, which traces its roots directly to James Naismith, the game's inventor.

Naismith coached at Kansas, and was succeeded by Dr. Forrest (Phog) Allen, whose 746 career victories Smith could surpass this sea-

son. Among Allen's players were reserves Rupp and, later, Smith, who was born the year Rupp finished the first of his 41 seasons as Kentucky's head coach. Attending Kansas on an academic scholarship, Smith played on teams that won the 1952 NCAA title and finished second in 1953.

Nearly four decades later, the former guard says he's as excited as ever about the upcoming season, and the seasons to come. "I'm lucky to be a coach his long," Smith says of his Tar Heel regime, which predates manned space flight, the Beatles' first recording contract, and nearly half the teams in major league baseball. "I'm happy. I'm working today."

We Salute The Tar Heels!

'More Than A Coach.'

It was the summer of 1961.

Roger Maris was overtaking Babe Ruth with 61 home runs. The Yankees were on the way to the second of five consecutive World Series, where they were to beat the Reds in five games.

Gus Grissom had joined Alan Shepard as the first Americans in space.

President John Kennedy accepted full responsibility for the failed Bay of Pigs invasion and then announced federal agents would be placed on some commercial airliners to prevent hijacking. JFK was also concerned that freedom riders were being attacked in Alabama.

TV had been labeled a "vast wasteland," and moviegoers were watching *West Side Story*, *Breakfast At Tiffany's*, *The Hustler* and *Guns of Navarone*.

We were dancing to the music of 19-year-old Ernest Evans, who was trying to teach us the Twist. He's better known as Chubby Checker.

And, in August, Carolina named a new basketball coach.

I had spent the summer working at a small radio station in my hometown of Albemarle and was getting ready to return to Chapel Hill for my junior year. The Associated Press wire carried the report that Frank McGuire had resigned at UNC to coach the NBA's Philadelphia Warriors.

Less than 48 hours later his replacement was named—Dean Smith, the 30-year-old assistant to McGuire. Not many fans knew him, but I did. As Sports Director at WUNC-TV, I had interviewed him several times when I could not get to McGuire.

Coach Smith would inherit a program on NCAA probation, and many felt that Carolina wanted to de-emphasize basketball. The University had imposed its own limitations, which allowed the team to play only two games outside the regular conference schedule and trimmed the number of scholarships to two. Plus, there would be no off-campus recruiting.

Chancellor William B. Aycock made the decision to hire the untested assistant. He told me later that Coach Smith's job would not depend on how many games he won because of the limitations imposed by the University.

"We knew the time would come," Chancellor Aycock recalled, "when he would prove what he could do."

Larry Brown, a classmate of mine who played and coached under Dean Smith, claims his mentor's best coaching job might have been that first year when the Tar Heels were only 8-9. "We were awful," Brown remembers, "but we were in every game. Coach Smith never gave up, he never complained. He certainly got the most out of the talent he had available."

There were some good early wins. I remember listening to Carolina play at Kentucky in December of 1962, Coach

BOBBY JONES:

"Everybody felt they had let the team down, especially me ... but [Coach Smith] stopped me and we walked over to a corner. He told me how much he appreciated everything I had put into the game. That meant more to me than winning any game."

Smith's second season, and then celebrating when the undermanned Tar Heels upset the Wildcats, 68-66. That was the first game in a series sought by Kentucky's veteran coach, Adolph Rupp, who must have thought the young Carolina coach and his teams would be no problem. Dean Smith managed to beat Rupp's Wildcats five times, losing twice.

However, the fans were still disenchanted. They didn't understand why the Tar Heels weren't doing better. In 1965, the students burned Coach Smith in effigy after a 22-point loss at Wake Forest. (Carolina came back to upset Duke in Durham three days later.)

I was now at WFMY-TV in Greensboro and handling the PA system for the basketball games in the Greensboro Coliseum. I distinctly remember how some fans would boo Coach Smith when he was introduced prior to the tapoff.

The talent was getting better. Larry Brown was followed by Billy Cunningham. Then came Bob Lewis and Larry Miller and finally the class that included Rusty Clark, Bill Bunting, Dick Grubar, Joe Brown and Gerald Tuttle. That group really turned things around, and people finally began to realize what Dean Smith was capable of doing.

During my undergraduate days at Carolina, I had the good fortune of working several ACC basketball telecasts, and by 1968 I had joined the regular crew with Jim Thacker and Bones McKinney. I followed Coach Smith's first three Final Four teams very closely. I was there for the championships, and I was there for the disappointments.

Even though I had followed the Tar Heels for a long time, doing the Carolina broadcasts had never been a personal goal of mine. Like most people, I expected Bill Currie to continue handling the play-by-play forever. So I was surprised in February of 1971, when he left for KDKA in Pittsburgh. Soon after the season, Homer Rice, who was then the athletic director at Carolina, called and invited me to come talk with him about the job.

I called both Bill Dooley and Dean Smith to ask for their support and got a positive response. After I was named the new "Voice of the Tar Heels," I remember Coach Smith telling me what a good job I had done being impartial on TV, but now it would be okay to pull for Carolina. That has never been a problem.

I thought I knew Dean Smith fairly well, but when I became closely associated with his basketball program it was necessary to get to know him all over again. At least, I had to become familiar with the rules of his program. It was a learning experience.

I'll never forget the first road trip in December, 1971. The Tar Heels won, 90-75, in Pittsburgh on Saturday night. Coach Smith and I flew home on a private plane to tape his TV show, and we flew to New Jersey then drove down to Princeton, where Carolina would play Monday night.

Practice was scheduled soon after we reached the hotel, and I wanted to go along. The team bus was ready to roll, but I needed to get my luggage put away. I ran by the bus, and asked the coaches and players to please wait for me. That was my first lesson. The bus waits for nobody, and everybody has their watches set five minutes ahead so as not to be late.

In the early days, before portable videotape cameras were available, Coach Smith's TV show was recorded early Sunday morning in a Durham studio. He only ran late a couple of times, but when he did, he treated each crew member to dinner at a local restaurant.

His record proves he puts everything he has into a basketball game, but afterwards he doesn't dwell on the victory or defeat. Bobby Jones has told me that his lasting impression of Coach Smith is not the many wins, but the way he handled disappointment.

Specifically, Jones remembers the dramatic 54-52 overtime loss to Wake Forest in the opening round of the 1973 ACC Tournament. Coach Smith was positive in defeat. "Everybody felt they had let the team down, especially me," Jones said. "Afterwards, I was walking out of the locker room and Coach Smith was visiting with some reporters, but he stopped me and we walked over to a corner. He told me how much he appreciated everything I had put into the game. That meant more to me than winning any game."

The following year, the Tar Heels staged a miracle comeback against Duke in Chapel Hill. Down eight points in the final 17 seconds of regulation, they came back to tie the game and won it in overtime.

This was another in a long line of classic examples of just how amazing Coach Smith is in stressful situations. John Kuester, a former player who got into coaching, still re-

Durham with King Rice, Pete Chilcutt and Rick Fox after the 1991 ACC Championship.

members his coach under control.

"During that Duke game, I really expected him to just call for fouls," Kuester says. "Instead, he almost planned every situation where we stole the ball, got a foul and did everything we needed as we rallied for the win."

Certainly, you would think I could learn from such situations. Not me. The very next year in the ACC Tournament, Carolina trailed Wake Forest by eight points with 50 seconds left. When the Deacons scored, I told listeners on the Tar Heel Sports Network "that should just about do it."

Well, the audio for the broadcast was going right onto the coaches' film, and after Carolina tied the game and pulled it out again in overtime, Coach Smith insisted my comment be included in the season's highlights!

It's still there for all to hear.

Dean Smith is legendary for taking care of the young men who play for Carolina — long after they've graduated. And there are times when he tends to those who didn't play for him. In December of 1974, the Tar Heels were flying to Spain for a Christmas tournament. I had difficulty sleeping on the long flight and walked to the back of the plane. I noticed Coach Smith's overhead light was on, and he was writing Christmas cards. I sat with him for

a few minutes and discovered he was addressing cards to some parents of players he recruited but didn't come to Carolina.

Dean Smith has been my friend since he was an assistant coach at Carolina, and he is now the best basketball coach I know. But I also think he is one of the most caring people I have ever known.

A few years ago, a writer penned Coach Smith's biography. It was entitled *Dean Smith: More Than a Coach.*

Indeed.

—*Woody Durham*

Can't Beat The Real Thing.

Former Tar Heel Charlie Shaffer (right) with fellow UNC grad Charles Battle (left) and Billy Payne helped bring the Olympics to Atlanta.

An Olympic Feat

by Darren M. Evans

A former Tar Heel co-captain, a forward under the tutelage of of Dean Smith, uniform No. 42 ... a description that brings to mind a certain All-Star forward for the Los Angeles Lakers.

Well, it's not James Worthy, but a man who has proven himself as succesful off the court as Worthy has been on it.

Charlie Shaffer has also had his share of athletic success. The 49-year-old Atlanta attorney is on the board of directors for the Atlanta Olympic Organizing Committee (AOC), which recently won a three-year bidding process to give Atlanta the honor of hosting the 1996 Summer Olympic Games.

It all began when AOC Chairman Billy Payne, a local attorney who spearheaded the Olympic bid with former Atlanta mayor Andrew Young, contacted fellow attorney Horace Sibley to ask for help in bringing the Games to the United States. Sibley, a partner of Shaffer's in the Atlanta firm of King and Spalding, knew whom to turn to next.

"I had known of Billy Payne," says Shaffer, who's been a partner King and Spalding since 1966. "He played football at the University of Georgia, went to Georgia Law School and began practicing law in Atlanta.

"Horace was the third or fourth person involved. He asked me if I wanted to work on it, and I told him I'd love to."

A group of nine, which would become known as the "Atlanta Nine," was ultimately brought together to undertake the enormous task. Shaffer says the intensity of the bid process was comparable to trying to defend a two-on-one fastbreak, with this one made tougher by the eventual five-on-one faceoff against finalist cities Athens, Belgrade, Melbourne, Stockholm and Toronto.

The games, so to speak, began.

Shaffer quickly developed a good working relationship with Matts Carlgren, a prominent businessman from Sweden who was acting as one of the Olympic delegates. On Carlgren's trip to Atlanta, it was no coincidence that he was taken to the symphony. Carlgren, it turns out, is chairman of the Stockholm Symphony. All was well until a week before the official announcement of the host city, when Carlgren was invited to spend a week in Melbourne, Australia.

"I was a little worried about that," Shaffer says. "So as

We Salute The Tar Heels!

Shaffer can keep one eye on Atlanta from his perch at the law offices of King and Spalding.

soon as he got to Tokyo right before the vote, I called him and arranged to meet with him." Over a cup of coffee, Carlgren assured Shaffer he was still going to cast his ballot for Atlanta.

"The next day, the Australian group invited Matts to play 18 holes of golf with Greg Norman," Shaffer says. The Australian contingent had not only flown in the "White Shark," but also the prime minister of the country to help influence Carlgren in favor of the Australian bid. But there is a silver lining in every cloud. The next day, it rained.

"Matts only got to play nine holes of golf," Shaffer says. "I still think he stayed with us and voted for Atlanta."

Of course, Shaffer was already used to competition. Growing up in Chapel Hill, the son of the director of development at UNC, he was an outstanding athlete who excelled in a variety of sports.

Shaffer's academic and athletic endeavors took him to Woodberry Forest High School in Orange, Va., where he was a three-sport star. An all-state football and baseball player, Shaffer also had a good enough tennis game to win the 1960 Eastern Interscholastic Championship.

One of Shaffer's idols growing up was former Tar Heel basketball great Lennie Rosenbluth. Ironically, it was Rosenbluth's record that Shaffer broke when he scored 45

points in the last game of his high school career. Rosenbluth had set the Woodberry Forest gymnasium scoring record several years before, when he played for Staunton (Va.) Military Academy.

When Shaffer accepted a football scholarship to play quarterback at UNC, he was also a Morehead Scholar who maintained a serious interest in basketball. If he had trouble choosing which sport to emphasize at the collegiate level, that decision was made for him in his second freshman football game.

"In those days, freshmen couldn't play on the varsity level," Shaffer says. "In a game against Clemson, I dropped back to pass and the defensive end hit me in the back and the tackle hit me in the front. It tore my knee up."

After Shaffer went through two surgeries to repair the damaged knee, he decided to withdraw from school for the rehabilitation process. "That was the end of my football career," he says.

Shaffer re-enrolled at Carolina in the fall of 1961, while continuing to rehabilitate his knee. He soon recovered and went on to play varsity basketball and varsity tennis for the Blue and White.

During Shaffer's basketball career, he had the opportunity to play with a couple of well-known Tar Heels who went on to make names for themselves in the NBA. Larry Brown, now coach of the San Antonio Spurs, and Billy

Cunningham, executive vice president of the Miami Heat, were both all-stars during their playing careers.

"Larry was one of the better playmaking guards in college basketball," Shaffer says. "He was a great ballhandler and passer. I had a lot of layups from passes I got from Larry Brown.

"Billy Cunningham was just an extraordinary athlete. He was a great competitor and he had a killer instinct. He was also an unbelievable leaper and scorer."

During Shaffer's junior year, UNC was scheduled for a road trip that would take the Tar Heels to Bloomington, Ind., to play the Indiana Hoosiers, and on to Lexington, Ky., to take on the Kentucky Wildcats.

The Hoosiers were led by the Van Arsdale twins, who had just made the cover of *Sports Illustrated* as the country's best sophomores. Well, Cunningham would have none of that.

"Although we lost by 10 or 15 points," Shaffer says, "it turned out that Cunningham outplayed both of them. He showed them who was the outstanding sophomore."

After the game, the Tar Heels had to make the long bus trip to Lexington. It was there that a young Dean Smith would claim one of his first big interconference victories. "Kentucky had a great team, and we were down based on our loss to Indiana," Shaffer says.

Carolina was to play the Wildcats on Monday night. Upon arriving at the arena, the players were awestruck by the large gathering that had already assembled just to watch the preliminary freshman game.

"That was the freshman team that featured 'Rupp's Runts,'" Shaffer says. "Players like Louis Dampier, Pat Riley, Larry Conley. They were beating the other team very badly and there were already 15,000 people in the arena. We were really concerned about that.

"We were in the dressing room before the game, and Coach Smith said, 'Look, when you go out there tonight, just act like you're playing Tennessee. Forget about Kentucky or who you're playing. You have to go out and play 40 minutes of basketball.'"

It was a pretty good idea. The Tar Heels pulled off a 69-68 victory over the Wildcats. "It got us in the right psychological frame of mind," Shaffer says. "Adolph Rupp was coaching on one side, and Dean Smith was just in his second year as the head coach in Chapel Hill. It was really one of the greatest thrills I've had in sports."

It was through tennis, however, that Shaffer met a young coed named Harriet Houston. It was love, you might say, at first sight.

"We met at a tennis tournament in her hometown of Greenville, South Carolina," Shaffer says. "I went down to play in the Southern Open tennis tournament, and a friend of mine, Ben Geer Keyes, who played tennis at North Carolina, came to the tournament. He got me a blind date with Harriet, and we were married 14 months later."

The Shaffers are the proud parents of three children. Charles, III, 24, is a Princeton graduate and a second-year law student at Duke. Caroline, 22, is a 1991 graduate of UNC, and Emi, 14, is in the ninth grade at Westminster School in Atlanta.

Back at Carolina, Shaffer went on to earn an A.B. in history. In his final year of basketball, he was named the most outstanding senior and received the Foy Roberson Award for leadership and sportsmanship. A Phi Beta Kappa in the classroom, he was also the president of the senior class.

The Shaffers (L-R): Harriet, Charles, Caroline, Charles III, Emi.

Shaffer enrolled in the UNC School of Law in September, 1964. He was not altogether without sports, however.

"Coach Smith arranged for me to be assistant freshman basketball coach for a couple of years," Shaffer says. "It was a lot of fun and also a good diversion. It gave me some involvement in athletics."

Law was also an influential part of Shaffer's life. His grandfather, John Wallace Winborne, himself a Carolina graduate, was chief justice of the North Carolina Supreme Court in the late 1950s and early '60s.

Shaffer came to Atlanta at the urging of his uncle, Wallace Winborne, UNC Class of 1939, who was with Trust Company Bank in Atlanta.

"I had come to Atlanta to work at King and Spalding as a summer associate in 1966," Shaffer says. "My uncle asked me during my second year of law school if I wouldn't like to come down and work in a large law firm."

So he and Harriet moved to Georgia for the summer. "We liked Atlanta and had a wonderful time," Shaffer says. "We always assumed we would settle down in North

❋•❖•❋•••

Carolina, but we had such a good time here that we decided to move here after I graduated."

After receiving his Juris Doctor degree in 1967, Shaffer passed the Georgia Bar Exam and "thought in a few years we would be back in North Carolina. We've been here 24 years."

Shaffer practiced law for King and Spalding for seven years before being elected partner in 1974. He specializes in trial work and commercial litigation.

This training served Shaffer well in his role as a member of the Atlanta Olympic Committee. There was a lot to do to prepare for the bidding process. First on the agenda was getting the U.S. nomination.

"We were competing against San Francisco, Minneapolis-St. Paul and Nashville," Shaffer says. "I was actually involved in that lobbying effort. We traveled to Colorado Springs, New York City and Washington, D.C., as part of our lobbying effort with the United States Olympic Committee."

The group went to Washington in April of 1988. By that time, it was narrowed down to Atlanta and Minneapolis-St. Paul. Atlanta edged Minneapolis in the final ballot, 55-45. It was then time for Shaffer and the Atlanta committee to move up to the international level.

"I was involved with entertaining a lot of them when they came to town," Shaffer says. "I also did a lot of international traveling to get our bid going."

Shaffer and his colleagues first went to the Calgary Winter Games in 1988. The group also went to Seoul for the Summer Games, a move that really set the international lobbying task in motion.

"We even spent one night in Russia," Shaffer says. "We went over to Tallin, which is the capital of Estonia. That's where the yachting events were held during the 1980 Olympics."

Shaffer was there visiting the Olympic Village. "That was right at the time when Estonia, Latvia and Lithuania, the three Baltic States, were thinking about seceding from the Soviet Union," Shaffer says. "That was an interesting time to be over there."

The committee's main strategy was to get to see all of the delegates and to make sure all of them got to come to Atlanta. As part of the plan, each visitor spent at least one night at a private home for a small dinner. Shaffer says much of the credit for the success of the bid can be attributed to good ol' Southern hospitality.

When it finally came time for the IOC's decision, the culmination of two years of hard work was filled with anxious moments. The final convention was held in September, 1990, at the New Takanawa Prince Hotel in Tokyo. All of the IOC delegates were there to vote for the city to host the Games.

The voting started at 5 p.m. on Sept. 18. The delegates were all in one room. They cast their votes round-by-round, and the city receiving the fewest votes from the previous ballot was dropped from consideration. This process would continue until there was only one city left.

"After the first ballot, they announced to the delegates what the vote was, who the low city was and who would

UNC SPORTS INFORMATION

Shaffer ranks in UNC's top 20 in career field goal percentage.

drop off," Shaffer says. "Nobody outside of that room knew any information."

By the third ballot, the three remaining cities were Athens, Toronto and Atlanta. The penultimate vote had 36 votes for Athens, 34 for Atlanta and 22 for Toronto.

Because this would be the centennial anniversary of the modern Olympic Games, Athens was the sentimental favorite. "So it finally came down to whichever city could get those last 22 votes," Shaffer says.

After the final vote was taken, a formal ceremony took place to announce the winning city. After the delegates were shown a five-minute film presentation of each of the bid cities, they marched into the auditorium for the announcement. IOC Chairman Juan Antonio Samaranch dramatically entered the room to the sounds of the Olympic and Japanese anthems. And then, it was time for the announcement. As Shaffer retells the story, one can tell it remains a special moment for him.

"Mr. Samaranch says, 'It is a great privilege for the International Olympic Committee to announce that the host city for the 1996 Summer Olympics will be the city of ATLANTA!!' "

"That was the first time the delegates or anyone else knew," says Shaffer. "Now, everybody in the world knew Atlanta had won. It was an incredibly exciting moment."

The cheering has died down now, and Shaffer enjoys his work and teaching Sunday school classes on theology and literature. He doesn't play sports competitively anymore, but he says he enjoys jogging, swimming and bike riding.

Shaffer has had his moments in the spotlight. Now, it's time for all his hard work and planning to come to fruition.

Superdome

NCAA Title to NBA Finals

James Worthy, Sam Perkins and Michael Jordan, who started on 1982 NCAA title team (with Matt Doherty and Jimmy Black), met nine years later in NBA Finals.

HUGH MORTON
BILL SMITH (INSETS)

to Superstars.

By Alfred T. Hamilton, Jr.

CHICAGO, Ill.—It seems so much longer than nine years ago when the skinny Carolina freshman from Wilmington sprung off the Louisiana Superdome floor, stuck his tongue out and took the left wing jumpshot that seemingly altered his life completely. Michael Jordan said a few years ago that the shot he made to kill off Georgetown in 1982 actually altered his viewpoint about himself. It is almost as if he went up to take that shot in New Orleans and never came down.

Only seconds after Jordan's shot gave Carolina its 63-62 lead back then, there was another tableau in front of the Tar Heel bench, frozen in memory. There, hanging together in the air at least three feet off the floor are James Worthy and Sam Perkins, celebrating in the sky as Matt Doherty looks up in wonder.

And Jimmy Black, the Tar Heels' fifth starter, stands nearby watching Coach Dean Smith, deciding how to lead this national championship team for just two more seconds.

The Tar Heels had finally removed the awful weight, presenting UNC with its first national title since 1957 and coming about as close to making Dean Smith weep with pride as he will get. Those Carolina fans who understood what an incredibly difficult win it was were the smart ones. Those who thought it could be won again and again were the silly ones.

Fourteen players had done it in the Carolina way, including special help from Jimmy Braddock, Buzz Peterson and Chris Brust. But as long as there is sports memorabilia, there will be those starters' names: Black, Worthy, Perkins, Doherty and Jordan.

Come across now the last nine years to dirty and steamy Madison Street on Chicago's harsh West Side to the huge block of granite and brick called Chicago Stadium. It is a Sunday, another in an unending string of fresh sunny days in this championship summer for the Windy City.

The Stadium was quivering that day with 20,000 or so souls stuffed into 18,676 seats for the opening game of the 1991 NBA title series between the Chicago Bulls and the Los Angeles Lakers. The five 1982 Carolina starters would also be together again, perhaps for the first time since the spring of 1982.

College coaches Doherty (Davidson) and Black (then South Carolina, now Notre Dame), intergalactic Bulls star Jordan, shoo-in Hall of Famer Worthy, and

Assistant coaches Fogler (behind) and Williams realize what's about to occur. . .

Subs, left to right, Makkonen, Brownlee, Brust, Braddock and Peterson celebrate. . .

Smith, being hugged by Robinson, and Guthridge still know two seconds remain in the game. . .

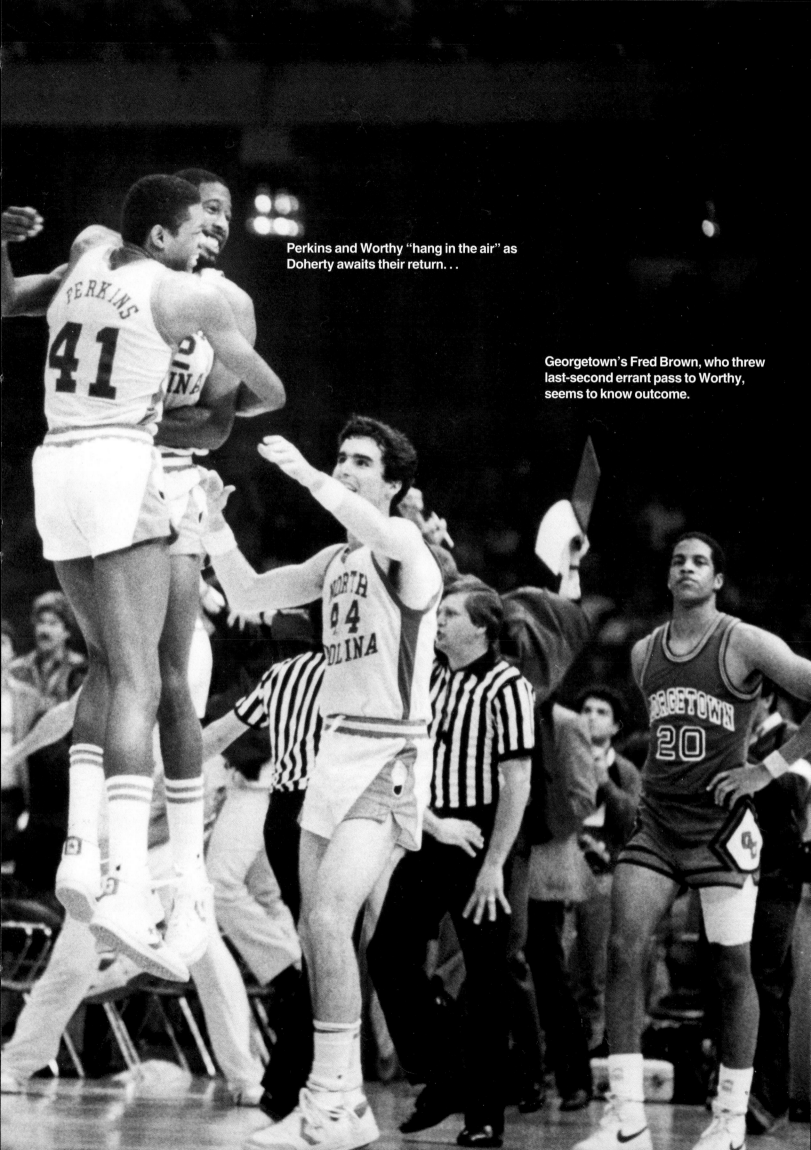

Perkins and Worthy "hang in the air" as Doherty awaits their return. . .

Georgetown's Fred Brown, who threw last-second errant pass to Worthy, seems to know outcome.

Smith says Tar Heels needed Doherty (44) and Black (21) to complement future NBA "first-rounders" Jordan, Perkins and Worthy.

HUGH MORTON

Hall candidate Perkins, the latter two Lakers. Now, with the luxury of hindsight, the special chemistry of the five is so very obvious.

Smith noted over the summer, "The interesting thing about the 1982 team is that we might not have won if we'd had two first-round draft choices [instead of Black and Doherty] to go with Michael, Sam and James."

Now, almost a decade later, Jordan, Perkins and Worthy became the first college teammates to appear together in an NBA final matchup. Mix in Scott Williams on the Bulls' bench and Assistant General Manager Mitch Kupchak of the Lakers, and this thing started to look like a pickup game at Granville Towers.

Former NBA player and current UNC assistant coach Phil Ford noted, "Even in a regular-season NBA game, it's unusual to have two players from the same school. To have four in a game is unheard of."

The *Chicago Sun-Times* went further, remarking, "This series might be the best testimony that the Atlantic Coast Conference is the premier nursery of college basketball," pointing out that Clemson's Horace Grant and Elden Campbell put six ACC alumni among the 24-player total.

But the Carolina players, and the NBA publicity pushers, understandably downplayed the strong UNC flavor in the finals. No group pictures were made, not even for posterity, and the Tar Heels were humble throughout about the old alma mater. As Williams later said, "I guess all of us could have gone out to dinner together, but I doubt if Michael or anybody else would have considered it proper. Anyway, neither group extended an invitation."

While the obvious media drumbeat was Michael vs. Magic Johnson, there was some notice of the Carolina Connection. CBS did a nice piece involving Black, Doherty and Smith (via telephone) at the Stadium and Jordan told the *Chicago Tribune*, "We have a lot of respect for one another because we played in college."

Perhaps more revealing was the Chicago TV station's tape of Worthy arriving at the Stadium for practice, retreating to what he thought was out of camera range, and embracing Jordan. For the most part, however, Williams described it best, "Let's get down to business now, and we'll see each other later in Chapel Hill."

The business they were conducting was Chicago's first title series in the team's 25-year history, and the Lakers' ninth such appearance in the last 12 years. Somehow, and there are basketball experts around even now who can't figure out how, the Bulls had won 61 regular-season games and swept the hated Detroit Pistons on their way to this game No. 1 in June.

Considering the duel between Magic and Michael, the "America's Team" role occupied by the Bulls, the matchup between two of our great cities and even all those Tar Heels, it was a championship ripe with potential.

Ripe for the incomparable Jordan, now a two-time MVP, winner of five consecutive scoring titles, and an all-league defenseman for the fourth straight season.

Ripe for the regal Worthy, a four-time world champion with a career scoring average of 18.6 during regular-season games that turns into 21.4 during his playoff career.

Ripe for the always-quiet Perkins, who had slipped into Los Angeles and worked the baseline for 13 points a game all season and served as the catalyst that the Lakers so badly needed in the winter of 1991.

And even ripe for the star-crossed Williams, a youngster who had dealt with nagging injuries and family tragedy in college, only to find himself undrafted, and then finally sitting near the end of the Bulls' bench eight months ago.

But regardless of age or stature, they are all Tar Heels. Says Worthy, "The age difference with Carolina players is never an issue in the NBA. There is a little arrogance associated with being a Carolina player in the pros . . . We all know we think alike. After all, we've all been raised by the same father."

GAME ONE

Jordan recently told Bob Greene of the *Tribune*, "When they introduce me at home, I never hear another word after 'Carolina.' Then I think that for some of the people in the Stadium, this might be the only time they'll be there." On June 2, 1991, Jordan's introduction went beyond words.

Horrendously for the home crowd, the Bulls panicked, going into that fire drill called "Watch Michael Heat Up." He too-quickly did, pouring in 36 points and distributing 12 assists, but it had that one-man show feel to it. After 25 lead changes and 14 ties, Perkins' rainbow 3-pointer with 14 seconds left produced the 93-91 final score.

Jordan almost won it back with a jumpshot over Perkins from just about the New Orleans spot on the left. It dished out, and he later said, "It took a Carolina guy to beat me."

The Tar Heels simply owned the game individually, Worthy and Perkins both scoring 22 points. The Carolina starters scored 24 of the game's first 37 points and, counting assists, were responsible for 44 of the first quarter's 59 points.

Perkins, who after the game said, "I may not have shown it, but I was excited," had the presence of mind to point to the assisting Johnson in the instant after his winning shot, just as Coach Smith must have preferred.

Worthy, often called Big Game James around the league, told the press at the series' beginning about his title incentive, "Once you've tasted honey, you're not interested in Sweet 'N' Low."

Maybe so, but James was noticeably low-key in Chicago, nursing a very shaky ankle. He seemed more eager to talk about the 1982 experience when given the chance.

"Our championship in New Orleans was the first thing I had ever won in basketball, if you don't count stuff down at the YMCA," he said, settling down with a single Amstel Light in a quiet hotel lobby. He might have immodestly added that he played like a man possessed in the Superdome nine years ago, bulling the Tar Heels through adversity, and scoring a career-high 28 points in his last college game.

He recalled, "Beating Georgetown that night was a must

JIMMY BLACK #21

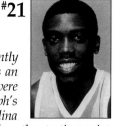

6-3 • Sr. • The Bronx, N.Y.

Lives in South Bend, Ind., where he recently joined the Notre Dame basketball staff as an assistant coach...Previous coaching stops were at UNC (graduate assistant, '84), St. Joseph's (Pa.) University ('85-90) and South Carolina ('91)...Dean Smith's "coach on the floor" as the starting point guard in '82...Most vivid memory: "Team meeting in December when we dedicated ourselves" to winning it...When the final buzzer sounded in '82, Smith and Black were the first Tar Heels to embrace..."We got it for you, Coach," Black said, tears streaming down his face. "I love you, Jimmy," Smith said.

Where Are

Following the 1982

10 years

MATT DOHERTY #44

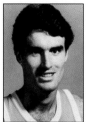

6-7 • So. • East Meadow, N.Y.

Lives in Davidson, N.C., with wife Kelly (Propst)...Married in May, 1991...At 29 years of age, entering his third season as an assistant coach at Davidson College...Says he's "fallen in love with coaching"...Worked as a stockbroker on Wall Street after graduating, but missed basketball...Found a niche as a color commentator for the Davidson Basketball Network and the Tar Heel Sports Network...A starter in '82, versatility earned him the nickname "Adaptable Matt"...Called "the ultimate team player" by Coach Eddie Fogler...Says the '82 Tar Heels had "the kind of chemistry every coach and team dreams about."

JEB BARLOW #43

6-7 • Sr. • Fuquay-Varina, N.C.

Lives in Little Rock, Ark., with wife Marilyn (Luke) of six years...Son Neal joined the family in 1991...Salesman, now in his sixth year with Standard Oxygen Service , a hospital supply company...One of three captains on the '82 team...Played two seasons at UNC, both ending in the NCAA championship game...Most vivid memory: "We were in the locker room after the game, and Coach Smith walks over to me and apologizes for not getting me [a senior] into the game. I couldn't believe it. Here we were, national champions, and he's more worried about me! It sounds crazy, but that's the kind of man he is."

JIM BRADDOCK #24

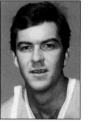

6-2 • Jr. • Chattanooga, Tenn.

Lives in Jacksonville, Fla....Athletic director and basketball coach at St. Matthew's School in Jacksonville...After graduating in 1983, played pro basketball in Ecuador and Holland before returning to the United States...The only non-starter on the '82 team who played in all 34 games...Usually the first Tar Heel off the bench...An outstanding outside shooter, recognized as Carolina's designated zone buster...Strange but true: once made 257 consecutive free throws in a practice session...Only Tar Heel on bench standing when Jordan took the winning jumper against Georgetown..."I knew it was going in."

CECIL EXUM #50

6-6 • So. • Dudley, N.C.

Lives in Victoria, Australia, where he plays professional basketball...Also directs the local junior basketball program in the province of Victoria...Basketball has helped take him around the world...Had previous stints in the professional ranks in both Europe and Scandinavia...Considered by his coaches one of the strongest practice players on the '82 team...Honored by his Tar Heel teammates for three consecutive years ('82-84) with North Carolina's Foy Roberson Award , given to the team's most inspirational player...Remains the only three-time winner in the 49-year history of the award.

JOHN BROWNLEE #32

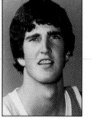

6-10 • Fr. • Fort Worth, Texas

Lives in Irving, Texas, (just outside Dallas) with wife Jennifer (Ott) of two years...Completed his college career at the University of Texas ...Played two years of pro hoops in Europe before returning home...Now works in commerical real estate for B.E.I Real Estate in Dallas...Says the '82 team doesn't come up in conversation too much out in The Lone Star State but, "Everyone knows that team and everyone remembers that game"...Most common question he's asked: These guys, Jordan, Perkins and Worthy, how good are they?...His response: "They were great then and they're great now."

WARREN MARTIN #54

6-11 • Fr. • Axton, Va.

Lives in Pittsboro, N.C....Teacher and basketball coach at Lee County High School...Saw only 20 minutes of action during the first three months of the '82 season, then played in 14 of the last 15 games...Incredible reaching height (9 feet, 5 inches) made him imposing practice competition for Sam Perkins and James Worthy...Holds the UNC records for most blocks in a game (nine) and a season (81)...Also fourth on the all-time list in career field goal percentage (59.4)...Most vivid memories: "James dunking on Sleepy Floyd's head and James and Sam jumping and hugging."

They Now?

National Champions later.

EDDIE FOGLER
Assistant Coach

Lives in Nashville, Tenn., with wife Robin (Sowell), also a Carolina grad...Daughter Emma is three years old...At 43, entering his third year as head coach at Vanderbilt, which he has led to a 38-27 record...Led the Commodores to the 1990 NIT championship...Compiled a 61-32 record as head man at Wichita State from '87-89...With the Tar Heels, played on two Final Four teams ('68, '69) amd coached on four others ('72, '77, '81, '82)...Served a total of 19 years under his mentor, Dean Smith...A key man in the recruiting of such players as Phil Ford, Mitch Kupchak, Michael Jordan, James Worthy and Sam Perkins.

CHRIS BRUST #45
6-9 • Sr. • Babylon, N.Y.

Lives in Chapel Hill with wife Mim (Sapp) of seven years...son Nicholas (4)...Now in his second year of administrative work for the UNC Athletic Department...Co-captain of the '82 team, backed up practice foes Worthy and Perkins...Laughs at memory of Patrick Ewing's intimidation attempts vs. Worthy and Perkins..."They weren't the kind of players to get worried about that kind of thing"...Most vivid memory: Last-second shot taken from midcourt by Georgetown's Sleepy Floyd..."It was right in front of our bench, and it was right on line. I was like 'Oh, no, it's going in,' but it fell about two feet short."

BILL GUTHRIDGE
Assistant Coach

Lives in Chapel Hill with wife Leesie...The couple has two sons, Jamie and Stuart, and a daughter, Megan...The 1991-92 season marks his 25th with the Tar Heels...Serves as Dean Smith's chief assistant...Has turned down a number of top-flight head coaching jobs over the years...Called "one of the top coaches in America" by Smith...Along with Smith and Georgetown's John Thompson, directed the 1976 U.S. Olympic team to the gold medal in Montreal...Has been involved in nine Final Four teams: one as the starting point guard at Kansas State ('58), one as an assistant at KSU ('64) and seven with the Tar Heels.

TIMO MAKKONEN #51
6-11 • Jr. • Lahti, Finland

Lives in Chicago with wife Mary (Bridger) of seven years...Works as a national accounting manager for Hyatt Hotels Corporation...Works "just down the road from Michael Jordan" on Madison Avenue...Earned an MBA degree from UNC in 1986...Says the Tar Heels' amazing run in '82 had a lot to do with the season-ending loss to Indiana in the NCAA finals the year before..."From day one, we were determined to get back at it. Finishing second was a disappointment"...Memories of the championship game: "It has an almost dream-like quality to it. Looking back, it all melts together as one big celebration."

ROY WILLIAMS
Assistant Coach

Lives in Lawrence, Kan., with wife Wanda, son Scott (14) and daughter Kimberly (12)...Native of Asheville, N.C....At 41, entering his third season as head coach at Kansas, the third-winningest program in the history of college basketball (behind UNC and Kentucky)...Led Jayhawks to the NCAA title game a year ago...Named National Coach of the Year in 1990...Selected National Rookie Coach of the Year in '89...Played for the Tar Heel freshman team in 1969...Earned his undergrad education degree from UNC in '72 and his master's in '73...Served 10 years ('79-88) under Dean Smith before moving on to Kansas.

BUZZ PETERSON #22
6-3 • Fr. • Asheville, N.C.

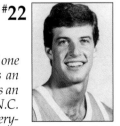

Lives in Raleigh with wife Jan (Maney) of one year...At 28, entering his second year as an assistant coach at N.C. State...Regarded as an excellent recruiter...Says "loyalties are to N.C. State right now, but you never forget everything you take away from the North Carolina basketball program"...Previously assisted at East Tennessee State...Missed first month of '82 season with a stress fracture, but played some crucial minutes in the backcourt down the stretch ...Roomed with fellow freshman "Mike" Jordan...After graduation, played professionally in Belgium and the Continental Basketball Association.

LYNWOOD ROBINSON #4
6-1 • Fr. • Mt. Olive, N.C.

Lives in Boone, N.C....Has been taking post-graduate classes at Appalachian State University...Immediate plans involve going to film school and working in the motion picture industry...Earned undergraduate degree (B.S.) in communications...Previously worked as a consumer credit consultant in Raleigh and as a salesman in Chapel Hill...Worked at the point guard position on the '82 team and played one more year with the Tar Heels before transferring to ASU...Played his high school ball at Southern Wayne High School, where he was on the same squad with '82 Tar Heel teammate Cecil Exum.

We Salute The Tar Heels!

win for us; it simply had to be done . . . The fact that Coach Smith had never won the title was certainly beginning to take its toll on the players."

He might have added the fans. Defending Carolina from fraudulent "choke" charges in the media was a full-time hobby in those days. Smith had one tiny Achilles heel left, and the ink-stained wretches loved to nip at it.

"After 1981 [the NCAA final loss to Indiana]," Worthy recalled, "we were expected to get back to the Final Four, and all of us had some anxiety." Sometime around the regular season's end, point guard and captain Black had finally blown the team's cover, publicly saying that it was time to win one for the coach. It may have worked, but you can be sure Smith still cringes at the memory .

"We couldn't have done it in New Orleans without Jimmy," said Worthy. "He was our link to Coach Smith, our version of Magic Johnson and the guy we looked to."

Worthy is also a believer in the Big Shot Theory, commenting then and now on Jordan, "I'm extremely happy for Michael, as I would be anytime a friend of mine can go to the top like he has. It has been a great story, and it all started with the shot in New Orleans."

Even in the middle of NBA Finals hysteria in Chicago, Worthy carried an air of gentleness mixed with fatigue. There have been peaks and valleys, for sure. Monstrous financial and athletic success, two career-threatening leg injuries, the string of championships, the heartbreak of his Houston arrest on solicitation charges earlier in the season.

He said simply, "It was difficult for me."

Perkins surely brightened Worthy's life by accepting Laker owner Jerry Buss' offer of $19.2 million (for six years) to come over from Dallas. Worthy said, "I have truly enjoyed playing with my old teammate . . . Sam is a safe and good friend. My eyes just lit up when we signed him. "

As for the task at hand in Chicago, Worthy was quietly confident during the Lakers' two-game trip to the Midwest. But even after L.A. swiped Game One, he called the Bulls "a team that will be upset, hungry and aggressive on Wednesday [Game Two]."

What Worthy perhaps knew better than most was that the Bulls never got in rhythm while losing Game One by a single basket, and that his own injury was not responding all that well to several hours of daily therapy. Only in hindsight would anyone remember a Chicago writer's opinion that Scottie Pippen would outplay Worthy because "Worthy's mobility may be hindered because of a sprained left ankle."

GAME TWO

In the game that actually turned the 1991 title momentum over to the Bulls, the once-jumpy Jordan & Company looked like your golfer friend who drinks two beers for his nerves, and then makes every putt all day long.

Jordan was downright ridiculous, hitting 13 in a row at

❀•❀•❀•••

one point, 15 of 18 for the game. By easing himself slowly into the offense, MJ made the necessary room for John Paxson (16), Scottie Pippen (20), Horace Grant (20) and Bill Cartwright (12). The group that a certain tiresome national magazine once called the Jordanaries responded with an NBA Finals record 61.7 percent team shooting performance.

The game is fast becoming a legend in Chicago, first because it is the only finals victory to date in town, second because it certified the Bulls as world title contenders, and third because it contained what is now known in Chicago as The Move.

There was 7:47 (yes, it's true) left in the Bulls' 107-86 romp when Jordan went up sort of mystically to his left, hung there as if deciding what to do, switched the ball to his left hand as Perkins' shadow hung above him and then in slow descent, dumped a little dropshot off the glass and in. The din in the Stadium left an indelible message with Magic, the rest of the Lakers, and most of all with the Bulls.

Williams: showed NBA glimpses. CHICAGO BULLS

The Chapel Hill Road Show continued to rave reviews, but Jordan had reached another level. He had 33 in Game Two with 13 assists, one of those to a jubilant Williams, who also got 15 key minutes and three rebounds. The truly bad news for the Lakers was that Jordan was outscored 68-33 by his fellow starters. On Sunday, those figures had been 37-36.

Michael was oh so loose. He is rumored to have gone out to dinner with Spike Lee, Ahmad Rashad and Denzel Washington, a known Lakers fan.

Scott Williams probably went out to dinner with his girlfriend. Whatever his dining routine, he may have had more to gain from this series than any of his more famous Carolina friends. To begin with the obvious, Jordan, Worthy and Perkins made at least $8 million among them in 1991 salary alone. Williams, we suppose, made the NBA minimum $120,000.

So, when the Bulls later divided their $828,125 winning share, it was a serious budgeting coup for the rookie Tar Heel.

On the other hand, the business realities of the NBA were proving unsettling for Williams at season's end. He said this summer, "The NBA has been a little less glamorous than I thought. Most of the guys in the league are interested mainly in the money, and that distracts me some."

Ignored in the draft much to the distress of his college coach, Williams made the Bulls roster as a free agent partially, he believes, because Jordan was particularly supportive. Williams played some quality minutes late in the season, averaging 2.5 points in 51 games, making 53 of his 104 floor shots.

His view of No. 23 sounds much like a typical fan. He said, "I just don't see how he does it, on the court and off. If he had hooked up with some knuckleheads in the beginning, it might have been different. But he has a lovely family and good people around him."

Williams admits readily to living in a different world than Jordan, and probably Worthy and Perkins. He said, "You might think that because you make this league that you can play with everybody. But I promise that some of these guys are on a higher plane than the other 200 of us in the league."

"The Carolina thing in the series was strong for me," he added, "and I loved being on the court with the men who won the 1982 championship, but I never really felt like I belonged in the foursome until I got some playing time [Games Two, Three, Four and Five]…I hope I showed some glimpses of one day playing on their level."

Williams believes the 1991 Bulls became champions largely because of highly competitive practices and a mission to beat Detroit, a team Williams describes as "definitely dirty." He added, "Everybody got along well on our team this year, and that's not all that common in the NBA."

His own struggle to make this team was a critical moment in his young life, especially now that an Italian team has offered him a seven-figure salary to come over for a couple of years. He recalled, "My brother and Coach Smith told me to be confident, that the right opportunity would come and to take advantage of it." He might well have been describing the Bulls.

GAME THREE

About the only thing the Bulls had not demonstrated in Game Two was how to come from behind. In the first California game, the Bulls cut a 13-point third period deficit to 72-66 with 12 minutes left and then tied the game at 92 with a Jordan jumper over Vlade Divac. The comeback by Chicago was particularly telling because it came in the Great Western Forum, and it came gradually with the Lakers absolutely powerless to stop it.

In overtime, some inescapable cracks began appearing in the proud Laker armor. Even gimpy with a sprained toe,

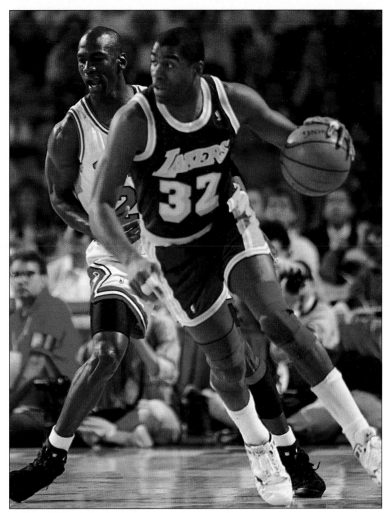

Magic now clearly in Michael's shadow.

BILL SMITH

Jordan ran pretty much free in the 104-96 overtime win on his way to 29 points and nine assists. Perkins worked the paint for 25 points and Worthy managed 19, but it took them 51 and 48 minutes respectively to do it.

The UNC production had exceeded even the wildest expectations by this time. Through three games, Jordan, Worthy and Perkins had scored 221 of the 577 points scored by everybody. A Carolina fan had a hard time sipping a beer without missing a basket. Perkins had made 22 of his 42 shots, Worthy was 29 of 57 and Jordan was (gulp) 40 for 70.

One of the series' more interesting TV moments was when commentator Mike Fratello dragged out that tired old joke about the only person capable of holding Michael Jordan under 20 points is Dean Smith. The joke never tells anybody about Jordan's passing game, his court vision, his defense, his desire to win.

Smith is too professional to argue the point, other than to say, "The obvious difference is in the rules. You can always stop a particular player in college with our rules. College rules are for balance and NBA rules are for stars."

With the Bulls' world title, Jordan passed into something akin to America's modern royalty, an echelon occupied by people like Elvis, Marilyn Monroe, Billy Graham, The Donald. Jordan can't quite walk on Lake Michigan, but there probably aren't many people around him telling him he can't.

Smith commented, "Winning it all was nice for Michael. Unfortunately, people say you need to win everything in order to be successful." The coach added, "I know Michael wanted to do it before very much longer, but I don't believe he thought it would be this year."

Smith, like most Carolina folks, had some very mixed emotions as the championship series unfolded. Obviously, the focus was on Jordan's chance to win one after seven years, and the growing worry that he would join Chicago's Ernie Banks as an immortal who never played for the whole enchilada.

At least one Carolina fan had another perspective, of course. Perkins doesn't say a whole lot, but he makes it count. He said to assembled reporters, "Everyone loves Michael and they want him to have his ring. But there are some others around who have been here just as long, and don't have one either."

Perkins was referring to the oft-forgotten fact that he was the next pick behind Michael in the 1984 draft. Even in eventual defeat for L.A., Smith believes the 1991 playoff served as something of a coming-out for Perkins. The UNC coach commented, "It is nice for people to finally know Sam's name. And getting into the NBA finals is the best way for people to hear your name."

There are not a lot of things left to say about Jordan the player, and to this point he has handled his unnatural fame with grace. While the camp followers and public fawning will continue to test Jordan's character, the man who made it possible for Jordan even to take that jumper in New Orleans believes he is up to it. Worthy said, "I knew he would be exciting as a pro, but I had no idea he would dominate the league this early . . . But we knew he was a man among boys as a player, and he has developed as a sociable person both on and off the court."

In this 1991 series, by the way, Jordan forever ended any reasonable discussion about the relative skills of himself and Magic Johnson. There will be some lingering talk about Johnson's championships, and his value as a huge point guard, but it is all nonsense. Just switch the two players between L.A. and Chicago, and see what would have happened over the last five years.

In the finals, Jordan scored 156 points, Magic 93. Jordan shot .558 from the floor against Magic's .431. Michael had 14 steals to Magic's six. Jordan blocked seven shots, Magic none. Magic committed 22 turnovers to Michael's 18. Magic did lead in assists, 62-57. They don't keep stats on important shots hit, but Jordan must have led 15 to 1. Not being as good as the best player who ever lived is hardly anything for Johnson to be ashamed of.

GAME FOUR

In moving out to their 3-1 series lead, the Bulls just slowly ground up the Lakers in front of a befuddled Jack Nicholson, Dyan Cannon and a Great Western Forum crowd that started leaving even earlier than usual. Jordan, changing shoes in midstream to compensate for his throbbing toe, passed out 13 assists and scored 28. The Bulls led by eight at the half and 16 after 36 minutes.

Worthy's ankle, pressed beyond endurance by too many minutes and the youngster Pippen, forced him to the bench, never to return in 1991. He admitted later, "It got to the point that I was unable to do anything I needed to do." The Bull defenders, able to trap Perkins underneath because the Lakers couldn't have thrown it in Marina del Rey from the perimeter, forced the ex-Carolina great into a 1-for-15 shooting night. Sam was to call it a "tough day at the office."

The Laker fans were mostly in the sunshine before the 97-82 hog killing ended. Southern Cal professor Dallas Willard tried his best to explain to the *Chicago Tribune*, "In Chicago, there is a sense of civic centeredness. You have a long history and people tie into that . . . Out here, the identification with the team is more ego-centered. There's no loyalty to the city."

◆ ◆ ◆

The great drama inspired by the 1991 NBA championship had largely drifted away by the morning of June 12, a few hours before the Forum crowd was to show up to watch the end. Back in Chicago, there were thousands of people who secretly hoped the Bulls would lose Game Five so they could finish the Lakers in the Stadium.

The hundreds of fans who had paid ticket brokers more than $1,000 each for Game Six tickets were unabashedly pulling for the Lakers, lest their tickets be redeemable for $50. NBC, which behind closed doors had worried about a Bulls sweep from the beginning, was now faced with the next worst option. The Lakers were prohibitive underdogs now, with the tentative announcement that neither Worthy nor shooting guard Byron Scott would play at all.

The Bulls kept their mouths shut as much as possible, and must have been none too happy when the Chicago papers covered a squabble between Mayor Richard Daley and a West Side alderman over how to route the Bulls' victory parade. Shades of 1986 when the Shea Stadium scoreboard congratulated the Boston Red Sox for "winning" the World Series.

By sundown of another glorious day in The City With Big Shoulders, the intersection of Chicago and Rush streets was virtually deserted two minutes before the 7 p.m. tipoff. At Rush and Delaware, a dozen horses of the Chicago P.D. Mounted Patrol shifted uneasily in their blue and white vans. An unmarked squad car sat in an alley, the cops catching the introductions on a Watchman and shooting the breeze with two shoeshine boys. Everybody was in this thing together.

You could hardly get through the door at Gingerman's on Division, where stainless steel buckets of Rolling Rock played a close second to the 10 television sets. The block's half-dozen bars were all jammed, and they all exploded when Paxson hit the Bulls' first basket. Paxson, for goodness sakes, had now hit 21 of his last 31 shots.

GAME FIVE
Because Los Angeles was relying on Terry Teagle, Elden

Hugh Morton's now-famous picture of Smith, UNC Sports Information Director Rick Brewer, Worthy and Black in locker room contemplating what had been accomplished.

MANNY MILLAN/SPORTS ILLUSTRATED

Worthy: "My most cherished moment."

went in.

Paxson hit 29 of his last 42 shots in the series, and when this happens on a team that already has Michael Jordan, Horace Grant and Scottie Pippen, you can plan the victory parade anytime you want. Scott Williams, by the way, played eight minutes, giving him 55 minutes in a world championship he dared not have dreamed about last summer.

Chicago's center city filled up, of course, and those magnificent horses kept everybody under control. Now there were television lights up on the roof of Mother's Bar, and all of Division was a champagne shower. The cops just blocked off the street for three blocks and counted on the horses.

Actually, the city was pretty quiet, given the rarity of a world championship in Chicago. There was an unusual pride in the Bulls, however, because this is a two-league baseball town, and you either pull for the Cubs or the Sox. Everybody loves the Bulls. About the loudest sounds into the morning of June 13 were thunderous chants about Detroit inhaling.

Two Tar Heel players won, and two lost. Nobody disagreed with Smith's thought, "I'm only sorry James could not have played at full steam."

Thoughts of Worthy and the street celebration in Chicago inevitably freshen memories of that damp and brusque night in New Orleans, when the Tar Heel bus rolled in front of the Monteleone Hotel in the French Quarter, and the finally-NCAA champion Tar Heels stepped down into that maelstrom on Bienville Street. Many of their parents rode in that bus, and pressed their faces to the windows as their sons were swept one by one up the hotel steps. How the mothers and fathers must have felt.

Okay, the NBA is the big time, with millions of dollars wearing sneakers, and so much riding on the outcome. No argument. But reflect on what Worthy said 10 days earlier as the four-time NBA champion sat with another Carolina guy in that Chicago hotel lobby.

"That night nine years ago in New Orleans seems bigger each year," Big Game James had said. "Maybe it is special because it touched so many hundreds of thousands of people, I don't know. I can tell you this, it is probably my most cherished moment in athletics."

Campbell and Tony Smith to hold off Chicago, and because the Bulls had the luxury of coming home happy even with a loss, this might have been the most intriguing game of all. The Lakers trailed by only one at halftime, and there were murmurs in Gingerman's, Mother's, Houlihan's, etc. in downtown Chicago. Coach Phil Jackson was having none of it, however, keeping both Jordan and Pippen in for 48 minutes. Pippen had the time of his life with 32 points, 13 rebounds and seven assists. Jordan had 30 with 10 assists, and a tiring Perkins hung in there with 22 points and nine rebounds in the Lakers' 108-101 loss.

The night's special quality, however, was centered on Paxson, the lowest paid starting guard in the NBA and a career-long darling of Chicago fans. If you want to feel your skin crawl, just sit in a Chicago Irish bar and watch a slow, white Notre Dame graduate hit five fourth-quarter jumpshots to win a world championship. Jordan seemed to enjoy it the most; once he started pumping his fist and bobbing his head even before one of the Paxson jumpers

1957

35 years later, the perfect season has become folklore in North Carolina. The back-to-back, triple-overtime wins on that March weekend in Kansas City are strictly storybook stuff. But it all happened, and it changed the lives of 10 young men who made it happen. "Not a week goes by without someone asking me," says Raleigh dentist Danny Lotz, a reserve on the 1957 National Champions, who finished 32-0.

Joe Quigg (41), shown playing Wake Forest, made the winning FTs against Kansas; Tommy Kearns (40) driving on Wilt Chamberlain; and Lotz (33) celebrates with teammates.

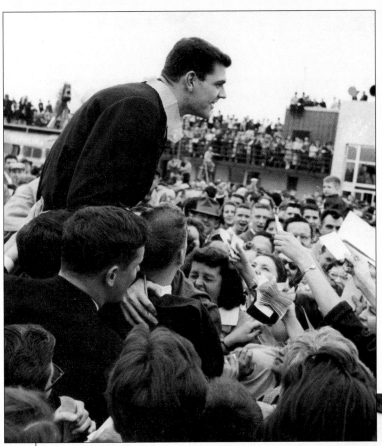

32-0

A crowd of 10,000 greeted the Tar Heels on their triumphant return to the Raleigh-Durham Airport. "Our feet never touched the ground," recalls Quigg, who was carried from the plane.

We Salute The Tar Heels!

'We Can Be Young Again.'

By Alfred T. Hamilton, Jr.

Looking back now over these nearly 40 years since he came to Chapel Hill, he must have been easy for the opposition to dislike. There was a sort of arrogance to this Rosenbluth guy, this New Yorker who came South in the early '50s to play basketball for Frank McGuire at Chapel Hill. Cocky and streetwise, he had a gunslinger quality to him, a bit of a sneer disguised as a smile, an attitude that seemed to say, "Let's start shooting and see who's standing when it's over."

But he never *looked* especially dangerous, lanky and sunken-chested with big feet and the long hands of a musician. If he ever got into a fight in a UNC uniform, it wasn't a very big fight. There was no physical intimidation from No. 10, possibly the best finesse basketball player ever at the University of North Carolina. He was almost effete in the center position on offense, delicately darting around the perimeter like some elusive insect looking for a meal.

But Lennie Rosenbluth, Class of 1957, was a killer in shorts. His right arm was a stiletto, and he specialized in fatal injections. The record is clear, 26.9 points per game over a 76-game career, taking shots from almost anywhere inside 25 feet, at any point in a game. The team scoring leadership in 27 of his last 32 games in college.

The last 32, by the way, were all wins. In his senior season, he became the central figure in what was the most dramatic season in the first century of college basketball. The 1957 national champions from UNC, 32-0 with six overtimes in the Final Four weekend, captured the hearts of Carolina people forever.

OK, the '57 Heels can't be compared to the great teams of the last 25 years in Chapel Hill, and for sure their old-fashioned style would wilt in today's thunderous, physical game. But there will never be a set of Carolina starters quite like Pete Brennan, Bob Cunningham, Tommy Kearns, Joe Quigg and Lennie Rosenbluth.

Least of all like Lennie Rosenbluth, the man who would shoot from the top of the key, tuck his elbows against his rib cage and then backpedal downcourt while his shot still descended. Almost all of those shots, it seems from 35 years away, went in.

He remembers, "Really, I never took a shot I didn't think was going in. I tried to do everything the same with every shot. Elbows in tight, hand and fingers extending straight to the basket. I rarely had a shot off line. When they did miss, they were either long or short."

Listen to Rosie, as he was called, describing again the simple act of shooting a basketball. Who could have imagined what Rosenbluth's shot, and the season his shooting artistry helped achieve, would someday mean? Certainly not Rosenbluth back then, when a hamburger steak at the Goody Shop was a delicacy, or a movie seemed a welcome substitute for a class.

But now Rosenbluth knows, long after the memories of the Tin Can's old running track, the dark-blue cardigan letter sweater and the wood-smoky chill of an autumn dusk in Chapel Hill are almost gone.

Now 57, he says, "We could not have known then what the season would finally mean to the school, the state,

maybe even the game, and to each of us. But I do now, and it seems to get bigger every year. When we hear from people who remember the season, it allows us to relive it. And as long as we can relive it, we can be young again."

The perfect season of 1956-57 took its first feeble step in March of '56 after a less than perfect performance against Wake Forest. It came in the ACC Tournament semifinals in Raleigh's Reynolds Coliseum, where Wake ripped the 18-4 Tar Heels, beating them far worse than the 77-56 score would indicate.

"This was a terrible whipping we took from Wake Forest," Rosenbluth recounts in his distinctive lispy Bronx accent, unchanged by 40 years in the South. "It was one of the worst defeats we ever had, and Coach wouldn't let us forget it the next year."

It was to be an important lesson, since the fundamentally sound and oh-so-well-coached Demon Deacons nearly drove North Carolina crazy in four games during the title season, all Wake losses by eight, three, five and two points. Coach Bones McKinney's team was patient, took care of the ball and made most of their big shots.

Rosenbluth's theory: "Wake Forest, I believe, really wanted to beat the guys from New York [all five UNC starters]. Wake's players were almost all from North Carolina, and I think the New York thing was very important to them."

While Rosenbluth remembers very little rancor in the UNC-Big Four rivalries, he is not overly happy with McKinney, whom Rosenbluth believes unfairly criticized his defensive skills. "Bones was always saying I couldn't play defense, but I consider it a bad rap. I wasn't terribly fast, but I got there. If teams changed their offenses to try and put a man where I played in the zone, I never saw it work."

Prior to the season's beginning, Rosenbluth was coping with some other critics closer to Woollen Gym, specifically the teammates who thought he had shot too much as a junior, and would likely gun again as a senior. One of only three seniors on the team, Rosie had been named captain by McGuire.

"There definitely was some complaining," he remembers, "and some of it was about me shooting too much. They gave their gripes and I listened.

"I think everybody on that team wanted to shoot, with the exception of Cunningham, who always preferred to pass the ball. But we got it talked out once and for all. And I still believe they wanted to go to me at the end of games."

Consistent shooting from several players, in the final analysis, was the essence of the team. Point guard Kearns made his open shot, Brennan and Quigg hit baseline jumpers in traffic or squared-up against zones, and Rosenbluth would make just about any shot he wanted unless he was double-teamed, and that tactic just played into McGuire's hands.

Rosenbluth notes, "Coach's whole idea was that the ball

Rosenbluth went to UNC after failing a tryout for legendary N.C. State coach Everett Case in Raleigh's Thompson Gymnasium.

is gold, and you don't waste gold. We played a very controlled freelance. Because both Quigg and I could go inside and outside, most people played zone against us. Then we just surrounded the zone and waited for the good shot.

"Let me tell you, basketball becomes a simpler game when you have a few people who can shoot."

By the time he was a college senior, Rosie was 25 years old and a veteran of maybe 1,000 YMCA and Catskill league games even before he came to Staunton Military Academy in Virginia, and then Chapel Hill. Because 21-year-olds could play high school ball in New York (accommodating Korean war vets), and with a season lost to a coaches' strike, Rosie had hardly any prep career.

But he was a playground scoring machine, learning to shoot from all five positions and playing at times exclusively with and against black players whose own legends were still locked away inside the mean fences of New York's playgrounds. Rosenbluth recalls, "When I was 17, I played on a team from the Carlton YMCA with Sihugo Green and Ray Felix. I bet we won 80 in a row."

After an unsuccessful audition for Everett Case in Raleigh's old Thompson Gymnasium (Rosenbluth admits he was out of shape and probably looked bad), Rosenbluth was advised by college scout Harry Gotkin to wait until then-St. John's coach Frank McGuire decided between Alabama and North Carolina. The rest, of course, is our story.

Rosenbluth remains philosophical about the rejection from the Silver Fox in Raleigh. He says, "Coach Case also turned down Dickie Hemric, so I never felt too bad. Shavlik (Ronnie), Hemric and Rosenbluth. That wouldn't have been a bad front line."

Nor, of course, was Quigg, Brennan and Rosenbluth a bad front line. The early-season feuding behind them, the ❀•❖•❖•••

Order more copies of CAROLINA COURT plus our other magazines, books and tapes!

Call 1-800-447-3649 For Credit Card Orders
Or Send a Check Payable to Village Sports (PO Box 3300, Chapel Hill, NC 27515).
Just copy this order form and mail in—do not tear out!

'57 Tar Heels took the first steps down the long run. For the record, the first five were Furman, Clemson, George Washington, South Carolina (overtime) and Maryland.

"We had talked our problems out at the beginning, and we had a meeting or two as the season went on," the captain recalls. "I don't believe it is possible for a team with a serious dissension problem to win. And we won."

Facts From '57

1. *Rosenbluth shared none of McGuire's superstitions, including the coach's preference for the team's white uniforms, and playing on rainy nights.*

2. *The blue and white basketball which Carolina opened warmups with somehow ended up in the Charles Rouse residence on Fairview Road in Raleigh. Years later, some teen-agers unknowingly dribbled all the paint and signatures off in the driveway.*

3. *Ken Rosemond, a 26-year-old married guard, was Rosie's best friend on the team. Rosemond often drove the "smoking car" on short road trips.*

4. *In 1952, Coach McGuire's office was also the ticket booth.*

5. *Rosie was engaged to the former Pat Oliver of Mt. Airy during the perfect season. Now, they have been married for 34 years.*

Rosenbluth on the toughest team rule: "We spent a lot of time dodging old Buck Freeman [McGuire's long-late assistant coach] because he didn't want us dating during the season. He said basketball and girls don't mix."

Rosenbluth, wife Pat, two grown children and a 14-month-old grandson are Miamians now. Since 1965, Rosie has been in Florida where he has had twin careers in high school teaching and coaching. He and Pat sometimes talk about moving back to North Carolina, maybe Chapel Hill. But then, the grandchildren will be Floridians.

His memories of Chapel Hill are as much centered on just being there as playing basketball. "I was pretty much just a normal kid; I roomed with whomever I got paired up with. I remember the players ate a lot of our meals at the Monogram Club, and then we were switched over to Lenoir Hall. We just got in line and waited like everybody else."

Rosie remembers feeling no pressure at all as the '57 Heels moved through their dream season. "I believe both coaches were feeling a lot of pressure; maybe they knew how much it all might mean. But the players just didn't seem to feel it."

But Carolina had been expected to be good, and by New Year's the Tar Heels were 14-0, Dixie Classic champions, and ranked second in the nation behind Kansas. It was time to load up the caravan, Rosemond behind the wheel in the smoking car, and drive over to Raleigh to play N.C. State. In retrospect, the last five minutes of this game defined the season.

Carolina burst open a close game and ravaged the Pack, 83-57, in front of 12,400 highly offended State fans. In the last few minutes, McGuire roamed in front of the bench, raving at the Tar Heels as if the game were close. Rosenbluth remembers, "We were killing them, and he wanted us to play even harder. We were laughing, but we made sure he didn't see us laugh."

Kansas had lost the night before and Carolina became No. 1. No T-shirts were printed, nobody made the front cover of *Sports Illustrated*. The best anybody could do was a little cardboard decal, and that didn't even have a sticky back. It is hard to remember college basketball as such a simple thing, but it was.

According to Rosenbluth, a calm settled over the All-American at this juncture. "Halfway through the year, I went ahead and predicted we would go all the way. Somehow, I just sensed we had a good chance. It seemed there was a different hero every night, and winning began to seem inevitable."

Games 16 and 17 tested that theory. First, there was Maryland leading by four with less than two minutes to play at College Park. Kearns mostly, along with Cunningham, got Carolina out of that mess. The 17th win

"Halfway through the year, I went ahead and predicted we would go all the way. . .It seemed there was a different hero every night, and winning began to seem inevitable."

was at home against Duke, 75-73 behind 35 points from Rosie.

When the 6-foot-5, 180-pound Rosenbluth got to running hot, there was something of a frenzy about it. Rosie always seized the moment, and defenders panicked. No. 10 would simply get open, get a pass and make one of about 12 kinds of shots he liked. Opponents' eyes would glaze over, and Rosie would just keep jabbing with the stiletto. The most outrageous was a turnaround, no-look jumpshot from the corner, maybe 19 feet away.

"It's really an easy shot," he says today. "Just because your back is to the basket doesn't mean you can't sense where it is. I just whirled, kept my right elbow in, and released the ball from the center of my forehead. I don't think there ever was a defensive player who was really ready for it."

The last two league games came against Wake Forest and Duke, the Wake game played on the road without a bed-ridden Quigg. Carolina escaped again from the Deacons, 69-64, and broke away at Duke after trailing with five minutes left. That left the Tar Heels at 24-0.

"When the season ended," Rosenbluth remembers, "I was in my hottest streak of the year. Over the next eight games, I felt relied on to score . . . I was comfortable with that."

Where Are They Now?

Following the 1957 team 35 years later.

FRANK McGUIRE
Head Coach

Lives in Columbia, S.C., with wife Jane...First wife, the former Patricia Johnson, died in 1967...Three children, Patricia, Carol Ann and Frank, Jr....Coached the Tar Heels for nine years (1952-61), between college stints at alma mater St. John's (1947-51) and South Carolina (1964-80) and one year in the pros with the Philadelphia Warriors...Remains active in USC athletics...Revered as a superb coach, psychologist and motivator...On the famous jump ball between the 7-foot Chamberlain and 5-11 Kearns to start the game: "We weren't going to win the tap anyway, so why not?"...On the title game: "I told them it wasn't North Carolina vs. Kansas. I told them it was our five against Wilt Chamberlain!"

ROY SEARCY   #22
6-4 • Jr. • Draper, N.C.

Lives in Winston-Salem with wife Rhoda (Moyer) of eight years...Two daughters, Robin and Courtney, from a previous marriage...An expecting first-time grandfather, October arrival...Has worked in real estate since '74, now a broker for Prudential Piedmont Triad Properties in Winston-Salem ...Says it amazes him that people still talk about a game played 35 years ago...Most vivid memory: "Seeing 10,000 people at the airport. It was mindboggling."...On the team: "We had a lot of fun. We were a loose group, and the off-court stuff we got into was just terrific." On the miracle season: "There are certain times in a game when you just have to have a bucket. At those times, we had Lennie Rosenbluth."

PETE BRENNAN   #35
6-6 • Jr. • Brooklyn, N.Y.

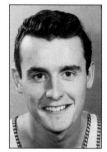

Lives in Spring Lake, N.J....President of his own men's clothing company in New York...Saved the Tar Heels' dream season in the Final Four game against Michigan State...At the end of the first overtime, with UNC trailing by two, he grabbed a missed FT and went the length of the floor to score and send the game into a second overtime...Strange but true: Brennan abandoned his old Buick in front of the Monogram Club on campus at the beginning of the '57 season. He thought it would be bad luck to move it during the winning streak. At various times during the season, it was painted blue by UNC students, red by N.C. State fans, then blue again. Finally, after the championship game, he put his lucky charm up for sale.

DANNY LOTZ   #33
6-7 • So. • Northport, N.Y.

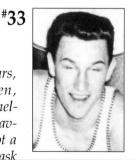

Lives in Raleigh with wife of 25 years, Anne (Graham)...Three children, Jonathan (20), Morrow (18) and Rachel-Ruth (16)...Dentist in Raleigh since leaving the Air Force in 1965...Says not a week goes by that a patient doesn't ask about playing against Wilt or playing for a national championship team...Most vivid memory: Standing at foul lane, opposite Pete Brennan, in final seconds of national semifinal vs. Michigan State and hoping for an MSU miss (Brennan grabbed missed FT, scored, UNC won)...On Lennie Rosenbluth:"If I had to pick a team today to start with, I'd pick Lennie first and Michael Jordan second. If they had the 3-point shot back then, Lennie would've scored 50 points a game."

BOB CUNNINGHAM   #32
6-4 • Jr. • New York, N.Y.

Lives in Westport, Conn., with wife Anne (Sklar) of three years...Three children, Robert, Margaret and Ellen, whose mother Frances passed away in 1982...In 13th year as national accounts manager for Sensormatic Electronic in New York after 12 years with IBM...Says sheer skill was key to the team..."There was a chemistry there, a lot of camaraderie and respect, but the bottom line is that there was a lot of talent on that team"...Says team's success helped him later in the business world..."A lot of senior managers in companies were in college at that time...They remember the team and the names very well"...On how underdog UNC topped mighty Wilt: "Five guys beat one. It's still a team sport."

BUCK FREEMAN

Assistant Coach

Long-time assistant to McGuire, passed away in 1974...Considered the perfect tactical strategist to complement McGuire's personal motivational expertise...Graduated from St. John's in 1927 and later served there as the head basketball coach, head baseball coach and athletic director...Coached McGuire, the player, at St. John's and later joined McGuire, the coach, at UNC...Called "a basketball genius" by a consensus of his former players...A true student of the game, once figured the exact number of rotations a free throw should have (2 1/2)..."He was married to basketball," says Danny Lotz. "He wanted you to think about nothing but basketball and studying all year long."

GEHRMANN HOLLAND #31

6-3 • So. • Beaufort, N.C.

Lives in Pine Knoll Shores, N.C....Four children: Laura (29), Hannah (27), Christian (22) and Glenn (18), a football player at UNC...Works just down the road in his hometown as owner/operator of the Beaufort House Restaurant...Says the '57 starters didn't really go undefeated: "We beat them all the time in practice"...Says McGuire kept the little-used reserves motivated: "He used to say, 'Not only does UNC have the No. 1 team in the country, we have the No. 2 team in the country, too'"...What made the championship team special? "We were a loose bunch of guys who didn't take ourselves too seriously, but on game days we always found a way to do whatever it took to win."

TOMMY KEARNS #40

5-11 • Jr. • Bergenfield, N.J.

Lives in Darien, Conn., with wife Betsy (Wright) of 33 years...Three children, Elizabeth (30), Tom (28) and Caroline (24)...Long-time investment banker with Bear Stearns, now a private consultant...Calls Frank McGuire "a great coach" and Buck Freeman "one of the greatest strategists of all time"..."We won games we shouldn't have; people don't remember we played only six games in Woollen Gym that year...winning back-to-back games in triple overtime changed all of our lives — it was very helpful in my business career"...On his famous jump ball with Wilt Chamberlain to start the game: "I'm always asked what was I doing when the ball went up. Watching it!"

KEN ROSEMOND #11

5-8 • Jr. • Hillsborough, N.C.

Lives in Palm City, Fla., with wife of 27 years, Barbara (Ballenger), when not taking care of business in Durham ...Owner of Ultralook, a manufacturer of ultra suede garments...Sons Kenny (33) and Kevin (30) work for his Durham office...Still plays a lot of golf in Chapel Hill...Before 18 years in the apparel business, coached for 16 years...Head coach at Georgia after assisting at UNC (seven years) and South Carolina (one)...Says perfect season almost ended at Maryland, UNC down five with less than two minutes to play..."McGuire called a timeout and told everyone to be good losers and shake hands after the game"...Says "never a month goes by" that he doesn't hear questions about 1957.

JOE QUIGG #41

6-9 • Jr. • Brooklyn, N.Y.

Lives in Fayetteville, N.C., with wife Carol (Moser) of 29 years...two children, Shannan (28) and Joe (25)...A practicing dentist in Fayetteville since 1966 ...Played with N.Y. Knicks for one year before suffering a broken leg...Returned to UNC to assist McGuire and Dean Smith on '59 squad...Spent three years in Germany with the Army after graduating from UNC dental school in '63...Most vivid memory: game-winning free throws vs. Kansas..."It was a question of mechanics. I wasn't nervous. Luckily, they went in."...On the 10,000-person reception at RDU: "Our feet never touched the ground. We were carried from the plane, carried to our cars. We felt like movie stars."

BOB YOUNG #20

6-6 • Sr. • New York, N.Y.

Divides his time between Manhattan, N.Y., and Naples, Fla., with wife Patricia (Alpert) of 27 years...Son Kevin is a doctor...Worked 24 years for New Yorker *magazine before entering into several publishing ventures of his own...Says '57 season often comes into conversation this way: "Where'd you go to school?" UNC. "Did you play basketball?" Yes. "When?" 1957. "You mean you were on THE TEAM?"...On the subsequent success of the '57 team: "It was basketball that gave us an opportunity to attend UNC when we couldn't have afforded it otherwise. But I think the educational experience itself had more to do with any future successes than winning the championship."*

The '57 Tar Heels (L-R): Searcy, Cunningham (32), Rosenbluth (10), Brennan, McGuire, Quigg (hidden) and Holland (31).

Facts from '57

1. Rosenbluth scored a school-record 47 points in the season opener against Furman. The figure held up until Billy Cunningham scored 48 against Florida State in 1964.

2. The 83-57 rout of the Wolfpack in mid-season that made Carolina No. 1 was only the third time UNC had ever beaten an Everett Case team, and the first time by more than four points.

3. The issue of four Catholic starters and one Jew (Rosenbluth) simply never came up on the team. Rosie says, "McGuire started that business for the media."

4. The '57 Heels finished the season with only 10 players, having lost Tony Radovich, Stan Groll and Billy Hathaway to either eligibility or academic problems.

5. Frank McGuire helped change the school's basketball nickname from White Phantoms to Tar Heels, although the exact year is still murky.

Rosenbluth on personal accomplishments: "Being chosen National Player of the Year in 1957 is certainly a highlight, but you have to remember that the award didn't have much fanfare beyond a little letter in the mail."

◆ ◆ ◆

The national champions played seven games in

Raleigh's Reynolds Coliseum in 1957, including the ACC Tournament opening-round game against Clemson. Rosenbluth scored a still-record 47 points against the Tigers, on the way to a still-record 106 points for the tournament.

A day later, the most remembered shot of Lennie Rosenbluth's career nudged the Tar Heels past tenacious Wake Forest for the fourth time, this one in the ACC semifinals. The moment was set up by Wake's big, red-headed Jim Gilley, who hit two free throws with 55 seconds left, giving the Deacons a 59-58 lead. The majority of the full house in Reynolds was thundering over the prospect of these cocky Carolina guys finally losing and getting the hell back to Chapel Hill.

The Carolina haters couldn't wait. There would be no NCAA now, no Team of Destiny, no hot shots from New York building the foundation of everything that was to come in Atlantic Coast Conference basketball.

Except that Rosenbluth came up from the baseline, took an entry pass from Cunningham, felt a little bump from Ralph Branca (oops, Wendell Carr) and whipped in *a 14-foot hookshot.* Looking back in the summer of 1991, he says, "I promise I would not have taken the shot if I hadn't felt the

❄ • ❄ • ❄ • • •

contact. I was determined to get two foul shots out of it."

But always the gunner, he quickly adds, "But if anybody had ever watched me warm up [most people did] they would have seen me take hook shots from the corner, and even from the top of the key. I will admit that McGuire probably would have killed me if I had taken those shots in a game."

Rosenbluth downplays the importance of the resulting three-point play and the 61-59 lead which held up as the final score. He explains, "If the shot hadn't gone in, or I hadn't been fouled, somebody else would have saved us. There was plenty of time left."

The victory over Wake Forest, so bitter for the Wake people that it may be central to the bilious hatred most

". . .If anybody had ever watched me warm up, they would have seen me take hook shots from the corner, and even from the top of the key. I will admit that Coach McGuire probably would have killed me if I had taken those shots in a game."

Deacon fans now seem to have for Carolina, springboarded UNC through the tournament and to regional NCAA playoff wins over Yale, Canisius and Syracuse.

The Municipal Auditorium in Kansas City still sits there today in K.C.'s center city. It still has the movie-house windowed doors, and dark lobby, but basketball left the arena maybe 15 years ago. On that gray, rainy weekend 35 years ago, Municipal Auditorium became the focus of North Carolina basketball history.

The day before the Friday night semifinal against Michigan State, Rosie remembers, the Tar Heels watched a film of the Spartans. "They didn't look good in the film, and I think we overlooked them . . . And I had a terrible game, although Johnny Green [MSU's great defensive center] had something to do with that."

Carolina's panicky play took the Tar Heels to the brink. In the game's second overtime, Green was on the foul line, MSU ahead 64-62 with 11 seconds left. Pete Brennan then made the most important individual effort of the year. He took down Green's miss, went the length of the floor and hit an off-balance jumpshot for the tie at two seconds.

Carolina won 74-70 in three overtimes. Rosie remembers, "I had the best view of Brennan's play. I was running right behind him going down the court and had my hands over the rim as his shot went in."

The championship game has been immortalized for all sorts of reasons. Another three overtimes, of course, which will always make the 1957 Final Four unlike any other in history. The completion of an undefeated season, the matchup of the two top-ranked teams in the nation, the first final televised into North Carolina.

But the game's real magic lies in Kansas center Wilt

Chamberlain, an amazing man of his time who retains much of that myth even now. Fans packed the baseline six deep to watch him take layups in Kansas City. It wasn't against the rules to dunk during warmups back then, and Chamberlain would sort of get on his tip-toes and just throw the ball down and through.

For Carolina, according to Rosenbluth, it was important to pay as little attention to Chamberlain as possible. He explains, "Most of us had seen him play in the Catskills, and we just weren't that much in awe of him. We figured those dunks only counted two points each, and we just tried to force him into taking his fadeaway."

Offensively, Rosenbluth and Chamberlain pretty much washed, Rosie with 20 and Chamberlain with 23, including 11 of 16 free throws. Rosenbluth committed some admittedly impatient fouls and ultimately was disqualified with 1:45 left in regulation. The game to that point had been an agonizing chess match between McGuire and Kansas coach Dick Harp, who later became an assistant coach under Dean Smith.

Rosenbluth is convinced that the Jayhawks had Carolina in deep trouble with a five-point lead and around eight minutes left. Kansas then chose to hold the ball, and McGuire dropped the exhausted Tar Heels back in their zone. Rosie says, "Their freeze cooled them off. If they had kept running, they may well have built a double-figure lead, and we would have been finished."

Carolina managed a 48 tie in regulation and then the teams struggled through three overtimes. Rosenbluth, of course, got to chew his fingernails and watch. With KU ahead, 53-52, Quigg was fouled in the act of shooting with six seconds left. It led to a surprising timeout called by McGuire, a calm huddle, McGuire saying, "Joe, after you make both shots, get back and play good defense."

And then, the most vivid moment of all for Rosenbluth.

"The strongest memory I have of the whole thing is Joe hitting those free throws," says Rosenbluth. "He carried the greatest pressure of all, and lived the dream of anyone who has ever played basketball by simply making the shots."

A few seconds later, Quigg slapped away a pass intended for Chamberlain in the lane. And then, almost in slow motion it seems, the team converged at mid-court and celebrated with maybe a dozen Carolina fans. Rosie recalls, "I remember especially the strange hush that came over the place, and then everybody just filed out."

◆ ◆ ◆

Facts From '57

1. McGuire and Rosenbluth missed the team's monster reception at Raleigh-Durham Airport the following day, when an estimated 10,000 people threatened to spill onto the runways. The coach and star made a 10-second appearance on the Ed Sullivan Show.

2. It was raining the night Carolina played Kansas, and the Tar Heels wore white. Maybe McGuire was onto something.

❈•⁛❈•••

Rosenbluth battled Chamberlain (left) to a standstill in the '57 title game.

Classic Rock

Rock Classic

Roll

The action and excitement of Tar Heel Basketball is on Rock 93.9! If you're watching at home, turn down the sound and tune in Woody and Mick on Rock 93.9 with all of the heart-stopping play-by-play and interesting commentary! Or take Rock 93.9 along with you to the Smith Center and listen in the stands! The Tar Heels mean excitement, and nobody covers 'em better than Rock 93.9!

Rock 93.9 FM
Classic Rock & Roll

Lennie and wife Pat now live in Coral Gables, Fla., where Lennie is a teacher and coach at the local high school.

3. Tommy Kearns went out to jump against Chamberlain to open the game, mostly because UNC did not want a quick Kansas layup. Later, businessman Kearns handled many investments for Chamberlain.

4. By some early accounts, Carolina went 33-0, counting an opener against the semi-pro McCray Eagles. Of course, 32-0 has prevailed.

5. Carolina was a classic McGuire "Iron Man" program in 1957. Roy Searcy, Bob Young, Danny Lotz and Ken Rosemond got a few minutes, but not many.

Rosenbluth on shooting Quigg's free throws himself: "The way it turned out, I'm glad it was Joe shooting them."

Rosenbluth has taught American History at Coral Gables High School for 27 years. Before his retirement from coaching two years ago, he coached both public and private school basketball teams, building a record of 425-140, and winning a private school state championship eight years ago.

Even as a Florida coach, his connection with North Carolina State continued, this time with a young Chris Corchiani, who played for Rosenbluth in the eighth and ninth grades, the latter on a state champion. Coach Rosie says, "He simply could not be defensed as a ninth grader, and he played the same way we later saw in college."

If there is a celebration next spring of the '57 team's 35th anniversary, Rosenbluth says he will come to Chapel Hill. He will be substantially over his playing weight, graying at the temples, but with the same toothy smile that must have infuriated opponents when he started sticking in all those exotic one-handers.

He has visited the Smith Center and still can't get over seeing his No. 10 hanging high in the light-blue overhead of the cavernous arena, so far removed from those temporary bleachers in Woollen Gym, the cheerleaders in bobby socks, the high-topped Converse shoes.

He said this summer, "I think retiring my jersey might be the nicest honor I have. It is very special for me to imagine it hanging there every night."

Carolina's all-time leading per game scorer looks back over life as a glass more than half full, punctuated by his senior year in college and that strange season's effect on his life. He has no regrets, save for the fact that the national championship was not accompanied by a ring, as it is now. He despairs, "I think they might have given us watches, but mine's long gone if they did."

The pressure of his life in whatever form is winding down now. He is five years from retirement as a teacher, a grandfather once and game for more, and the owner of a cozy, 23-foot power boat, Dream Season. He is far removed from that precious glory of 35 years ago, when so much happened to those young Carolina men.

He says, "I guess you could say that all Pat and I hope for now is clear weather on Biscayne Bay."

(As a 12-year-old boy, Alfred Hamilton watched the Tar Heels win the national championship in Kansas City. He was also in New Orleans in 1982 when they won it again.)

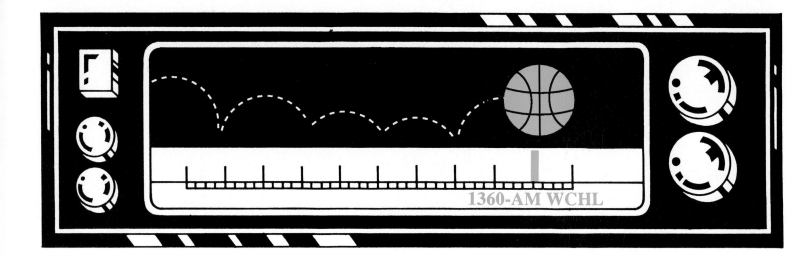

The Station To Turn To

WCHL has full coverage of Tar Heel basketball, from pre-game to the locker room and everything in between. Tune in to 1360AM WCHL for regularly scheduled Tar Heel sports coverage as well as total game coverage.

Game Day Coverage:
- **Early Tar Heel Preview, sponsored by Hello Deli!**
- **Woody Durham & Mick Mixon's Tar Heel play-by-play**
- **Coca-Cola Post Game Plus**

Regular Sports Coverage:
- Morning Sports with Woody Durham
- Afternoon Sports with Mick Mixon
- ACC Hotline with Woody Durham, Tuesday Nights at 8:00 pm
- Carolina Blue Line with Coach Dean Smith, Thursday Nights at 7:00 pm
- The Dean Smith Show, weekdays 12:50 pm and 7:05 pm

1360 WCHL
Non-Stop Chapel Hill

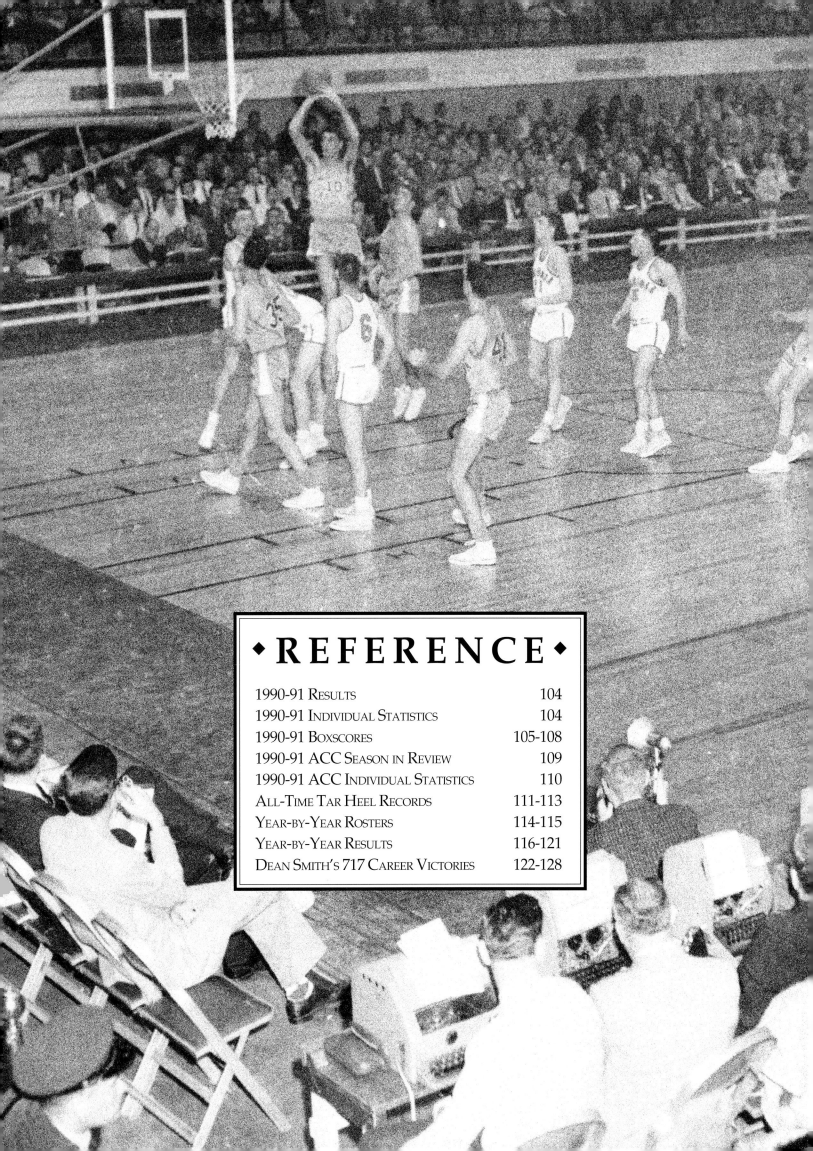

◆ REFERENCE ◆

1991 Tar Heels: 29-6 Overall, 10-4 ACC

RESULTS

San Diego State	W	99-63	Home	21,572	Nov. 24
Jacksonville	W	104-61	Home	18,103	Nov. 27
South Carolina	L	74-76	Charlotte, N.C.	22,680	Nov. 30
Iowa State	W	118-93	Charlotte, N.C.	20,384	Dec. 1
Connecticut	W	79-64	Home	21,572	Dec. 6
Kentucky	W	84-81	Home	21,572	Dec. 10
Alabama	W	95-79	Home	21,572	Dec. 15
Purdue	W	86-74	Away	14,123	Dec. 22
DePaul	W	90-75	Orlando, Fla.	6,027	Dec. 29
Stanford	W	71-60	Orlando, Fla.	4,841	Dec. 30
Cornell	W	108-64	Away	4,473	Jan. 3
Notre Dame	W	82-70	East Rutherford, NJ	12,702	Jan. 5
Maryland	W	105-73	Home	21,572	Jan. 9
Virginia	W	89-86	Away	8,864	Jan. 12
Duke	L	60-74	Away	9,314	Jan. 19
Wake Forest	W	91-81	Away	14,407	Jan. 23
Georgia Tech	L	86-88	Home	21,572	Jan. 27
Clemson	W	90-77	Away	10,500	Jan. 31
N.C. State	L	91-97	Away	12,400	Feb. 6
N.C. State	W	92-70	Home	21,572	Feb. 7
Virginia	W	77-58	Home	21,572	Feb. 9
Wake Forest	W	85-70	Home	21,572	Feb. 13
Maryland	W	87-75	Away	14,500	Feb. 16
The Citadel	W	118-50	Home	19,207	Feb. 18
Clemson	W	73-57	Home	20,148	Feb. 23
Georgia Tech	W	91-74	Away	10,113	Feb. 28
Duke	L	77-83	Home	21,572	March 3
Clemson	W	67-59	Charlotte, N.C.	23,532	March 8
Virginia	W	76-71	Charlotte, N.C.	23,532	March 9
Duke	L	96-74	Charlotte, N.C.	23,532	March 10
Northeastern	W	101-66	Syracuse, NY	17,206	March 15
Villanova	W	84-69	Syracuse, NY	17,523	March 17
Eastern Michigan	W	93-67	East Rutherford, NJ	19,544	March 22
Temple	W	75-72	East Rutherford, NJ	19,601	March 24
Kansas	L	73-79	East Rutherford, NJ	47,100	March 30

Player	G-GS	Min.-Avg.	FG	PCT.	3FG	PCT.	2FGPct.	FT	PCT.	Reb.-Avg.	PF-FO	A	TO	BS	ST	Pts.-Avg.
Cherry	20-1	58-2.9	10-14	.714	1-1	1.000	.692	9-13	.692	8-0.4	2-0	11	5	1	5	30-1.5
Chilcutt	35-33	937-26.8	175-325	.538	5-19	.263	.556	65-85	.765	231-6.6	38-0	47	60	35	41	420-12.0
Davis	35-20	851-24.3	161-309	.521	64-131	.489	.545	81-97	.835	85-2.4	35-0	66	37	9	30	467-13.3
Fox	35-32	999-28.5	206-455	.453	67-196	.342	.533	111-138	.804	232-6.6	103-3	131	102	17	70	590-16.9
Harris	27-1	118-4.4	14-42	.333	4-17	.235	.400	8-11	.727	21-0.8	14-0	12	18	0	7	40-1.5
Lynch	35-28	912-26.1	172-329	.523	7-10	.700	.517	85-135	.630	258-7.4	92-2	41	86	15	49	436-12.5
Montross	35-9	531-15.2	81-138	.587	0-0	.000	.587	41-67	.612	148-4.2	79-0	11	32	30	6	203-5.8
Phelps	30-4	293-9.8	25-51	.490	2-9	.222	.548	16-21	.762	33-1.1	30-0	58	40	3	27	68-2.3
Reese	33-2	291-8.8	56-105	.533	3-5	.600	.530	18-33	.545	54-1.6	14-0	17	20	2	9	133-4.0
Rice	35-30	984-28.1	91-199	.457	26-63	.413	.485	79-109	.725	62-1.8	51-0	207	76	1	38	287-8.2
Rodl	35-13	431-12.3	46-81	.568	12-27	.444	.630	23-37	.622	53-1.5	39-0	62	36	6	13	127-3.6
Rozier	34-1	317-9.3	64-136	.471	0-0	.000	.471	39-69	.565	101-3.0	41-1	18	30	17	12	167-4.9
Salvadori	31-0	102-3.3	18-35	.514	0-0	.000	.514	12-19	.632	27-0.9	13-0	0	5	8	1	48-1.5
Sullivan	34-1	167-4.9	10-23	.435	1-5	.200	.500	13-20	.650	22-0.6	18-0	18	10	1	6	34-1.0
Wenstrom	24-0	59-2.5	5-15	.333	0-0	.000	.333	7-12	.583	21-0.9	6-0	0	6	3	1	17-0.7
Team Totals	35	7050	1134-2257	.502	192-483	.398	.531	607-866	.701	1455-41.6	574-6	699	566	148	315	3067-87.6
Opponents	35	7050	974-2329	.418	197-622	.317	.455	362-568	.637	1225-35.0	708-21	519	635	115	270	2507-71.6

INDIVIDUAL CAREER STATS FOR RETURNING PLAYERS

PLAYER	YR	G	FIELD GOALS M-A	PCT	FREE THROWS M-A	PCT	REB	AVE	A	TO	S	PF-D	PTS	AVE
Cherry	Fr.	8	1-7	14.3	0-3	00.0	1	0.1	2	1	1	1-0	2	0.3
	So.	20	10-14	71.4	9-13	69.2	8	0.4	11	5	5	2-0	30	1.5
TOTALS		28	11-21	52.4	9-16	56.3	9	0.3	13	6	6	3-0	32	1.1
Davis	Fr.	35	44-86	51.2	24-31	77.4	27	0.8	9	12	3	10-0	116	3.3
	So.	34	111-249	44.6	59-74	79.7	60	1.8	52	31	33	42-0	325	9.6
	Jr.	35	161-309	52.1	81-97	83.5	85	2.4	66	37	30	35-0	467	13.3
TOTALS		104	316-644	49.1	164-202	81.2	172	1.6	127	80	66	87-0	908	8.7
Lynch	Fr.	34	112-215	52.1	67-101	66.3	183	5.4	34	66	37	105-6	292	8.6
	So.	35	172-329	52.3	85-135	63.0	258	7.4	41	86	49	92-2	436	12.5
TOTALS		69	284-544	52.2	152-236	64.4	441	6.4	75	152	86	197-8	728	10.6
Montross	Fr.	35	81-138	58.7	41-67	61.2	148	4.2	11	32	6	79-0	203	5.8
Phelps	Fr.	30	25-51	49.0	16-21	76.2	33	1.1	58	40	27	30-0	68	2.3
Reese	Fr.	33	56-105	53.3	18-33	54.5	54	1.6	17	20	9	14-0	133	4.0
Rodl	Fr.	34	27-55	49.1	12-24	50.0	24	0.7	21	28	13	24-0	79	2.3
	So.	35	46-81	56.8	23-37	62.2	53	1.5	62	36	13	39-0	127	3.6
TOTALS		69	73-136	53.7	35-61	57.4	77	1.1	83	64	26	63-0	206	3.0
Salvadori	Fr.	31	18-35	51.4	12-19	63.2	27	0.9	0	5	1	13-0	48	1.5
Sullivan	Fr.	34	10-23	43.5	13-20	65.0	22	0.6	18	10	6	18-0	34	1.0
Wenstrom	Fr.	32	10-19	52.6	9-14	64.3	20	0.6	2	7	1	17-0	29	0.9
	So.	24	5-15	33.3	7-12	58.3	21	0.9	0	6	1	6-0	17	0.7
TOTALS		56	15-34	44.1	16-26	61.6	41	0.7	2	13	2	23-0	46	0.8

CAREER THREE-POINT FIELD GOALS: Cherry 1-4, 25.0; Davis 112-255, 43.9; Lynch 8-13, 61.5; Phelps 2-9, 22.2; Reese 3-5, 60.0; Rodl 25-57, 43.9; Sullivan 1-5, 20.0.

UNC 99, San Diego State 63

Nov. 24, 1990 — Chapel Hill, NC

San Diego State	MP	TFG	3FG	FT	R	A	PF	TP
Thompson	22	2-4	0-0	1-2	0	2	4	5
Balzer	22	5-11	1-1	1-2	3	1	3	12
Dow	31	4-7	0-0	0-2	8	0	3	8
McKinney	16	1-3	0-2	0-1	2	3	1	2
Massey	38	6-18	1-3	5-7	8	7	1	18
McNaull	13	1-2	0-0	1-4	4	0	2	3
Steinly	17	1-2	0-0	1-3	4	0	3	3
Lewis	14	2-9	0-3	0-0	4	1	1	4
Barefield	7	0-0	0-0	0-0	0	0	0	0
Miller	4	1-2	0-1	2-4	0	0	1	4
Hamilton	8	1-2	0-0	0-0	0	0	1	2
Stewart	6	1-2	0-0	0-2	2	0	2	2
Pollard	2	0-0	0-0	0-0	0	0	0	0
Totals	**200**	**25-62**	**2-10**	**11-27**	**36**	**14**	**22**	**63**

UNC	MP	TFG	3FG	FT	R	A	PF	TP
Fox	23	3-8	1-3	0-0	9	2	3	7
Lynch	19	6-8	0-0	6-8	5	1	2	18
Chilcutt	20	5-11	0-0	0-1	5	2	0	10
Davis	17	6-9	2-3	2-2	2	1	2	16
Rice	20	1-4	1-2	0-0	1	9	0	3
Rodl	9	1-1	1-1	1-1	1	2	1	4
Rozier	13	5-6	0-0	0-0	7	2	5	10
Montross	18	2-4	0-0	2-8	6	2	3	6
Phelps	12	3-5	0-2	1-1	0	1	3	7
Sullivan	14	0-3	0-0	0-0	1	4	0	0
Harris	8	1-3	1-1	0-0	3	0	0	3
Reese	14	3-6	0-0	0-0	4	1	2	6
Salvadori	8	2-4	0-0	0-0	5	0	4	4
Cherry	5	2-2	0-0	1-2	0	0	0	5
Totals	**200**	**40-74**	**6-12**	**13-23**	**50**	**27**	**25**	**99**

San Diego State	**32**	**31**	**-**	**63**
UNC	**55**	**44**	**-**	**99**

Turnovers: SDSU 26, UNC 16.
Technical Fouls: None.
Officials: Dibler, Tate, Birk.
Attendance: 21,572.

UNC 104, Jacksonville 61

Nov. 27, 1990 — Chapel Hill, NC

Jacksonville	MP	TFG	3FG	FT	R	A	PF	TP
Hamilton	31	3-13	0-2	0-0	7	0	4	6
Law	26	8-15	0-0	0-1	5	3	3	16
Burroughs	24	7-9	0-0	1-2	5	0	4	15
Ivery	35	4-10	0-2	3-3	2	1	0	11
Tirado	33	1-2	0-1	0-2	2	4	2	2
Powell	20	0-7	0-0	2-2	2	0	3	2
Hanna	4	0-0	0-0	0-0	1	1	1	0
McDuffie	9	0-1	0-0	1-2	2	2	0	1
Shafer	9	2-3	0-0	0-0	0	0	0	4
Harris	9	2-4	0-0	0-0	4	1	1	4
Totals	**200**	**27-64**	**0-5**	**7-12**	**35**	**12**	**18**	**61**

UNC	MP	TFG	3FG	FT	R	A	PF	TP
Fox	21	8-17	3-8	0-0	4	2	1	19
Lynch	21	7-12	1-1	4-6	10	1	1	19
Chilcutt	17	2-4	0-0	0-0	2	1	2	4
Davis	14	0-4	0-3	1-2	2	0	2	1
Rice	18	2-5	1-3	0-0	1	7	1	5
Montross	17	3-3	0-0	2-2	6	0	0	8
Rodl	12	1-4	1-3	2-4	1	2	0	5
Rozier	18	9-12	0-0	4-6	8	1	3	22
Phelps	12	0-2	0-2	0-0	0	4	3	0
Sullivan	14	1-1	1-1	0-0	2	1	0	3
Harris	9	1-2	1-2	0-0	0	1	0	3
Reese	14	2-5	1-1	2-2	1	2	0	7
Salvadori	9	2-3	0-0	2-2	0	0	2	6
Cherry	4	1-1	0-0	0-0	0	2	0	2
Totals	**200**	**39-75**	**9-24**	**17-24**	**40**	**24**	**15**	**104**

Jacksonville	**23**	**38**	**-**	**61**
UNC	**49**	**55**	**-**	**104**

Turnovers: Jacksonville 29, UNC 15.
Technical Fouls: None.
Officials: Herring, Pitts, Wood.
Attendance: 18,103.

South Carolina 76, UNC 74

Nov. 30, 1990 — Charlotte, NC

South Carolina	MP	TFG	3FG	FT	R	A	PF	TP
Rhett	35	7-12	0-0	1-4	6	3	2	15
Glover	30	4-7	0-1	2-2	6	3	2	10
Roulston	15	1-2	0-0	0-0	3	0	3	2
English	24	5-12	1-1	2-3	3	9	5	13
Manning	34	7-14	1-2	0-0	3	3	3	15
Watson	25	3-7	1-2	3-5	4	2	2	10
Popovic	5	0-0	0-0	0-0	1	0	1	0
Wilson	5	2-2	0-0	1-2	2	0	1	5
Eggers	7	0-1	0-0	0-0	0	0	1	0
Leso	20	2-3	0-0	2-4	2	0	3	6
Totals	**200**	**31-60**	**3-6**	**11-21**	**32**	**20**	**23**	**76**

UNC	MP	TFG	3FG	FT	R	A	PF	TP
Chilcutt	24	4-8	0-0	1-2	3	2	2	9
Fox	28	4-10	1-3	6-6	6	2	4	15
Montross	19	0-1	0-0	0-0	1	0	2	0
Rodl	14	0-0	0-0	0-0	2	2	0	0
Rice	27	2-4	0-0	0-2	3	3	3	4
Sullivan	5	2-2	0-0	0-0	2	0	0	4
Harris	1	0-0	0-0	0-0	0	0	0	0
Phelps	12	3-5	0-0	1-1	1	1	2	7
Reese	4	0-1	0-0	0-2	0	1	1	0
Salvadori	1	0-1	0-0	0-0	1	0	1	0
Lynch	25	6-8	0-0	4-4	5	0	3	16
Davis	22	4-8	0-1	6-6	2	1	1	14
Rozier	18	2-5	0-0	1-1	4	0	3	5
Totals	**200**	**27-53**	**1-4**	**19-24**	**32**	**12**	**21**	**74**

South Carolina	**28**	**48**	**-**	**76**
UNC	**40**	**34**	**-**	**74**

Turnovers: South Carolina 24, UNC 28.
Technical Fouls: None.
Officials: Donaghy, Gordon, Donato.
Attendance: 22,680.

UNC 118, Iowa State 93

Dec. 1, 1990 — Charlotte, NC

Iowa State	MP	TFG	3FG	FT	R	A	PF	TP
Collins	24	4-9	0-2	3-6	2	5	3	11
Doerrfeld	20	2-3	0-0	1-2	4	0	4	5
Kunz	19	5-7	0-0	0-1	3	0	3	10
Pearson	38	6-12	5-10	1-2	4	5	4	18
Chappell	15	2-5	0-1	0-0	1	1	1	4
McKoy	2	0-0	0-0	0-1	0	2	0	0
Washington	1	0-0	0-0	0-0	0	0	1	0
Brown	1	0-0	0-0	0-0	1	0	0	0
Jackson	5	0-1	0-0	0-0	0	1	0	0
Thigpen	24	6-12	3-6	1-3	3	7	3	16
Bivens	9	1-1	0-0	1-2	1	0	1	3
Bergman	4	1-4	0-3	0-0	1	0	0	2
Pippett	7	1-2	0-0	0-0	1	0	1	2
Alexander	31	9-12	0-0	4-4	14	1	4	22
Totals	**200**	**37-68**	**8-22**	**11-21**	**41**	**22**	**25**	**93**

UNC	MP	TFG	3FG	FT	R	A	PF	TP
Lynch	29	8-16	0-1	4-8	8	3	4	20
Fox	22	5-13	1-3	4-4	11	1	2	15
Montross	15	4-5	0-0	0-0	5	0	4	8
Rodl	21	4-5	1-1	5-6	2	6	1	14
Phelps	12	2-3	0-0	0-0	0	1	1	4
Sullivan	6	0-1	0-1	1-2	1	1	0	1
Harris	4	3-3	1-1	1-1	0	0	3	8
Cherry	2	0-0	0-0	1-2	0	0	0	1
Rice	24	1-3	1-2	0-0	1	7	1	3
Reese	12	4-7	0-0	4-5	3	2	0	12
Chilcutt	20	4-10	0-0	1-2	5	0	1	9
Salvadori	7	1-4	0-0	0-0	1	0	1	2
Davis	13	4-8	0-0	1-1	2	2	0	9
Rozier	13	4-8	0-0	4-7	3	1	2	12
Totals	**200**	**44-86**	**4-9**	**26-38**	**46**	**24**	**20**	**118**

Iowa State	**40**	**53**	**-**	**93**
UNC	**60**	**58**	**-**	**118**

Turnovers: Iowa State 28, UNC 13.
Technical Fouls: None.
Officials: Donaghy, Scott, Gordon.
Attendance:

UNC 79, Connecticut 64

Dec. 6, 1990 — Chapel Hill, NC

UNC	MP	TFG	3FG	FT	R	A	PF	TP
Lynch	33	4-9	0-0	4-6	14	1	3	12
Fox	25	5-13	2-6	6-6	10	2	5	18
Chilcutt	25	4-8	0-0	3-5	6	1	1	11
Rodl	16	3-4	1-2	2-2	2	2	2	9
Phelps	10	0-1	0-1	0-0	0	2	0	0
Rice	29	0-1	0-1	0-0	3	4	2	0
Davis	22	2-8	1-5	6-6	0	1	1	11
Montross	18	2-5	0-0	0-0	7	0	2	4
Rozier	11	3-8	0-0	1-2	8	0	4	7
Sullivan	1	0-0	0-0	0-0	0	0	0	0
Harris	1	0-3	0-1	0-1	2	0	0	0
Reese	8	2-3	0-0	3-4	1	1	1	7
Salvadori	1	0-0	0-0	0-0	0	0	0	0
Totals	**200**	**26-63**	**4-16**	**25-32**	**54**	**14**	**21**	**79**

Connecticut	MP	TFG	3FG	FT	R	A	PF	TP
Sellars	29	3-6	0-0	3-9	8	1	5	9
Burrell	31	4-13	0-4	0-0	8	1	4	8
Cyrulik	13	2-6	0-0	0-0	2	0	5	4
Smith	34	8-21	3-6	2-4	3	2	2	21
Pikiell	25	1-7	0-2	2-2	3	3	4	4
Gwynn	22	5-10	0-0	1-4	1	1	1	11
Williams	19	0-2	0-0	1-4	2	1	4	1
DePriest	23	3-4	0-0	0-0	3	0	3	6
Katz	2	0-0	0-0	0-0	0	0	0	0
Suhr	1	0-0	0-0	0-0	0	0	1	0
Macklin	1	0-0	0-0	0-0	0	0	0	0
Totals	**200**	**26-69**	**3-12**	**9-23**	**32**	**9**	**29**	**64**

UNC	**33**	**46**	**-**	**79**
Connecticut	**40**	**24**	**-**	**64**

Turnovers: UNC 28, Connecticut 18.
Technical Fouls: None.
Officials: Higgins, Mingle, Rose.
Attendance: 21,572.

UNC 84, Kentucky 81

Dec. 10, 1990 — Chapel Hill, NC

Kentucky	MP	TFG	3FG	FT	R	A	PF	TP
Mashburn	28	7-12	1-2	0-0	10	1	4	15
Pelphrey	36	7-16	4-6	6-7	7	2	3	24
Hanson	26	5-11	0-0	0-0	4	2	4	10
Woods	34	3-12	0-0	0-0	1	5	1	6
Brassow	14	3-7	2-5	0-0	1	0	3	8
Farmer	23	3-9	3-6	0-0	1	3	3	9
Feldhaus	16	3-4	0-0	2-2	1	0	4	8
Martinez	8	0-1	0-0	0-0	1	0	2	0
Thompson	6	0-1	0-0	0-0	0	0	0	0
Braddy	4	0-0	0-0	0-0	1	0	0	0
Thomas	1	0-0	0-0	0-0	0	0	0	0
Davis	4	0-0	0-0	1-2	1	0	1	1
Totals	**200**	**31-73**	**10-19**	**9-11**	**32**	**13**	**25**	**81**

UNC	MP	TFG	3FG	FT	R	A	PF	TP
Chilcutt	26	6-11	0-0	2-3	10	0	0	14
Lynch	29	5-8	0-0	3-4	7	3	4	13
Montross	13	1-3	0-0	0-1	6	0	2	2
Fox	34	5-14	1-6	3-3	7	7	2	14
Rice	25	5-8	1-2	3-3	1	3	1	14
Rodl	15	1-1	0-0	3-4	3	2	1	5
Phelps	13	0-1	0-0	4-4	1	1	1	4
Rozier	12	0-3	0-0	1-4	2	1	1	1
Davis	20	5-9	1-1	2-4	0	2	1	13
Reese	5	1-1	0-0	0-0	1	0	1	2
Sullivan	2	0-0	0-0	2-2	1	0	0	2
Harris	2	0-2	0-0	0-0	1	1	0	0
Salvadori	2	0-0	0-0	0-0	0	0	0	0
Wenstrom	2	0-1	0-0	0-0	1	0	0	0
Totals	**200**	**29-62**	**3-9**	**23-32**	**45**	**20**	**14**	**84**

Kentucky	**41**	**40**	**-**	**81**
UNC	**33**	**51**	**-**	**84**

Turnovers: Kentucky 18, UNC 28
Technical Fouls: None.
Officials: Rutledge, Herring, Andrzejewski.
Attendance: 21,572

UNC 95, Alabama 79

Dec. 15, 1990 — Chapel Hill, NC

Alabama	MP	TFG	3FG	FT	R	A	PF	TP
Sprewell	22	1-7	0-1	0-0	4	2	2	2
Cheatum	35	7-18	0-1	0-1	11	0	5	14
Webb	17	1-2	0-0	0-0	1	1	0	2
Waites	22	2-4	1-1	0-0	2	5	4	5
Lancaster	23	3-12	0-2	0-0	5	2	2	6
Horry	30	8-16	4-6	3-3	10	0	4	23
Campbell	4	0-0	0-0	0-0	0	0	0	0
Jones	18	5-10	0-3	2-2	1	1	3	12
Robinson	26	6-15	1-3	2-2	7	3	3	15
Rich	1	0-0	0-0	0-0	0	0	0	0
Rice	2	0-0	0-0	0-0	0	0	1	0
Totals	**200**	**33-84**	**6-17**	**7-8**	**43**	**14**	**24**	**79**

UNC	MP	TFG	3FG	FT	R	A	PF	TP
Lynch	32	9-14	1-1	1-4	9	2	1	20
Fox	32	3-10	0-2	9-11	9	3	2	15
Chilcutt	30	9-10	0-0	4-4	8	1	1	22
Davis	28	4-6	0-0	6-8	3	4	0	14
Phelps	11	0-3	0-1	0-0	2	3	0	0
Rice	29	0-2	0-1	2-6	5	7	3	2
Montross	10	5-7	0-0	1-2	1	0	2	11
Rodl	12	1-3	0-1	0-0	3	1	1	2
Rozier	8	3-6	0-0	1-3	2	0	1	7
Reese	6	1-4	0-0	0-0	1	0	0	2
Sullivan	2	0-0	0-0	0-0	0	2	0	0
Totals	**200**	**35-65**	**1-6**	**24-38**	**46**	**23**	**11**	**95**

Alabama	**37**	**42**	**-**	**79**
UNC	**45**	**50**	**-**	**95**

Turnovers: Alabama 12, UNC 9.
Technical Fouls: None.
Officials: Clougherty, Scagliotta, Boudreaux.
Attendance: 21,572.

UNC 86, Purdue 74

Dec. 22, 1990 — Lafayette, Ind.

UNC	MP	TFG	3FG	FT	R	A	PF	TP
Lynch	33	6-13	1-2	3-6	6	3	4	16
Fox	28	7-14	3-6	5-5	5	2	4	22
Montross	16	0-1	0-0	1-2	3	1	3	1
Rodl	12	0-0	0-0	3-4	4	1	1	3
Rice	31	5-8	3-5	2-4	1	7	2	15
Chilcutt	31	5-7	0-0	5-7	8	0	1	15
Davis	25	4-7	2-3	2-2	3	1	0	12
Phelps	3	0-0	0-0	0-0	1	0	0	0
Rozier	8	0-1	0-0	0-0	0	1	0	0
Wenstrom	1	0-0	0-0	0-0	0	0	0	0
Salvadori	1	0-0	0-0	0-0	1	0	0	0
Sullivan	1	0-0	0-0	0-0	0	0	1	0
Reese	4	1-1	0-0	0-0	1	0	0	2
Harris	6	0-2	0-0	0-0	1	0	1	0
Totals	**200**	**28-54**	**9-16**	**21-30**	**34**	**16**	**17**	**86**

Purdue	MP	TFG	3FG	FT	R	A	PF	TP
White	29	1-4	0-0	3-4	5	3	5	5
Oliver	37	6-15	4-7	2-4	2	3	1	18
McNary	24	3-5	0-0	3-3	5	1	4	9
Trice	25	1-5	1-3	1-2	2	3	2	4
Austin	32	8-17	5-11	0-0	8	4	3	21
Barkett	14	1-2	0-1	0-0	0	3	1	2
Painter	5	0-1	0-1	0-0	1	1	0	0
Stanback	15	5-5	1-1	0-1	3	0	1	11
Riley	10	1-3	0-0	0-0	2	0	1	2
Darner	9	0-1	0-1	2-2	0	0	2	2
Totals	**200**	**26-58**	**11-25**	**11-16**	**30**	**18**	**20**	**74**

UNC	**35**	**51**	**-**	**86**
Purdue	**33**	**41**	**-**	**74**

Turnovers: UNC 19, Purdue 21.
Technical Fouls: UNC bench.
Officials: Paparo, Edsall, Corbin.
Attendance: 14,173.

UNC 90, DePaul 75

Dec. 29, 1990 — Orlando, Fla.

DePaul	MP	TFG	3FG	FT	R	A	PF	TP
Foster	29	4-11	0-2	1-2	5	2	1	9
Howard	23	2-6	0-0	2-4	5	2	1	6
Price	23	1-3	0-0	0-1	5	1	4	2
Davis	21	7-14	3-6	0-0	1	2	1	17
Booth	34	8-14	1-1	5-7	3	0	5	22
Daughrity	22	1-7	0-3	2-2	4	2	2	4
Murphy	2	0-0	0-0	0-0	0	2	0	0
Holland	9	1-3	0-0	0-0	0	1	1	2
Niemann	12	3-5	3-5	0-0	3	1	2	9
Stern	20	2-4	0-0	0-0	6	0	0	4
Ravizee	5	0-1	0-0	0-0	0	0	2	0
Totals	**200**	**29-68**	**7-17**	**10-16**	**35**	**13**	**19**	**75**

UNC	MP	TFG	3FG	FT	R	A	PF	TP
Rice	30	1-2	0-1	0-0	3	4	2	2
Chilcutt	24	5-9	0-0	4-4	11	2	0	14
Lynch	29	7-10	0-1	2-2	6	0	2	16
Davis	22	3-11	1-6	1-2	1	4	0	8
Rozier	11	4-5	0-0	3-7	8	2	1	11
Montross	13	3-6	0-0	0-0	5	0	2	6
Sullivan	4	0-0	0-0	0-0	0	1	1	0
Harris	4	0-1	0-1	0-0	0	0	0	0
Rodl	12	4-5	1-1	0-0	1	1	1	9
Cherry	1	0-0	0-0	0-0	0	0	0	0
Phelps	6	0-0	0-0	0-0	1	1	1	0
Reese	9	1-3	0-0	1-3	1	1	0	3
Salvadori	2	0-0	0-0	0-0	0	0	0	0
Fox	31	8-15	2-8	3-6	5	4	3	21
Wenstrom	2	0-1	0-0	0-0	0	0	0	0
Totals	**200**	**36-68**	**4-18**	**14-24**	**47**	**20**	**13**	**90**

DePaul	**37**	**38**	**-**	**75**
UNC	**44**	**46**	**-**	**90**

Turnovers: DePaul 17, UNC 15.
Technical Fouls: None.
Officials: Clougherty, Tanner, Patillo.
Attendance: 6,020.

UNC 71, Stanford 60

Dec. 30, 1990 — Orlando, Fla.

UNC	MP	TFG	3FG	FT	R	A	PF	TP
Rice	34	2-8	2-3	7-10	2	3	0	13
Lynch	22	2-8	0-0	0-1	8	1	4	4
Fox	36	7-16	3-7	3-5	6	5	2	20
Chilcutt	27	3-7	0-0	4-4	3	2	2	10
Davis	27	4-7	2-2	0-0	3	3	1	10
Montross	17	2-4	0-0	0-0	1	0	1	4
Sullivan	2	0-0	0-0	0-0	0	0	0	0
Harris	4	1-1	1-1	0-0	0	0	0	3
Rodl	11	1-1	0-0	0-0	1	1	0	2
Cherry	2	0-0	0-0	0-0	0	0	0	0
Reese	4	1-2	0-0	1-1	0	0	0	3
Salvadori	2	0-0	0-0	0-0	0	0	0	0
Rozier	10	1-3	0-0	0-0	2	0	2	2
Wenstrom	2	0-1	0-0	0-0	0	0	0	0
Totals	**200**	**24-58**	**8-13**	**15-21**	**29**	**15**	**12**	**71**

Stanford	MP	TFG	3FG	FT	R	A	PF	TP
Patrick	27	5-10	4-8	0-0	0	3	2	14
Ammann	16	1-5	0-2	0-0	1	0	3	2
Vlahov	28	0-5	0-1	2-2	5	4	4	2
Keefe	39	9-10	0-0	2-2	12	1	1	20
Wingate	35	7-12	0-0	2-2	12	2	3	16
Lollie	24	1-4	0-0	0-0	4	3	5	2
Hicks	15	2-5	0-1	0-0	0	2	1	4
Williams	3	0-1	0-0	0-0	0	0	0	0
Meyer	7	0-0	0-0	0-0	1	0	0	0
Morgan	6	0-1	0-0	0-0	0	1	0	0
Totals	**200**	**25-53**	**4-12**	**6-6**	**37**	**16**	**19**	**60**

UNC	**36**	**35**	**-**	**71**
Stanford	**30**	**30**	**-**	**60**

Turnovers: Stanford 20, UNC 9.
Technical Fouls: None.
Officials: Clougherty, Tanner, Day.
Attendance: 4,841.

UNC 108, Cornell 64

Jan. 3, 1991 — Ithaca, NY

UNC	MP	TFG	3FG	FT	R	A	PF	TP
Lynch	28	6-8	1-1	2-3	7	0	0	15
Fox	22	7-10	3-4	2-2	3	1	3	19
Chilcutt	19	4-7	0-0	1-2	4	1	0	9
Cherry	7	1-1	1-1	0-1	2	1	1	3
Rice	22	2-5	0-2	2-3	0	6	1	6
Davis	14	4-8	2-3	0-0	1	0	0	10
Montross	17	4-5	0-0	2-2	6	0	3	10
Rozier	16	3-8	0-0	4-6	5	1	1	10
Rodl	14	2-2	1-1	0-0	1	3	1	5
Harris	13	2-5	0-0	0-0	0	1	1	4
Reese	14	4-5	0-0	0-0	2	0	0	8
Sullivan	4	1-1	0-0	0-0	1	1	2	2
Salvadori	6	2-3	0-0	0-0	1	0	0	4
Wenstrom	4	1-1	0-0	1-2	2	0	0	3
Totals	**200**	**43-69**	**8-12**	**14-21**	**41**	**15**	**13**	**108**

Cornell	MP	TFG	3FG	FT	R	A	PF	TP
Dillard	20	2-6	1-4	0-0	2	0	2	5
Medina	28	6-9	0-0	4-4	4	1	1	16
Jackson	27	1-7	0-0	0-2	3	1	0	2
Johnson	20	0-4	0-3	0-0	2	2	3	0
Maharaj	24	5-9	2-6	2-2	0	0	4	14
Parker	18	2-7	1-4	0-0	3	0	3	5
Ableson	15	2-6	1-1	0-0	2	2	0	5
Hill	13	4-6	0-0	0-0	3	1	3	8
Gaca	17	2-10	1-4	0-1	4	1	1	5
McRae	17	1-1	0-0	2-4	5	0	0	4
Grant	17	0-1	0-0	0-0	0	0	1	0
Marshall	1	0-1	0-0	0-0	1	0	0	0
George	1	0-2	0-0	0-0	2	0	0	0
Treadwell	1	0-0	0-0	0-0	0	0	0	0
Totals	**200**	**25-69**	**6-22**	**8-13**	**37**	**8**	**18**	**64**

UNC	**53**	**55**	**-**	**108**
Cornell	**31**	**33**	**-**	**64**

Turnovers: Cornell 20, UNC 10.
Technical Fouls: None.
Officials: Corin, Cahill, McDonnell.
Attendance: 4,473.

UNC 82, Notre Dame 47

Jan. 5, 1991 — East Rutherford, NJ

UNC	MP	TFG	3FG	FT	R	A	PF	TP
Sullivan	11	2-3	0-0	2-4	4	2	0	6
Reese	13	2-5	0-0	1-2	6	2	2	5
Chilcutt	19	5-7	0-0	0-1	7	0	1	10
Rodl	9	0-2	0-2	0-0	0	0	0	0
Rice	27	0-3	0-2	0-0	1	9	1	0
Montross	16	3-3	0-0	1-2	3	1	3	7
Harris	8	0-2	0-1	0-2	1	0	1	0
Cherry	5	2-2	0-0	0-0	0	1	0	4
Salvadori	7	1-1	0-0	0-0	1	0	1	2
Lynch	22	1-4	0-0	3-6	4	2	2	5
Davis	23	5-8	4-6	0-0	2	1	1	14
Fox	26	5-12	4-9	8-8	4	3	1	22
Rozier	8	0-8	0-0	3-4	2	0	2	3
Wenstrom	6	0-0	0-0	4-4	3	0	0	4
Totals	**200**	**26-60**	**8-20**	**22-33**	**44**	**21**	**15**	**82**

Notre Dame	MP	TFG	3FG	FT	R	A	PF	TP
Ellis	28	5-11	1-1	3-6	8	1	5	14
Ellery	18	1-5	1-4	0-0	5	0	2	3
Ross, Jon	9	1-2	0-0	0-0	3	0	5	2
Bennett	36	1-12	0-4	0-0	5	10	4	2
Sweet	35	7-14	0-0	0-0	4	2	1	14
Tower	30	1-5	0-0	0-0	7	1	4	2
Boyer	30	4-7	2-4	0-0	0	0	4	10
Adamson	2	0-2	0-1	0-0	0	0	0	0
Cozen	5	0-1	0-1	0-0	1	1	1	0
Ross, Joe	7	0-1	0-0	0-0	0	0	1	0
Totals	**200**	**20-60**	**4-15**	**3-6**	**43**	**15**	**27**	**47**

UNC	**28**	**54**	**-**	**82**
Notre Dame	**24**	**23**	**-**	**47**

Turnovers: Notre Dame 19, UNC 8.
Technical Fouls: Ellery (intentional).
Officials: Mingle, Silvester, Valentine.
Attendance: 12, 702.

UNC 105, Maryland 73

Jan. 9, 1991 — Chapel Hill, NC

Maryland	MP	TFG	3FG	FT	R	A	PF	TP
Roe	30	10-19	2-6	1-1	5	0	2	23
Smith	18	0-4	0-0	1-4	4	1	3	1
Lewis	32	3-8	0-0	4-6	5	0	4	10
McLinton	27	6-14	0-1	1-1	7	4	3	13
Williams	37	7-21	1-6	1-3	8	8	4	16
Burns	18	0-2	0-0	2-3	3	1	3	2
Broadnax	15	1-1	0-0	3-5	1	0	3	5
Kjome	10	1-2	0-0	1-4	1	0	2	3
Downing	9	0-2	0-2	0-0	1	2	1	0
Thibeault	2	0-4	0-3	0-0	1	0	0	0
McGlone	2	0-1	0-0	0-0	0	0	0	0
Totals	**200**	**28-78**	**3-18**	**14-27**	**42**	**16**	**25**	**73**

UNC	MP	TFG	3FG	FT	R	A	PF	TP
Fox	28	1-9	1-4	6-8	11	4	2	9
Lynch	24	7-12	1-1	3-4	11	1	1	18
Chilcutt	23	7-10	0-0	3-4	9	1	1	17
Rodl	11	1-2	0-1	0-0	1	3	4	2
Rice	29	1-5	1-4	5-6	4	9	3	8
Montross	12	1-2	0-0	1-2	4	0	2	3
Davis	23	9-14	5-8	2-2	4	1	1	25
Rozier	9	2-4	0-0	1-2	3	0	0	5
Harris	11	1-3	0-2	2-2	2	2	3	4
Sullivan	12	2-4	0-1	3-4	1	0	1	7
Cherry	6	1-1	0-0	0-0	0	0	0	2
Salvadori	6	1-2	0-0	2-2	2	0	2	4
Wenstrom	6	0-0	0-0	1-2	3	0	1	1
Totals	**200**	**34-68**	**8-21**	**29-38**	**55**	**21**	**21**	**105**

Maryland	**28**	**45**	**-**	**73**
UNC	**47**	**58**	**-**	**105**

Turnovers: UNC 21, Maryland 20.
Technical Fouls: Maryland bench.
Officials: Wirtz, Croft, Herring.
Attendance: 21,572.

UNC 89, Virginia 86 (2 OT)

Jan. 12, 1991 — Charlottesville, Va.

UNC	MP	TFG	3FG	FT	R	A	PF	TP
Lynch	35	3-10	0-0	7-8	6	1	4	13
Fox	34	9-13	2-4	1-3	4	1	5	21
Chilcutt	38	10-17	0-0	5-6	11	2	2	25
Davis	38	0-6	0-4	6-8	4	1	1	6
Harris	4	0-1	0-1	0-0	1	1	2	0
Rice	43	5-9	0-1	4-6	3	8	2	14
Montross	21	4-9	0-0	0-2	5	0	0	8
Rodl	15	0-0	0-0	0-0	1	2	3	0
Rozier	8	1-2	0-0	0-2	2	0	0	2
Phelps	3	0-0	0-0	0-0	1	0	0	0
Salvadori	2	0-0	0-0	0-0	0	0	0	0
Wenstrom	2	0-0	0-0	0-0	0	0	0	0
Reese	5	0-2	0-0	0-0	1	0	1	0
Sullivan	2	0-0	0-0	0-0	0	0	1	0
Totals	**250**	**32-69**	**2-10**	**23-35**	**43**	**16**	**21**	**89**

Virginia	MP	TFG	3FG	FT	R	A	PF	TP
Turner	42	5-14	2-9	5-6	5	1	4	17
Stith	45	8-20	0-5	6-11	7	2	4	22
Jeffries	32	3-5	0-0	0-0	6	0	5	6
Oliver	36	4-12	0-1	0-0	4	2	2	8
Crotty	48	9-19	5-11	6-8	5	8	2	29
Blundin	31	1-3	0-1	1-2	7	1	4	3
Parker	14	0-1	0-0	1-2	6	1	2	1
Johnson	2	0-1	0-1	0-0	0	0	0	0
Totals	**250**	**30-75**	**7-28**	**19-29**	**45**	**15**	**23**	**86**

UNC	**33**	**38**	**7**	**11**	**89**
Virginia	**32**	**39**	**7**	**8**	**86**

Turnovers: Virginia 16, UNC 14.
Technical Fouls: Virginia bench.
Officials: Hartzell, Membo, Gordon.
Attendance: 8,864.

Duke 74, UNC 60

Jan. 19, 1991 — Durham, NC

UNC	MP	TFG	3FG	FT	R	A	PF	TP
Chilcutt	28	5-10	0-1	4-5	10	0	1	14
Fox	29	5-13	0-5	8-9	3	3	4	18
Montross	12	0-3	0-0	2-2	0	0	2	2
Rodl	13	1-2	0-0	0-0	0	1	0	2
Rice	30	0-3	0-0	2-4	2	6	1	2
Lynch	23	4-7	0-0	0-0	6	0	4	8
Davis	25	3-11	2-6	2-2	3	2	3	10
Harris	3	0-0	0-0	0-0	1	0	1	0
Rozier	8	0-1	0-0	0-0	2	0	4	0
Sullivan	8	0-1	0-0	2-2	3	0	1	2
Reese	10	1-3	0-1	0-0	2	0	1	2
Salvadori	2	0-0	0-0	0-0	2	0	0	0
Wenstrom	2	0-0	0-0	0-0	0	0	1	0
Phelps	7	0-0	0-0	0-0	1	0	1	0
Totals	**200**	**19-54**	**2-13**	**20-24**	**35**	**12**	**24**	**60**

Duke	MP	TFG	3FG	FT	R	A	PF	TP
Lang	14	2-4	0-0	2-2	2	0	2	6
Davis	10	1-3	0-0	0-0	2	0	1	2
Laettner	32	7-10	0-0	4-7	12	1	1	18
McCaffrey	32	3-12	0-3	3-4	2	2	2	9
Hurley	37	0-7	0-3	6-8	4	8	3	6
Hill, T.	23	7-9	1-1	5-7	1	1	2	20
Hill, G.	17	2-7	0-0	0-0	2	2	4	4
Palmer	16	0-1	0-0	0-0	1	1	3	0
Koubek	19	4-7	1-3	0-0	6	1	2	9
Totals	**200**	**26-60**	**2-10**	**20-28**	**35**	**16**	**20**	**74**

UNC	**28**	**32**	**-**	**60**
Duke	**24**	**50**	**-**	**74**

Turnovers: UNC 25, Duke 18.
Technical Fouls: Lynch.
Officials: Wirtz, Rose, Edsall.
Attendance: 9,314.

UNC 91, Wake Forest 81

Jan. 23, 1991 — Winston-Salem, NC

UNC	MP	TFG	3FG	FT	R	A	PF	TP
Chilcutt	29	4-8	0-0	0-1	7	1	3	8
Rodl	16	1-3	1-2	2-2	3	4	1	5
Montross	14	2-4	0-0	2-4	12	1	1	6
Reese	10	1-2	0-0	2-2	0	0	2	4
Rice	35	6-10	5-7	5-6	3	7	1	22
Sullivan	2	0-0	0-0	0-0	0	0	0	0
Harris	5	2-3	0-1	0-0	0	0	1	4
Cherry	1	0-0	0-0	0-0	1	0	0	0
Salvadori	2	0-0	0-0	0-0	0	0	0	0
Lynch	25	4-8	0-0	0-0	8	0	4	8
Davis	22	5-7	2-3	2-3	3	0	0	14
Fox	30	5-14	3-8	7-10	7	5	4	20
Rozier	7	0-1	0-0	0-0	2	0	0	0
Wenstrom	2	0-0	0-0	0-0	0	0	0	0
Totals	**200**	**30-60**	**11-21**	**20-28**	**47**	**18**	**17**	**91**

Wake Forest	MP	TFG	3FG	FT	R	A	PF	TP
King, C.	22	6-15	0-0	4-4	6	0	4	16
Tucker	34	8-16	1-2	0-0	5	1	3	17
Rogers	37	4-13	1-4	0-0	7	1	1	9
Siler	21	5-9	1-3	1-2	2	2	4	12
McQueen	34	3-6	2-3	2-2	4	9	4	10
Childress	26	4-11	3-6	4-7	2	4	3	15
Doggett	1	0-0	0-0	0-0	0	0	1	0
Owens	19	0-7	0-3	2-2	2	2	0	2
Medlin	4	0-0	0-0	0-0	1	1	2	0
King, S.	1	0-0	0-0	0-0	0	0	1	0
Hedgecoe	1	0-0	0-0	0-0	0	0	0	0
Totals	**200**	**30-77**	**8-21**	**13-17**	**30**	**20**	**23**	**81**

UNC	**39**	**52**	**-**	**91**
Wake Forest	**42**	**39**	**-**	**81**

Turnovers: UNC 16, Wake Forest 10.
Technical Fouls: UNC bench.
Officials: Donaghy, Higgins, Gordon.
Attendance: 14,407.

Georgia Tech 88, UNC 86

Jan. 27, 1991 — Chapel HIll, NC

Georgia Tech	MP	TFG	3FG	FT	R	A	PF	TP
Mackey	38	10-14	0-0	4-4	17	0	1	24
Hill	31	3-7	1-1	0-1	1	2	4	7
Geiger	31	7-12	0-0	3-4	6	2	4	17
Barry	40	9-25	2-12	0-0	3	1	2	20
Anderson	40	6-19	1-8	1-1	6	13	1	14
Newbill	16	2-4	0-0	0-0	2	0	1	4
Domalik	4	1-2	0-1	0-0	1	0	0	2
Totals	**200**	**38-83**	**4-22**	**8-10**	**37**	**18**	**13**	**88**

UNC	MP	TFG	3FG	FT	R	A	PF	TP
Lynch	27	6-16	0-0	4-4	13	2	3	16
Chilcutt	31	7-13	0-0	1-1	9	1	0	15
Montross	16	0-4	0-0	1-2	4	0	4	1
Fox	31	7-17	3-11	3-3	6	6	3	20
Rice	30	5-10	1-2	0-0	1	8	3	11
Davis	25	2-8	1-4	6-6	1	2	0	11
Phelps	6	0-1	0-0	2-2	2	1	0	2
Rozier	4	2-2	0-0	0-0	2	0	0	4
Rodl	10	1-1	1-1	0-0	4	1	1	3
Sullivan	3	0-1	0-0	1-2	0	0	0	1
Harris	3	0-0	0-0	0-0	2	0	0	0
Reese	8	0-1	0-0	0-0	3	0	0	0
Salvadori	3	1-2	0-0	0-0	2	0	0	2
Wenstrom	3	0-1	0-0	0-0	1	0	0	0
Totals	**200**	**31-77**	**6-18**	**18-20**	**51**	**21**	**14**	**86**

Georgia Tech	**34**	**54**	**-**	**88**
UNC	**45**	**41**	**-**	**86**

Turnovers: UNC 16, Georgia Tech 11.
Technical Fouls: None.
Officials: Moreau, Gray, Hartzell.
Attendance: 21,572.

UNC 90, Clemson 77

Jan. 31, 1991 — Clemson, SC

UNC	MP	TFG	3FG	FT	R	A	PF	TP
Rodl	16	2-7	0-3	0-0	3	4	1	4
Chilcutt	28	4-11	0-0	1-2	10	1	0	9
Montross	15	2-2	0-0	0-1	8	0	2	4
Rice	29	5-7	0-1	4-5	4	5	1	14
Davis	20	1-3	1-1	0-1	2	1	1	3
Lynch	26	5-8	0-0	4-8	7	0	0	14
Fox	28	10-21	4-10	2-3	6	5	2	26
Harris	3	0-0	0-0	0-0	1	2	0	0
Reese	8	2-5	0-1	0-0	1	0	0	4
Rozier	9	3-4	0-0	4-4	4	0	0	10
Sullivan	7	0-0	0-0	0-0	1	1	2	0
Phelps	9	1-1	0-0	0-0	3	2	0	2
Salvadori	2	0-0	0-0	0-0	1	0	1	0
Totals	**200**	**35-69**	**5-16**	**15-24**	**52**	**21**	**10**	**90**

Clemson	MP	TFG	3FG	FT	R	A	PF	TP
Harris	16	0-3	0-1	0-0	1	2	2	0
Jones	28	7-11	0-0	0-0	0	9	0	2	14
Davis	36	6-15	0-0	0-2	8	0	4	12
Mason	17	0-2	0-2	0-0	2	1	2	0
Young	33	6-16	3-12	0-0	1	3	4	15
Burks	25	4-8	1-5	2-2	1	6	2	11
Bovain	16	4-8	1-4	0-0	2	1	0	9
Tyson	19	4-10	0-2	0-0	6	2	4	8
Paul	3	0-0	0-0	0-0	0	1	0	0
Brown	1	0-0	0-0	0-0	1	0	0	0
Bruce	6	3-4	2-3	0-0	0	1	0	8
Totals	**200**	**34-77**	**7-29**	**2-4**	**33**	**17**	**20**	**77**

UNC	**42**	**48**	**-**	**90**
Clemson	**30**	**47**	**-**	**77**

Turnovers: UNC 25, Clemson 19.
Technical Fouls: Clemson bench; Rozier.
Officials: Scagliotta, Herring, Edsall.
Attendance: 10,500.

N.C. State 97, UNC 91

Feb. 6, 1991 — Raleigh, NC

UNC	MP	TFG	3FG	FT	R	A	PF	TP
Lynch	22	5-11	1-1	2-4	8	1	4	13
Fox	34	8-17	6-14	0-0	2	7	3	22
Chilcutt	32	7-10	2-2	3-4	5	3	3	19
Rice	28	3-7	2-3	0-0	1	10	1	8
Davis	26	7-12	3-5	0-2	4	2	3	17
Montross	17	1-3	0-0	2-2	4	0	0	4
Rodl	11	2-2	0-0	0-0	0	2	1	4
Rozier	5	0-0	0-0	0-0	1	2	1	0
Phelps	9	1-1	0-0	0-0	1	3	3	2
Sullivan	3	0-0	0-0	0-0	0	0	0	0
Harris	3	0-0	0-0	0-0	0	0	0	0
Reese	4	1-1	0-0	0-0	0	0	1	2
Salvadori	3	0-0	0-0	0-0	0	0	0	0
Wenstrom	3	0-0	0-0	0-0	0	0	0	0
Totals	**200**	**35-64**	**14-25**	**7-12**	**31**	**30**	**20**	**91**

N.C. STATE	MP	TFG	3FG	FT	R	A	PF	TP
Gugliotta	40	10-14	5-8	3-5	10	4	4	28
Feggins	33	5-8	0-0	1-2	3	2	2	11
Thompson	38	3-5	0-0	1-4	8	2	3	7
Corchiani	37	3-8	1-3	3-4	1	12	2	10
Monroe	40	12-24	6-11	7-7	4	2	2	37
Bakalli	12	1-3	0-1	2-2	0	1	1	4
Totals	**200**	**34-62**	**12-23**	**17-24**	**28**	**23**	**14**	**97**

UNC	45	46	-	91
N.C. State	53	44	-	97

Turnovers: UNC 17, N.C. State 11.
Technical Fouls: None.
Officials: Donaghy, Gray, Crowley.
Attendance: 12,400.

UNC 92, N.C. State 70

Feb. 7, 1991 — Chapel Hill, NC

N.C. State	MP	TFG	3FG	FT	R	A	PF	TP
Gugliotta	38	2-10	1-9	2-2	5	0	4	7
Feggins	24	3-9	0-0	0-0	2	0	5	6
Thompson, K.	20	2-2	0-0	2-4	4	1	3	6
Monroe	32	7-20	5-12	1-2	1	2	5	20
Corchiani	38	3-6	0-1	7-8	1	9	2	13
Robinson	5	0-0	0-0	0-0	1	0	1	0
Bakalli	32	4-8	2-5	3-4	6	2	2	13
Ritter	4	0-3	0-2	0-0	1	0	1	0
Lewis	2	1-1	0-0	0-0	0	0	0	2
Fletcher	2	0-0	0-0	1-2	0	1	0	1
Lee	1	0-0	0-0	2-2	0	0	0	2
Campion	1	0-0	0-0	0-0	0	0	0	0
Thompson, T.	1	0-0	0-0	0-0	0	0	0	0
Totals	**200**	**22-59**	**8-29**	**18-24**	**25**	**15**	**23**	**70**

UNC	MP	TFG	3FG	FT	R	A	PF	TP
Fox	30	4-8	1-4	7-8	10	8	4	16
Lynch	27	5-12	1-1	2-4	6	3	1	13
Chilcutt	27	5-7	0-0	2-2	4	3	1	12
Rodl	21	5-5	1-1	1-1	1	4	3	12
Rice	28	3-7	1-1	3-4	1	2	2	10
Phelps	12	0-2	0-0	1-3	1	0	3	1
Reese	5	2-3	0-0	0-0	4	0	0	4
Montross	12	4-5	0-0	0-0	3	0	3	8
Davis	17	4-8	1-4	1-1	6	2	2	10
Rozier	8	0-3	0-0	1-2	1	0	0	1
Sullivan	5	0-0	0-0	0-0	0	1	1	0
Salvadori	4	1-3	0-0	1-2	2	0	1	3
Cherry	2	0-1	0-0	0-0	1	1	1	0
Wenstrom	2	1-1	0-0	0-0	1	0	0	2
Totals	**200**	**34-65**	**5-11**	**19-27**	**46**	**24**	**22**	**92**

N.C. State	39	31	-	70
UNC	45	47	-	92

Turnovers: UNC 18, N.C. State 16.
Technical Fouls: Corchiani; UNC bench.
Officials: Paparo, Hartzell, Gordon.
Attendance: 21,572.

UNC 77, Virginia 58

Feb. 9, 1991 — Chapel Hill, NC

Virginia	MP	TFG	3FG	FT	R	A	PF	TP
Stith	27	6-13	0-1	2-2	5	0	4	14
Turner	31	2-11	0-5	0-0	4	4	3	4
Jeffries	29	1-4	0-0	2-4	6	3	3	4
Parker	26	4-6	1-1	6-8	4	1	4	15
Crotty	29	4-13	1-2	2-2	1	1	2	11
Kirby	17	2-7	1-3	0-0	0	1	2	5
Smith	10	1-2	0-1	0-0	0	1	1	2
Blundin	20	1-1	0-0	1-2	6	1	2	3
Wilson	4	0-1	0-0	0-0	1	0	1	0
Katstra	5	0-0	0-0	0-0	0	1	0	0
Floriani	1	0-0	0-0	0-0	0	0	0	0
Stewart	1	0-1	0-0	0-0	1	0	0	0
Totals	**200**	**21-59**	**3-13**	**13-18**	**32**	**13**	**22**	**58**

UNC	MP	TFG	3FG	FT	R	A	PF	TP
Fox	27	4-6	3-4	3-4	5	0	3	14
Lynch	21	2-9	0-0	1-3	7	3	1	5
Chilcutt	29	6-8	0-0	0-0	7	2	1	12
Davis	24	5-7	4-6	5-6	3	6	1	19
Rice	29	0-3	0-3	4-6	0	3	1	4
Rodl	14	0-3	0-1	0-0	0	2	1	0
Reese	10	3-4	1-1	2-2	4	0	0	9
Montross	14	3-5	0-0	0-1	6	1	4	6
Rozier	11	1-4	0-0	1-1	1	0	2	3
Phelps	11	0-0	0-0	0-0	0	4	1	0
Salvadori	4	1-2	0-0	1-2	1	0	0	3
Sullivan	4	0-0	0-0	0-0	0	0	0	0
Cherry	1	1-1	0-0	0-0	0	0	0	2
Wenstrom	1	0-0	0-0	0-0	0	0	0	0
Totals	**200**	**26-52**	**8-15**	**17-25**	**36**	**21**	**15**	**77**

Virginia	26	32	-	58
UNC	42	35	-	77

Turnovers: Virginia 18, UNC 15.
Technical Fouls: None.
Officials: Paparo, Lembo, Edsall.
Attendance: 21,572.

UNC 85, Wake Forest 70

Feb. 13, 1991 — Chapel Hill, NC

Wake Forest	MP	TFG	3FG	FT	R	A	PF	TP
Tucker	30	4-8	0-0	0-0	1	1	2	8
King	34	7-13	0-1	2-2	9	2	3	16
Rogers	37	5-13	0-0	3-4	11	2	3	13
Siler	20	2-7	0-3	0-0	4	1	2	4
McQueen	34	4-8	1-2	0-0	6	7	3	9
Medlin	7	1-1	0-0	0-2	1	1	1	2
Childress	29	7-16	3-9	0-1	3	2	4	17
Owens	7	0-5	0-0	1-2	1	0	0	1
Wise	1	0-0	0-0	0-0	0	1	0	0
Doggett	1	0-0	0-0	0-0	0	0	0	0
Totals	**200**	**30-71**	**4-15**	**6-11**	**39**	**17**	**18**	**70**

UNC	MP	TFG	3FG	FT	R	A	PF	TP
Fox	32	8-17	2-7	3-4	9	3	4	21
Lynch	25	6-8	0-0	5-8	4	2	2	17
Chilcutt	26	4-9	0-0	0-0	3	3	0	8
Rodl	13	2-3	0-1	0-2	1	1	2	4
Rice	30	3-5	0-0	4-4	2	8	1	10
Montross	18	1-3	0-0	0-0	6	0	2	2
Phelps	10	0-1	0-0	2-2	2	3	1	2
Davis	27	5-8	1-3	1-2	1	3	0	12
Rozier	10	2-3	0-0	1-2	2	1	1	5
Sullivan	4	0-0	0-0	0-0	0	0	0	0
Reese	4	2-2	0-0	0-0	0	0	0	4
Salvadori	1	0-0	0-0	0-0	0	0	0	0
Totals	**200**	**33-59**	**3-11**	**16-24**	**33**	**24**	**13**	**85**

Wake Forest	35	35	-	70
UNC	45	40	-	85

Turnovers: Wake Forest 17, UNC 12.
Technical Fouls: None.
Officials: Moreau, Croft, Gordon.
Attendance: 21,572.

UNC 87, Maryland 75

Feb. 16, 1991 — College Park, Md.

UNC	MP	TFG	3FG	FT	R	A	PF	TP
Lynch	27	6-9	0-0	0-1	9	0	4	12
Fox	26	9-16	1-6	0-0	5	7	3	19
Chilcutt	32	7-14	0-1	0-0	9	2	0	14
Rice	29	5-7	0-0	1-1	2	7	3	11
Davis	28	5-9	1-3	0-0	3	2	2	11
Rodl	11	1-2	0-0	1-2	3	0	1	3
Phelps	10	0-1	0-0	0-0	1	3	0	0
Montross	10	4-4	0-0	1-1	1	0	4	9
Reese	11	2-4	0-0	0-0	2	0	0	4
Rozier	7	1-2	0-0	2-4	3	1	0	4
Sullivan	3	0-0	0-0	0-0	0	0	0	0
Salvadori	3	0-0	0-0	0-0	2	0	0	0
Cherry	1	0-1	0-0	0-0	0	0	0	0
Wenstrom	1	0-0	0-0	0-0	0	0	0	0
Harris	1	0-2	0-2	0-0	1	0	0	0
Totals	**200**	**40-71**	**2-12**	**5-9**	**43**	**22**	**17**	**87**

Maryland	MP	TFG	3FG	FT	R	A	PF	TP
Smith	28	2-8	0-0	0-1	9	2	1	4
Broadnax	32	3-8	0-0	0-2	4	3	3	6
Lewis	32	8-13	0-0	4-6	5	0	3	20
Roe	32	4-15	2-11	1-2	4	0	0	11
McLinton	38	9-12	0-1	3-6	3	4	2	21
Burns	18	2-5	0-0	2-2	2	0	2	6
Downing	12	2-5	1-3	0-0	2	1	1	5
Thibeault	6	1-4	0-2	0-0	1	0	2	2
Kjome	1	0-1	0-0	0-0	2	0	0	0
McGlone	1	0-0	0-0	0-0	0	0	0	0
Totals	**200**	**31-71**	**3-17**	**10-19**	**36**	**10**	**14**	**75**

UNC	45	42	-	87
Maryland	43	32	-	75

Turnovers: UNC 16, Maryland 15.
Technical Fouls: None.
Officials: Scagliotta, Corbin, Herring.
Attendance: 14,500.

UNC 118, The Citadel 50

Feb. 18, 1991 — Chapel Hill, NC

The Citadel	MP	TFG	3FG	FT	R	A	PF	TP
Mosay	24	1-7	0-1	0-0	5	2	5	2
Holstein	25	2-4	0-0	1-1	3	1	1	5
Van Schaardenburg	28	1-8	0-0	0-0	3	2	1	2
Wright	33	6-13	2-4	0-0	4	2	2	14
Campbell	30	4-14	4-8	0-0	4	1	3	12
Hodges	4	1-1	1-1	0-0	0	1	0	3
Harris	17	3-9	1-3	0-0	4	0	0	7
McDowell	15	2-4	0-0	0-0	4	0	4	4
Braggs	10	0-4	0-1	1-2	1	0	2	1
Williamson	9	0-3	0-1	0-0	0	0	1	0
Stowers	3	0-1	0-1	0-0	0	1	0	0
Ishie	2	0-0	0-0	0-0	0	0	0	0
Totals	**200**	**20-68**	**8-20**	**2-3**	**30**	**10**	**19**	**50**

UNC	MP	TFG	3FG	FT	R	A	PF	TP
Fox	18	5-9	2-4	1-2	7	3	1	13
Lynch	13	3-5	0-0	0-0	4	1	0	6
Chilcutt	17	4-5	1-1	0-0	3	1	0	9
Rodl	12	2-4	0-0	0-0	1	4	1	4
Rice	15	4-8	0-0	1-1	1	4	0	9
Davis	14	6-8	3-5	0-0	2	1	0	15
Montross	14	4-4	0-0	3-5	5	0	2	11
Phelps	9	0-0	0-0	0-0	3	8	1	0
Reese	12	5-6	0-0	1-1	2	4	0	11
Rozier	16	7-8	0-0	1-3	4	0	0	15
Salvadori	12	2-3	0-0	2-5	3	0	0	6
Sullivan	14	1-3	0-1	0-0	2	2	2	2
Harris	14	3-4	0-0	3-3	3	4	0	9
Cherry	11	1-2	0-0	4-4	2	3	0	6
Wenstrom	9	1-3	0-0	0-2	4	0	1	2
Totals	**200**	**48-72**	**6-11**	**16-26**	**46**	**35**	**8**	**118**

The Citadel	21	29	-	50
UNC	62	56	-	118

Turnovers: The Citadel 31, UNC 15.
Technical Fouls: None.
Officials: Hartzell, Nobles, Hess.
Attendance: 19,207.

UNC 73, Clemson 57

Feb. 23, 1991 — Chapel Hill, NC

Clemson	MP	TFG	3FG	FT	R	A	PF	TP
Jones	24	1-4	0-0	5-9	3	1	3	7
Brown	22	2-7	0-0	0-0	5	0	5	4
Davis	37	7-13	0-0	5-8	15	0	3	19
Bruce	30	3-10	1-6	0-0	1	1	3	7
Burks	12	1-3	0-1	0-0	0	0	1	2
Bovain	32	5-10	2-5	0-1	2	1	0	12
Mason	11	0-1	0-0	0-0	1	1	1	0
Young	28	3-9	0-4	0-0	1	7	5	6
Lastinger	3	0-0	0-0	0-1	1	0	0	0
Paul	1	0-0	0-0	0-0	0	0	0	0
Totals	**200**	**22-57**	**3-16**	**10-19**	**34**	**10**	**22**	**57**

UNC	MP	TFG	3FG	FT	R	A	PF	TP
Fox	31	5-12	0-5	2-4	5	2	3	12
Lynch	26	2-10	0-0	5-6	7	1	3	9
Chilcutt	29	4-5	0-0	1-1	4	1	1	9
Davis	27	5-8	1-3	2-2	0	0	4	13
Phelps	13	3-3	1-1	0-0	0	0	0	7
Rice	26	2-5	0-0	4-4	1	4	1	8
Montross	14	1-3	0-0	5-6	3	0	2	7
Rodl	12	0-1	0-1	0-0	3	2	2	0
Reese	7	1-2	0-0	0-1	1	0	1	2
Rozier	8	0-0	0-0	1-2	6	1	0	1
Salvadori	2	1-1	0-0	0-0	0	0	0	2
Sullivan	2	0-0	0-0	0-0	1	1	0	0
Harris	1	0-0	0-0	0-0	1	0	0	0
Cherry	1	0-0	0-0	1-2	0	1	0	1
Wenstrom	1	1-1	0-0	0-0	0	0	1	2
Totals	**200**	**25-51**	**2-10**	**21-28**	**32**	**13**	**18**	**73**

Clemson	22	35	-	57
UNC	31	42	-	73

Turnovers: Clemson 26, UNC 20.
Technical Fouls: None.
Officials: Paparo, Moreau, Gordon.
Attendance: 20,148.

UNC 91, Georgia Tech 74

Feb. 28, 1991 — Atlanta, Ga.

UNC	MP	TFG	3FG	FT	R	A	PF	TP
Lynch	28	7-12	0-0	3-4	12	1	1	17
Fox	29	6-11	2-4	4-4	6	2	3	18
Chilcutt	30	2-8	1-1	4-4	8	4	2	9
Rice	31	2-5	0-0	1-2	1	7	2	5
Davis	29	5-10	3-5	3-4	3	4	0	16
Montross	14	4-5	0-0	0-1	3	0	1	8
Rozier	6	2-6	0-0	0-0	4	2	1	4
Rodl	10	1-2	1-1	0-0	2	0	1	3
Phelps	8	1-2	0-0	1-2	1	2	2	3
Sullivan	2	1-1	0-0	0-0	0	0	1	2
Reese	9	2-5	0-0	0-0	1	1	0	4
Harris	1	0-1	0-1	0-0	0	0	0	0
Cherry	1	1-1	0-0	0-0	0	0	0	2
Salvadori	1	0-0	0-0	0-0	0	0	0	0
Wenstrom	1	0-0	0-0	0-0	0	0	0	0
Totals	**200**	**34-69**	**7-12**	**16-21**	**43**	**23**	**14**	**91**

Georgia Tech	MP	TFG	3FG	FT	R	A	PF	TF
Barry	37	6-19	5-13	0-0	4	3	4	17
Mackey	36	6-12	0-0	1-1	10	1	3	13
Munlyn	5	1-4	0-0	0-0	5	0	0	2
Domalik	8	1-2	1-2	0-0	0	0	1	3
Anderson	40	6-19	0-6	3-5	3	8	2	15
Geiger	23	6-9	0-1	0-0	8	0	4	12
Hill	34	3-8	3-6	2-3	6	7	3	11
Newbill	16	0-0	0-0	1-2	3	0	2	1
Balanis	1	0-1	0-0	0-0	0	0	0	0
Totals	**200**	**29-74**	**9-28**	**7-11**	**41**	**19**	**19**	**74**

UNC	43	48	-	91
Georgia Tech	21	53	-	74

Turnovers: Georgia Tech 11, UNC 6.
Technical Fouls: None.
Officials: Wirtz, Lembo, Edsall.
Attendance: 10,113.

Duke 83, UNC 77

March 3, 1991 — Chapel Hill, NC

Duke	MP	TFG	3FG	FT	R	A	PF	TP
Hill, G.	32	7-8	0-0	2-5	5	3	2	16
Davis	25	1-4	0-0	3-5	7	1	2	5
Laettner	36	7-13	0-0	4-4	4	5	4	18
Hill, T.	31	2-6	0-1	6-6	7	1	0	10
Hurley	34	7-12	4-6	0-0	1	6	5	18
McCaffrey	22	1-5	0-0	2-2	2	5	2	4
Koubek	17	3-6	3-4	1-2	3	1	2	10
Buckley	3	1-1	0-0	0-0	0	0	0	2
Totals	**200**	**29-55**	**7-11**	**18-24**	**33**	**22**	**17**	**83**

UNC	MP	TFG	3FG	FT	R	A	PF	TP
Fox	32	5-14	1-5	3-6	10	7	3	14
Lynch	17	3-4	0-0	2-3	4	0	5	8
Chilcutt	32	7-15	1-6	3-3	4	1	0	18
Rodl	9	1-2	0-0	0-0	1	1	2	2
Rice	32	3-6	0-1	1-2	0	5	2	7
Davis	31	5-10	1-4	5-5	2	1	1	16
Rozier	14	1-3	0-0	0-0	3	0	3	2
Montross	12	2-2	0-0	2-2	2	0	1	6
Phelps	9	0-1	0-1	0-0	0	1	1	0
Reese	8	2-2	0-0	0-2	2	0	0	4
Sullivan	3	0-0	0-0	0-0	0	0	2	0
Wenstrom	1	0-0	0-0	0-0	0	0	0	0
Totals	**200**	**29-59**	**3-17**	**16-23**	**30**	**16**	**20**	**77**

Duke	46	37	-	83
UNC	36	41	-	77

Turnovers: UNC 17, Duke 16.
Technical Fouls: None.
Officials: Paparo, Donaghy, Hartzell.
Attendance: 21,572.

UNC 67, Clemson 59

March 8, 1991 — Charlotte, NC

Clemson	MP	TFG	3FG	FT	R	A	PF	TP
Bovain	26	2-6	0-2	0-0	1	2	1	4
Jones	30	7-9	0-0	2-2	6	1	0	16
Davis	34	7-15	0-0	2-2	6	1	0	16
Bruce	23	2-7	1-4	0-0	6	2	0	5
Harris	24	2-3	0-0	0-0	2	5	5	4
Young	16	3-6	1-4	0-0	1	3	3	7
Burks	31	4-8	0-4	0-1	1	1	2	8
Brown	16	0-3	0-1	0-0	4	1	3	0
Totals	**200**	**27-57**	**2-15**	**3-6**	**33**	**15**	**19**	**59**

UNC	MP	TFG	3FG	FT	R	A	PF	TP
Fox	34	4-10	3-6	3-4	6	2	2	14
Lynch	31	2-9	0-0	1-3	8	3	2	5
Chilcutt	36	6-14	0-2	0-0	3	0	1	12
Davis	30	6-7	3-4	0-0	1	2	3	15
Rice	32	3-8	1-4	6-8	3	6	2	13
Montross	12	1-2	0-0	2-2	2	0	3	4
Sullivan	6	0-0	0-0	2-2	0	0	0	2
Rodl	10	0-0	0-0	0-0	3	0	0	0
Phelps	8	1-1	0-0	0-0	0	0	1	2
Salvadori	1	0-0	0-0	0-0	0	0	0	0
Totals	**200**	**23-51**	**7-16**	**14-19**	**27**	**13**	**14**	**67**

Clemson	42	17	-	59
UNC	36	31	-	67

Turnovers: Clemson 17, UNC 12.
Technical Fouls: None.
Officials: Donaghy, Moreau, Edsall.
Attendance: 23,532.

UNC 76, Virginia 71

March 9, 1991 — Charlotte, NC

Virginia	MP	TFG	3FG	FT	R	A	PF	TP
Stith	38	8-24	1-6	4-6	4	4	4	21
Turner	36	6-18	0-3	2-4	9	0	3	14
Jeffries	21	2-4	0-0	0-0	2	0	2	4
Crotty	39	8-11	3-6	4-6	2	1	1	23
Oliver	32	3-10	0-0	0-0	4	0	3	6
Smith	1	0-0	0-0	0-0	0	0	0	0
Blundin	23	0-0	0-0	1-2	3	0	3	1
Parker	10	1-3	0-0	0-0	2	0	0	2
Totals	**200**	**28-70**	**4-15**	**11-18**	**29**	**5**	**16**	**71**

UNC	MP	TFG	3FG	FT	R	A	PF	TP
Fox	31	6-12	1-2	0-1	15	6	3	13
Lynch	20	5-10	0-0	0-0	5	1	4	10
Chilcutt	30	5-12	0-2	3-4	11	4	2	13
Davis	28	4-11	1-3	0-0	2	1	1	9
Rice	29	2-5	1-1	2-3	3	1	1	7
Montross	17	3-4	0-0	1-1	6	1	4	7
Rodl	12	1-3	0-1	0-0	1	1	1	2
Phelps	11	2-4	1-1	0-0	0	2	0	5
Reese	9	1-2	0-0	0-0	2	1	0	2
Rozier	13	3-5	0-0	2-2	2	0	1	8
Totals	**200**	**32-68**	**4-10**	**8-11**	**51**	**18**	**17**	**76**

Virginia	29	42	-	71
UNC	43	33	-	76

Turnovers: UNC 16, Virginia 9.
Technical Fouls: UNC bench.
Officials: Herring, Moreau, Gray.
Attendance: 23,532.

UNC 96, Duke 74

March 10, 1991 — Charlotte, NC

UNC	MP	TFG	3FG	FT	R	A	PF	TP
Fox	27	10-16	2-3	3-3	6	3	4	25
Lynch	27	2-6	0-0	2-4	7	2	4	6
Chilcutt	29	2-5	0-0	4-4	8	1	2	8
Davis	29	7-14	3-4	0-0	4	2	0	17
Rice	26	5-7	1-2	1-2	1	7	1	12
Montross	15	3-3	0-0	1-2	3	0	2	7
Sullivan	1	0-1	0-1	0-0	0	0	0	0
Harris	1	0-0	0-0	0-0	0	0	0	0
Rodl	12	1-2	1-1	3-4	0	1	2	6
Phelps	13	2-3	0-0	1-1	2	3	0	5
Reese	12	2-3	0-0	0-0	0	1	0	4
Salvadori	1	1-1	0-0	0-0	0	0	0	2
Rozier	5	1-3	0-0	0-0	4	0	0	2
Cherry	1	0-0	0-0	2-2	0	1	0	2
Wenstrom	1	0-0	0-0	0-0	0	0	0	0
Totals	**200**	**36-64**	**7-11**	**17-22**	**37**	**21**	**15**	**96**

Duke	MP	TFG	3FG	FT	R	A	PF	TP
Hill, G.	29	4-9	0-0	2-2	7	1	1	10
Davis	17	2-2	0-0	4-4	3	0	1	8
Laettner	30	9-18	1-2	3-4	5	2	4	22
Hill, T.	22	1-11	0-2	0-0	2	0	0	2
Hurley	36	0-4	0-4	2-2	0	3	1	2
Clark	1	0-1	0-0	0-0	0	0	0	0
McCaffrey	23	2-4	1-1	0-0	0	3	1	5
Lang	3	1-3	0-0	0-0	1	0	0	2
Koubek	27	7-13	5-7	2-3	4	1	2	21
Palmer	2	0-0	0-0	0-0	0	0	1	0
Buckley	9	1-1	0-0	0-0	1	0	3	2
Ast	1	0-0	0-0	0-0	0	0	0	0
Totals	**200**	**27-66**	**7-16**	**13-15**	**28**	**10**	**14**	**74**

UNC	49	47	-	96
Duke	36	38	-	74

Turnovers: Duke 19, UNC 17.
Technical Fouls: Duke bench; Laettner.
Officials: Wirtz, Paparo, Donaghy, Herring (standby).
Attendance: 23,532.

Rick Fox won MVP for the ACC Tournament and led UNC to the Final Four.

UNC 101, Northeastern 66

March 15, 1991 — Syracuse, NY

Northeastern	MP	TFG	3FG	FT	R	A	PF	TP
Anderson	31	3-5	0-0	3-3	4	1	5	9
Lacy	31	5-10	0-1	2-2	4	3	4	12
Carney	31	9-19	0-0	4-4	9	2	2	22
Robinson	24	0-5	0-3	0-0	3	8	2	0
Jenkins	23	4-15	1-2	0-1	3	3	3	9
Harlee	21	0-5	0-3	0-0	1	0	4	0
Hodge	13	2-3	0-0	0-2	0	0	3	4
Hough	12	3-9	2-6	0-0	2	0	2	8
McBride	1	0-0	0-0	0-0	0	0	0	0
Callahan	6	0-0	0-0	0-0	1	0	0	0
Brighthaupt	2	1-1	0-0	0-0	1	0	0	2
Battle	4	0-0	0-0	0-0	0	0	0	0
Spokas	1	0-0	0-0	0-0	0	0	0	0
Totals	**200**	**27-72**	**3-15**	**9-12**	**32**	**17**	**25**	**66**

UNC	MP	TFG	3FG	FT	R	A	PF	TP
Fox	26	6-8	2-2	2-2	6	3	0	16
Chilcutt	21	6-8	0-0	0-0	4	0	0	12
Montross	18	2-7	0-0	1-1	5	2	2	5
Davis	21	5-9	1-4	5-5	1	5	1	16
Rice	23	3-5	0-1	2-2	1	6	1	8
Lynch	24	5-6	0-0	2-2	7	0	2	12
Rodl	16	2-2	0-0	0-5	2	3	1	4
Phelps	12	1-2	0-0	0-0	3	5	0	2
Rozier	9	4-8	0-0	2-3	4	0	2	10
Reese	9	3-5	0-0	0-1	3	0	0	6
Sullivan	9	0-1	0-0	0-0	1	0	0	0
Harris	4	0-1	0-0	2-2	1	0	1	2
Cherry	4	0-0	0-0	0-0	1	1	0	0
Salvadori	4	1-2	0-0	4-6	0	0	0	6
Wenstrom	4	1-3	0-0	0-0	2	0	2	2
Totals	**200**	**39-67**	**3-7**	**20-29**	**47**	**25**	**12**	**101**

Northeastern	29	37	-	66
UNC	50	51	-	101

Turnovers: Northeastern 21, UNC 20.
Technical Fouls: None.
Officials: Wolkow, McDonald, Carr.
Attendance: 17,206.

UNC 84, Villanova 69

March 17, 1991 — Syracuse, NY

Villanova	MP	TFG	3FG	FT	R	A	PF	TP
Bain	24	2-7	0-2	2-2	3	1	4	6
Miller, L.	35	6-12	1-2	4-4	7	3	1	17
Dowdell	26	3-8	0-0	2-2	6	3	5	8
Woodard	32	5-11	3-7	2-2	3	1	3	15
Walker	21	4-9	3-6	0-0	1	1	3	11
Byrd	28	1-4	0-0	0-0	2	0	1	2
Bryson	7	0-0	0-0	0-0	0	0	0	0
Mumford	12	3-4	2-2	2-2	0	2	2	10
Pelle	11	0-0	0-0	0-0	4	0	1	0
Miller, D.	1	0-1	0-1	0-0	0	0	0	0
Masotti	1	0-1	0-0	0-0	1	0	0	0
Vrind	1	0-0	0-0	0-0	0	0	1	0
Muller	1	0-1	0-1	0-0	0	0	0	0
Totals	**200**	**24-55**	**9-21**	**12-12**	**34**	**11**	**21**	**69**

UNC	MP	TFG	3FG	FT	R	A	PF	TP
Fox	32	6-12	2-7	0-0	2	8	3	14
Lynch	32	8-11	0-0	3-4	10	0	1	19
Chilcutt	26	4-10	0-1	3-5	5	1	3	11
Davis	31	6-11	3-4	3-4	3	4	0	18
Rice	28	3-8	1-1	1-2	1	9	1	8
Rodl	6	1-1	0-0	0-0	0	2	0	2
Montross	13	2-3	0-0	0-0	5	1	1	4
Phelps	11	2-4	0-0	3-4	3	2	0	7
Reese	10	0-0	0-0	0-0	1	0	2	0
Rozier	6	0-1	0-0	1-2	0	0	1	1
Sullivan	1	0-0	0-0	0-0	0	0	0	0
Harris	1	0-0	0-0	0-0	0	0	0	0
Cherry	1	0-0	0-0	0-0	0	0	0	0
Salvadori	1	0-0	0-0	0-0	0	0	0	0
Wenstrom	1	0-0	0-0	0-0	1	0	0	0
Totals	**200**	**32-61**	**6-13**	**14-21**	**35**	**27**	**12**	**84**

Villanova	32	37	-	69
UNC	44	40	-	84

Turnovers: Villanova 22, UNC 16.
Technical Fouls: None.
Officials: Wulkow, Harmon, MacDonald.
Attendance: 17,523.

HUGH MORTON

UNC 93, Eastern Michigan 67

March 22, 1991 — East Rutherford, NJ

Eastern Michigan	MP	TFG	3FG	FT	R	A	PF	TP
Thomas, Carl	33	10-16	5-10	2-2	5	2	3	27
Hallas	31	4-9	0-0	1-2	2	2	3	9
Kennedy	37	8-14	0-0	3-6	6	1	4	19
Neely	33	0-4	0-0	0-0	4	5	0	0
Thomas, Charles	37	3-11	2-9	0-0	5	6	2	8
Felder	7	0-0	0-0	0-0	0	1	0	0
Frasor	1	1-1	0-0	0-0	1	0	0	2
Lewis	10	0-1	0-1	0-0	0	1	3	0
Nickleberry	1	0-2	0-0	0-0	0	0	1	0
Pearson	2	0-1	0-0	0-0	0	0	0	0
Boykin	7	1-2	0-0	0-0	3	0	0	2
Pangas	1	0-0	0-0	0-0	0	0	0	0
Totals	**200**	**27-61**	**7-20**	**6-10**	**30**	**18**	**16**	**67**

UNC	MP	TFG	3FG	FT	R	A	PF	TP
Lynch	30	5-11	0-0	0-1	7	0	3	10
Fox	24	3-10	0-2	0-0	6	0	4	6
Chilcutt	24	8-9	0-0	2-2	5	2	0	28
Rice	25	4-6	1-2	3-3	3	6	2	12
Davis	29	5-6	5-5	3-3	4	1	1	18
Montross	18	5-7	0-0	7-8	6	0	3	17
Sullivan	4	0-0	0-0	0-2	1	1	0	0
Harris	2	0-1	0-0	0-0	0	0	0	0
Rodl	9	1-2	0-0	0-0	0	1	0	2
Cherry	2	0-1	0-0	0-0	1	0	0	0
Phelps	13	2-2	0-0	0-0	0	4	1	4
Reese	12	1-4	0-0	1-2	0	0	0	3
Salvadori	2	1-3	0-0	0-0	2	0	0	2
Rozier	4	0-2	0-0	0-0	0	1	0	0
Wenstrom	2	0-2	0-0	1-2	3	0	0	1
Totals	**200**	**35-66**	**6-9**	**17-23**	**40**	**16**	**14**	**93**

Eastern Michigan	42	25	-	67
UNC	44	40	-	84

Turnovers: Eastern Michigan 16, UNC 12.
Technical Fouls: None.
Officials: Dibler, Bair, Allen, Monje (standby).
Attendance: 19,544.

UNC 75, Temple 72

March 24, 1991 — East Rutherford, NJ

Temple	MP	TFG	3FG	FT	R	A	PF	TP
Kilgore	40	7-15	3-6	1-5	5	4	4	18
Strickland	37	3-7	0-0	2-2	6	1	2	8
Hodge	39	3-7	0-0	1-2	6	0	1	7
Carstarphen	35	3-11	2-9	0-0	3	5	5	8
Macon	38	12-23	4-9	3-3	9	1	3	31
Harden	5	0-0	0-0	0-0	1	1	1	0
Spears	3	0-2	0-0	0-0	1	0	0	0
Totals	**200**	**28-65**	**9-24**	**7-12**	**35**	**12**	**16**	**72**

UNC	MP	TFG	3FG	FT	R	A	PF	TP
Lynch	30	5-9	0-0	0-0	8	0	3	10
Fox	32	8-16	2-7	1-1	7	5	3	19
Chilcutt	32	3-10	0-1	1-2	9	0	1	7
Rice	32	2-4	2-2	6-6	2	7	0	12
Davis	30	7-13	2-6	3-3	3	2	1	19
Montross	15	0-3	0-0	1-2	2	0	3	1
Sullivan	3	0-0	0-0	0-0	0	0	0	0
Rodl	7	2-3	1-1	0-0	0	0	1	5
Phelps	8	0-1	0-0	0-0	2	0	0	0
Reese	10	1-1	0-0	0-0	2	0	0	2
Rozier	1	0-1	0-0	0-0	0	1	0	0
Totals	**200**	**28-61**	**7-17**	**12-14**	**40**	**15**	**12**	**75**

Temple	30	42	-	72
UNC	35	40	-	75

Turnovers: UNC 7, Temple 6.
Technical Fouls: None.
Officials: Harrington, Range, Mingle, Monje (standby).
Attendance: 19,601.

Kansas 79, UNC 73

March 30, 1991 — Indianapolis, IN

Kansas	MP	TFG	3FG	FT	R	A	PF	TP
Jamison	25	4-8	0-0	1-3	11	2	4	9
Maddox	27	4-10	0-0	2-2	4	2	3	10
Randall	34	6-11	0-0	4-6	11	4	1	16
Brown	24	1-10	1-6	0-0	4	1	2	3
Jordan	36	4-11	2-6	6-13	4	7	2	16
Richey	10	1-1	0-0	2-2	1	0	2	4
Woodbery	6	0-0	0-0	2-2	1	0	1	2
Tunstall	20	1-5	1-2	2-5	2	1	2	5
Wagner	2	0-1	0-0	0-0	1	0	0	0
Scott	16	6-9	0-0	2-3	6	0	3	14
Johanning	0	0-0	0-0	0-0	1	0	0	0
Totals	**200**	**27-66**	**4-14**	**21-36**	**51**	**17**	**20**	**79**

UNC	MP	TFG	3FG	FT	R	A	PF	TP
Lynch	30	5-8	0-0	3-6	5	2	5	13
Fox	29	5-22	0-7	3-3	9	7	5	13
Chilcutt	27	2-8	0-1	0-0	11	1	3	4
Rice	30	1-6	0-3	3-4	0	3	2	5
Davis	31	9-16	2-4	5-5	5	1	0	25
Montross	19	3-4	0-0	0-1	3	1	4	6
Sullivan	0	0-0	0-0	0-0	0	0	3	0
Harris	2	0-2	0-2	0-0	0	0	0	0
Rodl	8	0-1	0-0	0-0	2	0	1	0
Phelps	10	1-1	0-0	0-1	1	1	4	2
Reese	11	2-5	1-1	0-3	2	0	0	5
Rozier	3	0-0	0-0	0-0	0	0	0	0
Totals	**200**	**28-73**	**3-18**	**14-23**	**42**	**16**	**27**	**73**

Kansas	43	36	-	79
UNC	34	39	-	73

Turnovers: Kansas 18, UNC 15.
Technical Fouls: 2 – UNC bench.
Officials: Donaghy, Hightower, Pavia, Harrington (standby).
Attendance: 47,100.

1990-91 ACC Season In Review

1991 ATLANTIC COAST CONFERENCE STANDINGS

Team	CONFERENCE GAMES					ALL GAMES				
	W	L	Pct.	Off.	Def.	W	L	Pct.	Off.	Def.
Duke	11	3	.786	84.4	73.4	32	7	.821	87.7	73.7
*North Carolina	10	4	.714	85.3	75.9	29	6	.829	87.6	71.6
N.C. State	8	6	.571	83.5	85.2	20	11	.645	89.3	83.5
Wake Forest	8	6	.571	81.9	79.8	19	11	.633	80.5	74.9
Virginia	6	8	.429	73.4	74.4	21	12	.636	74.3	68.5
Georgia Tech	6	8	.429	78.6	79.1	17	13	.567	82.5	77.0
Maryland	5	9	.357	78.6	86.7	16	12	.571	80.2	79.4
Clemson	2	12	.167	67.2	78.6	11	17	.393	73.7	76.7

(*Won Championship in Conference Tournament)
RECORD AGAINST NON-CONFERENCE TEAMS: Won 101, Lost 27 — 78.9%

ACC TOURNAMENT RESULTS

Charlotte Coliseum, Charlotte, North Carolina
1st Round: North Carolina 67, Clemson 59; N.C. State 82, Georgia Tech 68; Virginia 70, Wake Forest 66.
Semifinals: Duke 93, N.C. State 72; North Carolina 76, Virginia 71.
Championship: North Carolina 96, Duke 74.

NCAA RESULTS

East Regional (Syracuse, N.Y.)
1st Round: North Carolina 101, Northeastern 66
2nd Round: North Carolina 84, Villanova 69
East Regional (College Park, Md.)
1st Round: N.C. State 114, Southern Mississippi 85
2nd Round: Oklahoma State 73, N.C. State 64
Midwest Regional (Minneapolis, Minn.)
1st Round: Duke 102, Northeast Louisiana 73
2nd Round: Duke 85, Iowa 70
Midwest Regional (Dayton, Ohio)
1st Round: Georgia Tech 87, DePaul 70
2nd Round: Ohio State 65, Georgia Tech 61
Southeast Regional (Atlanta, Ga.)
1st Round: Wake Forest 71, Louisiana Tech 65
2nd Round: Alabama 96, Wake Forest 88
West Regional (Salt Lake City, Utah)
1st Round: Brigham Young 61, Virginia 48
East Regional (East Rutherford, N.J.)
Semifinals: North Carolina 93, Eastern Michigan 67
Finals: North Carolina 75, Temple 72
Midwest Regional (Pontiac, Mich.)
Semifinals: Duke 81, Connecticut 67
Finals: Duke 78, St. John's 61
Final Four (Indianapolis, Ind.)
Semifinals: Duke 79, UNLV 77; Kansas 79, North Carolina 73
Finals: Duke 72, Kansas 65

NCAA ALL-REGION TEAMS

East — Hubert Davis, North Carolina; Rick Fox, North Carolina
Midwest — Bobby Hurley, Duke (MVP); Christian Laettner, Duke; Thomas Hill, Duke
Final Four — Christian Laettner, Duke (MVP); Bobby Hurley, Duke; Billy McCaffrey, Duke

FINAL 1991 POLLS

AP	UPI	USA/CNN
4. North Carolina	4. North Carolina	4. North Carolina
6. Duke	6. Duke	7. Duke

(NOTE: Final polls are published prior to NCAA Tournament)

NBA DRAFTEES

First Round — Kenny Anderson, Georgia Tech (New Jersey/2nd overall); Dale Davis, Clemson (Indiana/13th); Rick Fox, North Carolina (Boston/24th); Pete Chilcutt, North Carolina (Sacramento/27th)
Second Round — Rodney Monroe, N.C. State (Atlanta/30th); Chris Corchiani, N.C. State (Orlando/36th)

ALL-AMERICA SELECTIONS

Kenny Anderson (Georgia Tech) — 1st Team — Associated Press, United Press International, U.S. Basketball Writers Association, National Association of Basketball Coaches. 2nd Team — The Sporting News.
Christian Laettner (Duke) — 2nd Team — Associated Press, United Press International, U.S. Basketball Writers Association, National Association of Basketball Coaches, The Sporting News.
Rodney Monroe (N.C. State) — 1st Team — The Sporting News. 2nd Team — United Press International, National Association of Basketball Coaches. 3rd Team — Associated Press.
Rick Fox (North Carolina) — 3rd Team — The Sporting News. HM — United Press International.
Chris Corchiani (N.C. State) — 3rd Team — National Association of Basketball Coaches. HM — United Press International.
Bryant Stith (Virginia) — HM — Associated Press, United Press International.
Dale Davis (Clemson) — HM — Associated Press.

NATIONAL HONORS

Rodney Rogers (Wake Forest) — National Freshman of the Year — U.S. Basketball Writers Association, Basketball Times. Freshman All-America — Basketball Weekly.
Matt Roe (Maryland) — Academic All-America — College Sports Information Directors of America.

ALL-TOURNAMENT TEAM

FIRST TEAM: Rick Fox, North Carolina; Hubert Davis, North Carolina; Christian Laettner, Duke; John Crotty, Virginia; Rodney Monroe, N.C. State.
SECOND TEAM: Pete Chilcutt, North Carolina; King Rice, North Carolina; Greg Koubek, Duke; Chris Corchiani, N.C. State; Grant Hill, Duke.
TOURNAMENT MOST VALUABLE PLAYER: Rick Fox

1991 ASSOCIATED PRESS ALL-ACC TEAM

(Selected by Panel of Sports Writers and Broadcasters from ACC Area)

Player, School	Hgt.	Wgt.	Class	Hometown
FIRST TEAM				
Kenny Anderson, Georgia Tech	6-2	168	So.	Rego Park, NY
Christian Laettner, Duke	6-11	235	Jr.	Angola, NY
Rodney Monroe, N.C. State	6-3	185	Sr.	Hagerstown, MD
Bryant Stith, Virginia	6-5	204	Jr.	Freeman, VA
Rick Fox, North Carolina	6-7	231	Sr.	Nassau, Bahamas
SECOND TEAM				
Chris Corchiani, N.C. State	6-1	186	Sr.	Miami, FL
Dale Davis, Clemson	6-11	230	Sr.	Toccoa, GA
Rodney Rogers, Wake Forest	6-7	235	Fr.	Durham, NC
Tom Gugliotta, N.C. State	6-9	230	Jr.	Huntington Station, NY
Malcolm Mackey, Georgia Tech	6-11	248	So.	Chattanooga, TN
THIRD TEAM				
John Crotty, Virginia	6-1	184	Sr.	Spring Lake, NJ
Pete Chilcutt, North Carolina	6-10	232	So.	Eutaw, AL
Bobby Hurley, Duke	6-0	160	So.	Jersey City, NJ
Matt Roe, Maryland	6-6	201	Sr.	Manlius, NY
Thomas Hill, Duke	6-4	195	So.	Lancaster, TX

PLAYER OF THE YEAR: Rodney Monroe (N.C. State)
ROOKIE OF THE YEAR: Rodney Rogers (Wake Forest)
COACH OF THE YEAR: Dave Odom (Wake Forest)

PLAYER/ROOKIE OF THE WEEK

Player-Of-Week	Rookie-Of-Week
1st Week—Kenny Turner, Virginia	Rodney Rogers, Wake Forest
2nd Week—Bobby Hurley, Duke	Rodney Rogers, Wake Forest
3rd Week—Thomas Hill, Duke	Rodney Rogers, Wake Forest
4th Week—Malcolm Mackey, GA Tech	Garfield Smith, Maryland
5th Week—Thomas Hill, Duke	Randolph Childress, Wake Forest
6th Week—Randolph Childress, WF	Rodney Rogers, Wake Forest
7th Week—Jon Barry, GA Tech	Randolph Childress, Wake Forest
8th Week—Rodney Monroe, N.C. State	Rodney Rogers, Wake Forest
9th Week—Chris Corchiani, N.C. State	Grant Hill, Duke
10th Week—Rick Fox, North Carolina	Rodney Rogers, Wake Forest

FINAL 1990-91 ATLANTIC COAST CONFERENCE
MEN'S INDIVIDUAL BASKETBALL STATISTICS

SCORING

Player, School	FG	3Pt.	FT	Pts.	Avg.
Rodney Monroe, N.C. State	285	104	162	836	27.0
Kenny Anderson, Georgia Tech	278	65	155	776	25.9
Bryant Stith, Virginia	228	38	159	653	19.8
Christian Laettner, Duke	271	18	211	771	19.8
Dale Davis, Clemson	191	0	119	501	17.9
Matt Roe, Maryland	170	48	109	497	17.8
Rick Fox, North Carolina	206	61	111	590	16.9
Chris Corchiani, N.C. State	160	51	134	505	16.3
Rodney Rogers, Wake Forest	199	10	81	489	16.3
Jon Barry, Georgia Tech	180	77	41	478	15.9
John Crotty, Virginia	176	46	115	513	15.5
Malcolm Mackey, Georgia Tech	190	0	80	460	15.3
Tom Gugliotta, N.C. State	170	66	65	471	15.2
Chris King, Wake Forest	179	17	77	452	15.1
Kenny Turner, Virginia	179	33	93	484	14.7
Randolph Childress, WF	123	64	95	405	14.0
Hubert Davis, North Carolina	161	64	81	467	13.3
Bryant Feggins, N.C. State	174	0	65	413	13.3
George Lynch, North Carolina	172	7	85	436	12.5
Pete Chilcutt, North Carolina	175	5	65	420	12.0

STEALS

Player, School	Games	No.	Avg.
Kenny Anderson, Georgia Tech	30	89	3.0
Chris Corchiani, N.C. State	31	91	2.9
Rick Fox, North Carolina	35	70	2.0
Christian Laettner, Duke	39	75	1.9
Rodney Rogers, Wake Forest	30	53	1.8
Jon Barry, Georgia Tech	30	53	1.8
Tom Gugliotta, N.C. State	31	53	1.7
Thomas Hill, Duke	38	59	1.6
Bryant Stith, Virginia	33	51	1.5
Randolph Childress, Wake Forest	29	44	1.5

REBOUNDS

Player, School	Games	No.	Avg.
Dale Davis, Clemson	28	340	12.1
Malcolm Mackey, Georgia Tech	30	321	10.7
Tom Gugliotta, N.C. State	31	281	9.1
Christian Laettner, Duke	39	340	8.7
Cedric Lewis, Maryland	28	233	8.3
Rodney Rogers, Wake Forest	30	237	7.9
Kevin Thompson, N.C. State	31	240	7.7
George Lynch, North Carolina	35	258	7.4
Kenny Turner, Virginia	33	245	7.4
Rick Fox, North Carolina	35	232	6.6

ASSISTS

Player, School	Games	No.	Avg.
Chris Corchiani, N.C. State	31	299	9.6
Bobby Hurley, Duke	29	289	7.4
King Rice, North Carolina	35	207	5.9
Kenny Anderson, Georgia Tech	30	169	5.6
John Crotty, Virginia	33	169	5.1
Derrick McQueen, Wake Forest	29	142	4.9
Kevin McLinton, Maryland	28	123	4.4
Rick Fox, North Carolina	35	131	3.7
Jon Barry, Georgia Tech	30	110	3.7
David Young, Clemson	28	100	3.6

BLOCKED SHOTS

Player, School	Games	No.	Avg.
Cedric Lewis, Maryland	28	143	5.1
Dale Davis, Clemson	28	74	2.6
Malcolm Mackey, Georgia Tech	30	54	1.8
Kevin Thompson, N.C. State	31	49	1.6
Christian Laettner, Duke	39	44	1.1
Tom Gugliotta, N.C. State	31	34	1.1
Matt Geiger, Georgia Tech	27	29	1.1
Pete Chilcutt, North Carolina	35	35	1.0
Chris King, Wake Forest	30	30	1.0
Ricky Jones, Clemson	27	25	0.9

FIELD GOAL PERCENTAGE
(Minimum 5 FGs Scored Per Game)

Player, School	Games	FGM	FGA	Pct.
Christian Laettner, Duke	39	271	471	.575
Rodney Rogers, Wake Forest	30	199	349	.570
Malcolm Mackey, Georgia Tech	30	190	345	.551
Pete Chilcutt, North Carolina	35	175	325	.538
Bryant Feggins, N.C. State	31	174	325	.535
Dale Davis, Clemson	28	191	359	.532
Tom Gugliotta, N.C. State	31	170	340	.500
Chris King, Wake Forest	30	179	366	.489
Bryant Stith, Virginia	33	228	484	.471
Chris Corchiani, N.C. State	31	160	343	.466

FREE THROW PERCENTAGE
(Minimum 2.5 FTs Scored Per Game)

Player, School	FTM	FTA	Pct.
Rodney Monroe, N.C. State	162	183	.885
Kenny Anderson, Georgia Tech	155	187	.829
Chris Corchiani, N.C. State	134	163	.822
Rick Fox, North Carolina	111	138	.804
Christian Laettner, Duke	211	263	.803
Matt Roe, Maryland	109	136	.801
Bryant Stith, Virginia	159	201	.791
John Crotty, Virginia	115	148	.777
Randolph Childress, Wake Forest	95	123	.772
Kenny Turner, Virginia	93	124	.750

3-POINT FIELD GOAL PERCENTAGE
(Minimum 1 Made Per Game)

Player, School	3PM	3PA	Pct.
Hubert Davis, North Carolina	64	131	.489
Rodney Monroe, N.C. State	104	239	.435
Robert Siler, Wake Forest	46	109	.422
Bobby Hurley, Duke	76	188	.404
Tom Gugliotta, N.C. State	66	166	.398
Randolph Childress, Wake Forest	64	166	.386
Chris Corchiani, N.C. State	51	135	.378
Jon Barry, Georgia Tech	77	209	.368
David Young, Clemson	50	142	.352
Kenny Anderson, Georgia Tech	65	185	.351

3-POINT FG PER GAME
(Minimum 1 Made Per Game)

Player, School	Games	No.	Avg.
Rodney Monroe, N.C. State	31	104	3.36
Jon Barry, Georgia Tech	30	77	2.57
Randolph Childress, Wake Forest	29	64	2.21
Kenny Anderson, Georgia Tech	30	65	2.17
Tom Gugliotta, N.C. State	31	66	2.13
Bobby Hurley, Duke	39	76	1.95
Rick Fox, North Carolina	35	67	1.91
Hubert Davis, North Carolina	35	64	1.83
David Young, Clemson	28	50	1.79
Matt Roe, Maryland	28	48	1.74

FINAL 1990-91 ATLANTIC COAST CONFERENCE TEAM STATISTICS

SCORING OFFENSE

Team	G	(W-L)	Pts.	Avg.
N.C. State	31	(20-11)	2769	89.3
Duke	39	(32-7)	3421	87.7
North Carolina	35	(29-6)	3067	87.6
Georgia Tech	30	(17-13)	2474	82.5
Wake Forest	30	(19-11)	2415	80.5
Maryland	28	(17-11)	2245	80.2
Virginia	33	(21-12)	2453	74.3
Clemson	28	(11-17)	2063	73.7

SCORING DEFENSE

Team	G	Pts.	Avg.
Virginia	33	2262	68.5
North Carolina	35	2507	71.6
Duke	39	2864	73.7
Wake Forest	30	2248	74.9
Clemson	28	2147	76.7
Georgia Tech	20	2310	77.0
Maryland	28	2222	79.4
N.C. State	31	2587	83.5

FIELD GOAL PERCENTAGE

Team	FGM	FGA	Pct.
Duke	1227	2401	.511
North Carolina	1134	2257	.502
Wake Forest	909	1859	.489
N.C. State	993	2045	.486
Georgia Tech	944	1995	.473
Clemson	801	1735	.462
Virginia	904	1987	.455
Maryland	814	1795	.453

FIELD GOAL PERCENTAGE DEFENSE

Team	FGM	FGA	Pct.
North Carolina	974	2329	.418
Duke	864	2051	.421
Clemson	748	1728	.433
Virginia	844	1908	.442
Duke	1087	2445	.445
Wake Forest	820	1773	.462
N.C. State	1021	2092	.488

3-POINT FIELD GOAL PERCENTAGE

Team	3PM	3PA	Pct.
N.C. State	267	644	.415
North Carolina	192	483	.398
Duke	176	459	.383
Wake Forest	171	449	.381
Georgia Tech	183	504	.363
Clemson	121	406	.298
Virginia	132	444	.297
Maryland	90	309	.291

3-POINT FIELD GOAL PERCENTAGE DEFENSE

Team	FGM	FGA	Pct.
North Carolina	197	622	.317
Maryland	161	465	.346
N.C. State	172	489	.352
Duke	165	464	.356
Virginia	132	364	.363
Georgia Tech	181	497	.364
Wake Forest	163	440	.370
Clemson	184	463	.397

SCORING MARGIN

Team	Off.	Def.	Margin
North Carolina	87.6	71.6	+16.0
Duke	87.7	73.7	+14.3
N.C. State	89.3	83.5	+5.8
Virginia	74.3	68.5	+5.8
Wake Forest	80.5	74.9	+5.6
Georgia Tech	82.5	77.0	+5.5
Maryland	80.2	79.4	+0.8
Clemson	73.7	76.7	-3.0

REBOUNDING MARGIN

Team	Own	Opp.	Margin
North Carolina	41.6	35.0	+6.6
Virginia	35.9	33.3	+2.6
Wake Forest	35.5	33.1	+2.4
Georgia Tech	41.8	39.4	+2.4
Duke	36.3	34.0	+2.3
Clemson	38.4	37.1	+1.3
N.C. State	36.9	35.8	+1.1
Maryland	39.2	39.0	-0.6

FREE THROW PERCENTAGE

Team	FTM	FTA	Pct.
N.C. State	516	677	.762
Duke	791	1089	.726
Virginia	513	712	.721
North Carolina	607	866	.701
Wake Forest	426	619	.688
Maryland	527	772	.683
Georgia Tech	403	603	.668
Clemson	340	543	.626

All-Time Tar Heels: 1,513 Wins

COMPLETE THROUGH THE 1991 SEASON

ALL-TIME RECORD: 1513-550 (73.3)

RECORD SINCE 1962, UNDER DEAN SMITH: 717-209 (77.4)

NON-CONFERENCE RECORD PAST 22 YEARS: 327-61 (84.3)

ATLANTIC COAST CONFERENCE CHAMPIONSHIPS (12)
1957, 1967, 1968, 1969, 1972, 1975, 1977, 1979, 1981, 1982, 1989, 1991

ALL-TIME TOURNAMENT RECORD: 55-25 (68.8)

ACC REGULAR SEASON FIRST-PLACE FINISHES (20)
1956 (tie), 1957, 1959 (tie), 1960 (tie), 1961, 1967, 1968, 1969, 1971, 1972, 1976, 1977, 1978, 1979 (tie), 1982 (tie), 1983 (tie), 1984, 1985 (tie), 1987, 1988

NCAA TOURNAMENT APPEARANCES (25)
1941, 1946 (2nd), 1957 (1st), 1959, 1967 (4th), 1968 (2nd), 1969 (4th), 1972 (3rd), 1975, 1976, 1977 (2nd), 1978, 1979, 1980, 1981 (2nd), 1982 (1st), 1983, 1984, 1985, 1986, 1987, 1988, 1989, 1990, 1991

NATIONAL CHAMPIONSHIPS
1924 (pre-NCAA), 1957, 1982

ALL-TIME NCAA TOURNAMENT RECORD: 54-26 (67.5)

NIT APPEARANCES (4)
1970, 1971 (1st), 1973 (3rd), 1974

ALL-TIME NIT RECORD: 7-3 (70.0)

NOTES
– Carolina has finished first, second or third in the ACC regular season for 27 straight years.
– Carolina has appeared in 17 consecutive NCAA Tournaments, the longest streak in the nation.
– Carolina has reached the NCAAs Final 16 for 11 consecutive years, the longest streak in the NCAA.

INDIVIDUAL—CAREER

Scoring Average
26.9 – Lennie Rosenbluth, 1955-57
24.8 – Billy Cunningham, 1963-65
22.12 – Bob Lewis, 1965-67
22.05 – Charlie Scott, 1968-70
21.78 – Larry Miller, 1966-68

Rebound Average
15.4 – Billy Cunningham, 1963-65
10.6 – Doug Moe, 1959-61
10.5 – Pete Brennan, 1956-58
10.4 – Lennie Rosenbluth, 1955-57
10.2 – Rusty Clark, 1967-69

Assist Average
6.12 – Phil Ford, 1975-78
6.05 – Kenny Smith, 1984-87
5.2 – Larry Brown, 1961-63
4.6 – Walter Davis, 1974-77
4.5 – King Rice, 1988-91
4.4 – Jeff Lebo, 1986-89

Games Played
140 – Pete Chilcutt, 1988-91
140 – Rick Fox, 1988-91
140 – King Rice, 1988-91
138 – Scott Williams, 1987-90
136 – Jimmy Braddock, 1979-83
135 – Sam Perkins, 1980-84
135 – Brad Daugherty, 1982-86
134 – Dave Popson, 1983-87
134 – Kevin Madden, 1986, 1988-90
133 – Jeff Lebo, 1986-89

Field Goals
865 – Phil Ford, 1975-78
825 – Al Wood, 1978-81
786 – Sam Perkins, 1981-84
765 – Larry Miller, 1966-68
760 – Brad Daugherty, 1983-86

Free Throws
603 – Lennie Rosenbluth, 1955-57
561 – Sam Perkins, 1981-84
560 – Phil Ford, 1975-78
512 – Bob Lewis, 1965-67
506 – Pete Brennan, 1956-58

INDIVIDUAL—SEASON

Points
895 – Lennie Rosenbluth, 1957
740 – Bob Lewis, 1966
731 – Charlie Scott, 1970
721 – Michael Jordan, 1983
717 – Larry Miller, 1968

Scoring Average
28.0 – Lennie Rosenbluth, 1957
27.4 – Bob Lewis, 1966
27.1 – Charlie Scott, 1970
26.7 – Lennie Rosenbluth, 1956
26.0 – Billy Cunningham, 1964
25.5 – Lennie Rosenbluth, 1955
25.4 – Billy Cunningham, 1965
23.1 – York Larese, 1961
22.7 – Billy Cunningham, 1963
22.4 – Larry Miller, 1968
22.3 – Charlie Scott, 1969
21.9 – Larry Miller, 1967
21.3 – Pete Brennan, 1958
20.8 – Phil Ford, 1978
20.4 – Doug Moe, 1961
20.2 – Brad Daugherty, 1986
20.0 – Michael Jordan, 1983

Rebounds
379 – Billy Cunningham, 1964
349 – Brad Daugherty, 1985
348 – Bobby Jones, 1973
344 – Billy Cunningham, 1965
341 – Rusty Clark, 1968

Rebound Average
16.1 – Billy Cunningham, 1963
15.8 – Billy Cunningham, 1964
14.3 – Billy Cunningham, 1965
14.0 – Doug Moe, 1961
11.71 – Lennie Rosenbluth, 1955
11.65 – Pete Brennan, 1958

Assists
235 – Kenny Smith, 1985
217 – Phil Ford, 1977
217 – King Rice, 1990
213 – Jimmy Black, 1982
210 – Kenny Smith, 1986
209 – Kenny Smith, 1987
207 – King Rice, 1991

Assist Average
7.0 – Phil Ford, 1976
6.6 – Phil Ford, 1977
6.5 – Kenny Smith, 1985
6.4 – King Rice, 1990
6.3 – Jimmy Black, 1982
6.2 – Kenny Smith, 1986

Field Goals
305 – Lennie Rosenbluth, 1957
290 – Charlie Scott, 1969
284 – Brad Daugherty, 1986
282 – Michael Jordan, 1983
281 – Charlie Scott, 1970

Field Goal Attempts
631 – Lennie Rosenbluth, 1957
611 – Charlie Scott, 1970
577 – Charlie Scott, 1969
553 – Larry Miller, 1967
545 – Larry Miller, 1968

Field Goal Percentage
.668 – Bobby Jones, 1972
.648 – Brad Daugherty, 1986
.643 – Mike O'Koren, 1978
.626 – Sam Perkins, 1981
.625 – Brad Daugherty, 1985

Free Throws
285 – Lennie Rosenbluth, 1957
222 – Bob Lewis, 1966
214 – Pete Brennan, 1958
189 – Lennie Rosenbluth, 1955
185 – Pete Brennan, 1957

Free Throw Attempts
376 – Lennie Rosenbluth, 1957
291 – Pete Brennan, 1958
274 – Bob Lewis, 1966
262 – Pete Brennan, 1957
256 – Larry Miller, 1968

Free Throw Percentage
.878 – Jeff Lebo, 1988
.876 – Steve Hale, 1985
.871 – Darrell Elston, 1974
.868 – York Larese, 1960
.864 – Jeff Lebo, 1989

INDIVIDUAL—GAME

Points
49 – Bob Lewis vs. Florida State, 12-16-65
48 – Billy Cunningham vs. Tulane, 12-10-64
47 – Lennie Rosenbluth vs. Furman, 12-3-56
45 – George Glamack vs. Clemson, 2-10-41
45 – Lennie Rosenbluth vs. Clemson, 1-1-56
45 – Lennie Rosenbluth, vs. William & Mary, 2-7-56
45 – Lennie Rosenbluth vs. Clemson, 3-3-57
41 – Charlie Scott vs. Virginia, 3-6-70
41 – Kenny Smith vs. Clemson, 1-28-87
40 – Charlie Scott vs. Duke, 3-8-69

Rebounds
30 – Rusty Clark vs. Maryland, 2-21-68
28 – Billy Cunningham vs. Maryland, 1-13-64
27 – Billy Cunningham vs. Clemson, 2-16-63
25 – Lennie Rosenbluth vs. South Carolina, 12-9-54
25 – Lennie Rosenbluth vs. Virginia, 1-11-55
25 – Billy Cunningham vs. Tulane, 12-10-64

Assists
17 – Jeff Lebo vs. UTC, 11-18-88
14 – Phil Ford vs. Howard, 1-11-75
14 – Phil Ford vs. Brigham Young, 12-20-76
14 – Phil Ford vs. N.C. State, 2-23-77
13 – Larry Brown vs. South Carolina, 2-28-63
13 – Steve Hale vs. Duke, 3-3-84
13 – Kenny Smith vs. Oral Roberts, 12-8-84
13 – Kenny Smith vs. SMU, 1-13-85
13 – Kenny Smith vs. The Citadel, 2-1-85
13 – Steve Hale vs. Clemson, 2-23-85
13 – Kenny Smith vs. UCLA, 11-24-85
13 – Jeff Lebo vs. Manhattan, 12-27-85
13 – Kenny Smith vs. Miami (Fla.), 12-6-86

TEAM—SEASON

Victories
32-0, 1957
32-2, 1982
32-4, 1987
30-5, 1946
29-6, 1991
29-8, 1981
29-8, 1989

Scoring Average
91.25, 1987
90.0, 1989
89.10, 1972
88.87, 1969
88.85, 1970
87.63, 1991
87.04, 1974

Average Winning Margin
17.7, 1972 (89.1-71.4)
17.6, 1986 (86.6-69.0)
17.5, 1945 (53.0-35.5)
16.5, 1946 (56.3-39.8)
16.4, 1987 (91.3-74.9)
16.0, 1991 (87.6-71.6)

Field Goal Percentage
.559, 1986
.543, 1984
.540, 1985
.5374, 1977
.5373, 1987
.5365, 1982

Free Throw Percentage
.783, 1984
.761, 1985
.758, 1960
.751, 1976
.746, 1977

TEAM—GAME

Points
129 vs. Manhattan, 12-27-85
128 vs. Dartmouth, 12-5-72
127 vs. Richmond, 12-8-65
127 vs. Rice, 12-2-71
123 vs. Loyola Marymount, 3-19-88
122 vs. Miami (Fla.), 12-6-86
121 vs. Kentucky, 12-27-89
121 vs. Niagara, 12-30-78
118 vs. Furman, 1-8-72
118 vs. Georgia Tech, 2-12-72
118 vs. Hawaii Loa, 12-29-87
118 vs. E. Tennessee State, 12-18-87
118 vs. Iowa State, 12-1-90
(UNC has scored 100 or more points 107 times.)

Fewest Points
8 vs. N.C. State, 1926
13 vs. Roanoke, 1916
14 vs. Durham YMCA, 1915
14 vs. Virginia Tech, 1919
14 vs. Duke, 1930

Opponent Points
110 by Kentucky, 12-27-89
107 by Indiana, 12-12-64
107 by Wake Forest, 2-9-65
106 by Duke, 2-23-63
106 by Tulane, 2-14-76 (4 OT)
106 by Maryland, 2-16-83
106 by Virginia, 1-15-89
(UNC opponents have scored 100 or more points 18 times)

Fewest Opponents Points
5 by Elon, 1912
5 by Hampden-Sydney, 1927
5 by Durham YMCA, 1927
7 by Davidson, 1929
8 by Davidson, 1913
8 by Tulane, 1928
8 by South Carolina, 1931

Victory Margin
84 vs. Manhattan, 12-27-85 (129-45)
69 vs. Davidson, 2-7-45 (89-20)
68 vs. The Citadel, 2-18-91 (118-50)
65 vs. Florida Southern, 12-1-69 (112-47)
63 vs. Greensboro YMCA, 1930 (88-25)
59 vs. Hampden-Sydney, 1927 (64-5)

Defeat Margin
43 vs. Lynchburg Elks, 1915 (63-20)
42 vs. Kentucky, 1-9-50 (86-44)
40 vs. N.C. State, 2-19-49 (79-39)
39 vs. N.C. State, 2-3-48 (81-42)
37 vs. Norfolk N.A.S., 1-12-45 (59-22)

CAREER FIELD GOAL PERCENTAGE LEADERS
50 PERCENT OR BETTER (AT LEAST 150 MADE)

	M	A	Pct.
1. Brad Daugherty (83-86)	760	1226	61.99
2. Bobby Jones (72-74)	522	859	60.77
3. J.R. Reid (87-89)	584	972	60.08
4. Warren Martin (82-86)	256	431	59.39
5. Dennis Wuycik (70-72)	519	880	58.97
6. Mitch Kupchak (73-76)	651	1110	58.65
7. Tommy LaGarde (74-77)	367	630	58.25
8. Kevin Madden (86, 88-90)	519	893	58.12
9. Sam Perkins (81-84)	786	1364	57.62
10. Mike O'Koren (77-80)	643	1124	57.21
11. Dave Chadwick (69-71)	179	315	56.82
12. Curtis Hunter (83-87)	201	357	56.30
13. Al Wood (78-81)	825	1474	55.97
14. John Virgil (77-80)	233	419	55.61
15. Scott Williams (87-90)	595	1080	55.09
16. Joe Wolf (84-87)	511	928	55.06
17. Charlie Shaffer (62-64)	221	406	54.43
18. James Worthy (80-82)	485	896	54.13
19. Bill Chamberlain (70-72)	389	720	54.02
20. Michael Jordan (82-84)	720	1333	54.01
21. John O'Donnell (72-74)	178	322	53.61
22. Pete Chilcutt (88-91)	483	904	53.43
23. Walter Davis (74-77)	754	1420	53.10
24. Phil Ford (75-78)	865	1640	52.74
25. Donn Johnston (71-73)	161	308	52.27
26. George Lynch	284	544	52.21
27. Dave Popson (84-87)	329	632	52.06
28. Steve Hale (83-86)	359	690	52.02
29. Rick Fox (88-91)	633	1221	51.84
30. Robert McAdoo (71-72)	243	471	51.59
31. Bill Bunting (67-69)	398	774	51.42
32. Ray Harrison (73-74)	153	298	51.34
33. George Karl (71-73)	494	964	51.25
34. Kenny Smith (84-87)	628	1226	51.22
35. Rusty Clark (67-69)	513	1003	51.14
36. Larry Miller (66-68)	765	1498	51.06
37. Jimmy Black (79-82)	258	512	50.39
38. Rich Yonakor (77-80)	226	449	50.33
39. Ranzino Smith (85-88)	304	605	50.25
40. Darrell Elston (72-74)	310	617	50.24

CAREER FREE THROW PERCENTAGE LEADERS
70 PERCENT OR BETTER (AT LEAST 100 MADE)

	M	A	Pct.
1. Jeff Lebo (86-89)	308	367	83.92
2. Jim Braddock (80-83)	106	127	83.46
3. Dennis Wuycik (70-72)	431	517	83.37
4. Darrell Elston (72-74)	125	150	83.33
5. Ed Stahl (73-75)	124	149	83.22
6. Ranzino Smith (85-88)	136	165	82.42
7. Kenny Smith (84-87)	293	356	82.30
8. Steve Hale (83-86)	230	283	81.27
9. Hubert Davis	164	202	81.19
10. Phil Ford (75-78)	560	693	80.81
11. York Larese (59-61)	351	441	79.59
12. Sam Perkins (81-84)	561	705	79.57
13. Larry Brown (61-63)	221	282	78.37
14. Tony Radovich (53-56)	216	276	78.26
15. Ray Respess (63-65)	110	141	78.01
16. George Karl (71-73)	305	391	78.00
17. Bob Lewis (65-67)	512	660	77.57
18. Walter Davis (74-77)	355	459	77.34
19. Lee Shaffer (58-60)	253	330	76.66
20. Joe Wolf (84-87)	186	243	76.54
21. King Rice (88-91)	252	330	76.36
22. Al Wood (78-81)	365	478	76.36
23. Tommy LaGarde (74-77)	273	358	76.26
24. Matt Doherty (81-84)	309	406	76.11
25. Harvey Salz (58-60)	246	324	75.92
26. Rick Fox (88-91)	284	375	75.73
27. John Kuester (74-77)	146	193	75.65
28. Dave Popson (84-87)	102	135	75.56
29. Steve Bucknall (86-89)	237	314	75.48
30. Michael Jordan (82-84)	314	420	74.76
31. Lennie Rosenbluth (55-57)	603	815	73.98
32. Jimmy Black (79-82)	212	289	73.36
33. Dave Colescott (77-80)	110	150	73.33
34. Mike O'Koren (77-80)	479	660	72.58
35. Charlie Scott (68-70)	397	547	72.57
36. Rich Yonakor (77-80)	145	201	72.13
37. Ray Stanley (58-60)	100	139	71.94
38. Al Lifson (52-55)	368	518	71.04
39. Pete Chilcutt (88-91)	164	231	71.00
40. Pete Brennan (56-58)	506	715	70.76
41. Robert McAdoo (71-72)	118	167	70.65
42. Curtis Hunter (83-87)	104	148	70.27
43. Bill Chamberlain (70-72)	179	255	70.19
44. Brad Daugherty (83-86)	392	560	70.00

CAREER SCORING LEADERS

	Pts.
1. Phil Ford (75-78)	2,290
2. Sam Perkins (81-84)	2,145
3. Lennie Rosenbluth (55-57)	2,045
4. Al Wood (78-81)	2,015
5. Charlie Scott (68-70)	2,007
6. Larry Miller (66-68)	1,982
7. Brad Daugherty (83-86)	1,912
8. Walter Davis (74-77)	1,863
9. Bob Lewis (65-67)	1,836
10. Michael Jordan (82-84)	1,788
11. Mike O'Koren (77-80)	1,765
12. Billy Cunningham (63-65)	1,709
13. Rick Fox (88-91)	1,703
14. Kenny Smith (84-87)	1,636
15. Mitch Kupchak (73-76)	1,611
16. Jeff Lebo (86-89)	1,567
17. J.R. Reid (87-89)	1,552
18. Scott Williams (86-90)	1,508
19. Dennis Wuycik (70-72)	1,469
20. Rusty Clark (67-69)	1,339
21. Pete Brennan (56-58)	1,332
22. Al Lifson (52-55)	1,322
23. Kevin Madden (86, 88-90)	1,296
24. George Karl (71-73)	1,293
25. Bobby Jones (72-74)	1,264

CAREER REBOUND LEADERS

1. Sam Perkins (81-84)	1,167
2. Billy Cunningham (63-65)	1,062
3. Mitch Kupchak (73-76)	1,006
4. Brad Daugherty (83-86)	1,003
5. Rusty Clark (67-69)	929
6. Scott Williams (87-90)	861
7. Pete Brennan (56-58)	854
8. Larry Miller (66-68)	834
9. Bobby Jones (72-74)	817
10. Mike O'Koren (77-80)	815
11. Lennie Rosenbluth (55-57)	790
12. Pete Chilcutt (88-91)	766
13. J.R. Reid (87-89)	731
14. Lee Dedmon (69-71)	729
15. Joe Wolf (84-87)	707
16. Jerry Vayda (53-56)	687
17. Walter Davis (74-77)	670
18. Bud Maddie (51, 53-54)	651
19. Charlie Scott (68-70)	649
20. Doug Moe (59-61)	635
21. James Worthy (80-82)	620
22. Bill Bunting (67-69)	612
23. Lee Shaffer (58-60)	606

CAREER ASSIST LEADERS

1. Kenny Smith (84-87)	768
2. Phil Ford (75-78)	753
3. King Rice (88-91)	629
4. Jeff Lebo (86-89)	580
5. Jimmy Black (79-82)	525
6. Steve Hale (83-86)	503
7. Matt Doherty (81-84)	446
8. Walter Davis (74-77)	409
9. George Karl (71-73)	394
10. Steve Bucknall (86-89)	382
11. John Kuester (74-77)	370
12. Mike O'Koren (77-80)	348
13. Rick Fox (88-91)	323
14. Charlie Scott (68-70)	310
15. Larry Miller (66-68)	309
16. Dick Grubar (67-69)	296
17. Larry Brown (61-63)	292
18. Steve Previs (70-72)	286
19. Bobby Jones (72-74)	285
20. Bob Lewis (65-67)	272
21. Darrell Elston (72-74)	259
22. Eddie Fogler (68-70)	249
23. Joe Wolf (84-87)	243

YEAR-BY-YEAR RESULTS

Year	W	L	UNC Pts.	Opp. Pts.	Coach
1911	7	4	343	265	Nat Cartmell
1912	4	5	244	208	Nat Cartmell
1913	4	7	276	231	Nat Cartmell
1914	10	8	584	555	Nat Cartmell
1915	6	10	386	447	Charles Doak
1916	12	6	527	426	Charles Doak
1917	5	4	313	280	Howell Peacock
1918	9	3	456	307	Howell Peacock
1919	9	7	542	458	Howell Peacock
1920	7	9	471	472	Fred Boye
1921	12	8	674	487	Fred Boye
1922	15	6	734	597	No Coach
1923	15	1	575	363	No Coach
1924	26	0	959	520	Norman Shepard
1925	20	5	794	505	Monk McDonald
1926	20	5	937	569	Harlan Sanborn
1927	17	7	787	518	James Ashmore
1928	17	2	650	424	James Ashmore
1929	17	8	750	613	James Ashmore
1930	14	11	806	643	James Ashmore
1931	15	9	705	518	James Ashmore
1932	16	5	678	517	George Shepard
1933	12	5	651	494	George Shepard
1934	18	4	730	528	George Shepard
1935	23	2	828	606	George Shepard
1936	21	4	887	720	Walter Skidmore
1937	18	5	864	670	Walter Skidmore
1938	16	5	828	670	Walter Skidmore
1939	10	11	817	804	Walter Skidmore
1940	23	3	1200	934	Bill Lange
1941	19	9	1336	1050	Bill Lange
1942	14	9	941	789	Bill Lange
1943	12	10	894	834	Bill Lange
1944	17	10	1173	1020	Bill Lange
1945	22	6	1483	993	Ben Carnevale
1946	30	5	1970	1392	Ben Carnevale
1947	19	8	1433	1250	Tom Scott
1948	20	7	1452	1219	Tom Scott
1949	20	8	1605	1484	Tom Scott
1950	17	12	1652	1596	Tom Scott
1951	12	15	1767	1790	Tom Scott
1952	12	15	1741	1794	Tom Scott
1953	17	10	2012	1877	Frank McGuire
1954	11	10	1439	1335	Frank McGuire
1955	10	11	1590	1599	Frank McGuire
1956	18	5	1839	1633	Frank McGuire
1957	32	0	2537	2098	Frank McGuire
1958	19	7	1867	1688	Frank McGuire
1959	20	5	1797	1629	Frank McGuire
1960	18	6	1756	1494	Frank McGuire
1961	19	4	1765	1512	Frank McGuire
1962	8	9	1230	1235	Dean Smith
1963	15	6	1608	1487	Dean Smith
1964	12	12	1861	1859	Dean Smith
1965	15	9	1915	1862	Dean Smith
1966	16	11	2184	2005	Dean Smith
1967	26	6	2630	2277	Dean Smith
1968	28	4	2680	2316	Dean Smith
1969	27	5	2844	2421	Dean Smith
1970	18	9	2399	2128	Dean Smith
1971	26	6	2706	2297	Dean Smith
1972	26	5	2762	2213	Dean Smith
1973	25	8	2796	2393	Dean Smith
1974	22	6	2437	2108	Dean Smith
1975	23	8	2623	2417	Dean Smith
1976	25	4	2474	2155	Dean Smith
1977	28	5	2759	2396	Dean Smith
1978	23	8	2513	2192	Dean Smith
1979	23	6	2218	1898	Dean Smith
1980	21	8	2124	1971	Dean Smith
1981	29	8	2660	2344	Dean Smith
1982	32	2	2269	1885	Dean Smith
1983	28	8	2909	2469	Dean Smith
1984	28	3	2483	2010	Dean Smith
1985	27	9	2647	2376	Dean Smith
1986	28	6	2945	2346	Dean Smith
1987	32	4	3285	2695	Dean Smith
1988	27	7	2791	2490	Dean Smith
1989	29	8	3331	2949	Dean Smith
1990	21	13	2808	2650	Dean Smith
1991	29	6	3067	2507	Dean Smith

81-Season Totals: 1513-550

A
Aiken, Ben ... 1939, 1941 (M)
Aitken, Stewart "Snooks" ... 1933-35
Allen, Bill ... 1945
Altemose, Bob ... 1943-44
Alvarez, Manny ... 1945
Anderson, Don ... 1944-46
Austin, John ... 1971

B
Baines, Greg ... 1990-91 (M)
Baldwin, Janet ... 1986-87 (M)
Barlow, Jeb ... 1981-82
Barrett, Jon ... 1971-72 (M)
Beale, W.F. ... 1933-34
Bell, Mickey ... 1973-75
Bennett, Benton ... 1949-50
Bennett, Bob ... 1964-66
Bershak, Andy ... 1937-38
Black, Jimmy ... 1979-82
Blood, E.B. ... 1934-35
Boone, Pete ... 1938
Bostick, Jim ... 1967
Bowers, Bruce ... 1962
Bowman, Dave ... 1940
Box, Boyce ... 1944
Braddock, Jim ... 1980-83
Bradley, Dudley ... 1976-79
Brandt, G.F. ... 1933
Branson, Les ... 1939
Brennan, Pete ... 1956-58
Brown, Bill ... 1963-65
Brown, Joe ... 1967-69
Brown, Larry ... 1961-63
Brown, Lou ... 1959-60
Brownlee, John ... 1982-83
Brust, Chris ... 1979-82
Buckley, Bruce ... 1974-77
Bucknall, Steve ... 1986-89
Budko, Pete ... 1978-81
Bunting, Bill ... 1967-69
Burch, Michael ... 1987-88
Burke, Edmund ... 1962 (M)
Burns, Charlie ... 1962-63

C
Callahan, Peppy ... 1962-63
Campbell, Greg ... 1966
Carson, Coy ... 1948-49
Carter, Jippy ... 1951,1953
Chadwick, Dave ... 1969-71
Chamberlain, Bill ... 1970-72
Chambers, Bill B. ... 1973-76
Chambers, Bill L. ... 1970-72
Chandler, S.M. ... 1933
Cherry, Scott ... 1990-91
Chilcutt, Pete ... 1988-91
Clark, Buddy ... 1955
Clark, Rusty ... 1967-69
Cochrane, Bill ... 1965-66 (M)
Cohen, John ... 1976-77 (M)
Cole, Mervin ... 1948
Coleman, Bob ... 1968-69 (M)
Colescott, Dave ... 1977-80
Coley, Woody ... 1975-77
Conlon, Martin ... 1961
Cooke, Mike ... 1962-64
Corson, Craig ... 1970-72
Cox, John ... 1971
Creticos, Soc ... 1944
Crompton, Geff ... 1974, 1978
Crotty, John ... 1958-60
Cuneo, Frank ... 1940
Cunningham, Billy ... 1963-65
Cunningham, Bob ... 1956-58

D
Dalton, Julie ... 1982-83 (M)
Daly, David ... 1981-82 (M)
Daugherty, Brad ... 1983-86
Davis, Hubert ... 1989-91
Davis, Walter ... 1974-77
Daye, James ... 1985-86
Deasy, Howard ... 1949-52
Dedmon, Lee ... 1969-71
Delany, Jim ... 1968-70
Denny, Jeff ... 1987-90
Dewell, John ... 1944
Dillon, John "Hook" ... 1945-48
Dilworth, Ben ... 1938-40
Doherty, Matt ... 1981-84
Donald, Doug ... 1972-73 (M)
Donnan, Dick ... 1944
Donohue, Hugh ... 1959-60, 62
Doughton, Ged ... 1976-79
Duckett, Chuck ... 1980-82 (M)
Duckett, Ricky ... 1977-79 (M)

E
Earey, Mike ... 1970
Eggleston, Don ... 1969-71
Ellis, Chris ... 1989 (M)
Ellis, Mike ... 1986-88 (M)
Elston, Darrell ... 1972-74
Elstun, Doug ... 1988
Emmerson, Fred ... 1967 (M)
Engle, Fred ... 1961 (M)
Exum, Cecil ... 1981-84

F
Ferraro, Hal ... 1949-51
Fitch, Jack ... 1944
Fleishman, Adam ... 1985-87 (M)
Fleishman, Joel ... 1957 (M)
Fletcher, Ralph ... 1966-68
Fogler, Eddie ... 1968-70
Ford, Phil ... 1975-78
Forehand, Randy ... 1968-69 (M)
Fox, Rick ... 1988-91
Freedman, Ellis ... 1943
Frye, Jim ... 1966-68

G
Galantai, Bill ... 1963-64
Garvin, Dick ... 1945
Gauntlett, Tom ... 1965-67
Gersten, Bobby ... 1940-42
Gilliam, Gid ... 1944 (M)
Gipple, Dale ... 1969-71
Glace, Ivan "Jack" ... 1933-35
Glamack, George ... 1939-41
Glancy, Gene ... 1953
Goodwin, Frank ... 1955
Greene, Hilliard ... 1955-56
Greene, John ... 1989-90
Gribble, Dickson ... 1966
Grimaldi, Vince ... 1951-53
Grubar, Dick ... 1967-69
Grubb, Foy ... 1937-38

H
Hale, Steve ... 1983-86
Hamilton, Jim ... 1947
Hanners, Dave ... 1974-76
Harris, Kenny ... 1990-91
Harris, W.C. ... 1935
Harrison, Ray ... 1973-74
Harry, Eric ... 1975-76
Hart, David ... 1982-84 (M)
Hartley, Dick ... 1943, 1947
Hassell, Pud ... 1964-65
Hassell, Ray ... 1964-65
Hayworth, Jim ... 1946-47
Hayworth, Lewis ... 1942-44
Henderson, Willis ... 1955
Henry, D.P. ... 1933
Hensley, Marty ... 1987, 1989-90
Hines, Wilmer ... 1933
Hite, Ray ... 1972-74
Hoffman, Brad ... 1973-75
Holland, Gehrmann ... 1957, 1959
Hopkins, Jerry ... 1989-91 (M)
Howard, Curtis ... 1942 (M)
Howard, Jimmy ... 1939-41
Huband, Kim ... 1970-72
Hudock, Jim ... 1960-62
Hughes, Red ... 1946
Hunter, Curtis ... 1983, 1985-87
Hunter, H.B. ... 1943 (M)
Hyatt, Rodney ... 1987-88

I
Isley, Mark ... 1984-86 (M)

J
Jenkins, Joe ... 1988
Johnston, Donn ... 1971-73
Jones, Bobby ... 1972-74
Jones, Harry ... 1961-62
Hones, Holly ... 1984 (M)
Jordan, Jim ... 1945-46
Jordan, Michael ... 1982-84

K
Kappler, Hugo ... 1949-51
Karl, George ... 1971-73
Katz, Art ... 1962-64
Kaveny, P.F. ... 1935
Kearns, Tommy ... 1956-58
Kenny, Eric ... 1979-81
Kepley, Dick ... 1958-59, 1961
Kocornik, Dick ... 1954
Kohler, Norm ... 1947-48
Krafcisin, Steve ... 1977
Krause, Dieter ... 1961-63
Kuester, John ... 1974-77
Kupchak, Mitch ... 1973-76
Kuralt, Justin ... 1988-91 (M)

L
LaGarde, Tommy ... 1974-77
Larese, York ... 1959-61
Lebo, Jeff ... 1986-89
Lee, Kenny ... 1978-80 (M)
Lewis, Bob ... 1965-67
Lifson, Al ... 1952-55
Likins, Paul ... 1952-55
Loftus, Michael ... 1947 (M)
Long, Albert ... 1954
Long, M.H. ... 1933-34
Lotz, Danny ... 1957-59
Lougee, Edgar ... 1943
Lubin, Ben ... 1955 (M)
Lutz, Loren ... 1976
Lynch, George ... 1990-91

M
Madden, Kevin ... 1986, 1988-90
Maddie, Bud ... 1951, 1953-54
Makkonen, Timo ... 1982-84
Markin, Walter ... 1945
Marks, Don ... 1943
Martin, Warren ... 1982-83, 1985-86
Mason, Jeff ... 1976-78 (M)
Mathes, Albert ... 1940
May, David ... 1988-89
McAdoo, Robert ... 1972
McCabe, Gerry ... 1954-56
McCachren, Bill ... 1937, 1939
McCachren, Dave ... 1933-34
McCachren, George ... 1943
McCachren, Jim ... 1934-35
McComb, Ken ... 1961
McCord, Dean ... 1984-85 (M)
McDavid, James ... 1958 (M)
McIntyre, Maria ... 1989-91 (M)
McKee, E.L. ... 1937 (M)
McKinney, Bones ... 1946
McSweeney, Bryan ... 1962-64
Meekins, Ralph ... 1981-83 (M)
Meroney, David ... 1937
Miles, Greg ... 1973-74 (M)
Miller, Larry ... 1966-68
Minor, W.T. ... 1935
Mirken, Mark ... 1965-67
Mock, Bernie ... 1944
Moe, Doug ... 1959-61
Moe, Donnie ... 1966-67
Montross, Eric ... 1991
Moore, Jim ... 1966
Morris, Cliff ... 1984-85
Morrison, Ian ... 1965
Mullis, Pete ... 1937-38
Murnick, Elliott ... 1963-64 (M)

N
Nagy, Fritz ... 1943
Nathan, Mark ... 1948
Nearman, Sherman "Nemo" ... 1947-50
Nelson, Melvin ... 1934-35
Norfolk, Ira ... 1945
Norwood, Michael ... 1986-87
Nyimicz, Dan ... 1948-49

O
O'Donnell, John ... 1972-74
O'Koren, Mike ... 1977-80

P-Q
Paine, George ... 1941-42
Parrish, Lannie ... 1984-86 (M)
Parsons, Kendra ... 1987-88 (M)
Patseavouras, John ... 1951 (M)
Patterson, Richard ... 1950-51
Paxton, Bob ... 1945-48
Pepper, Mike ... 1978-81
Perkins, Sam ... 1981-84
Pessar, Hank ... 1940-41
Peterson, Buzz ... 1982-85
Phelps, Derrick ... 1991
Phillips, Bob ... 1951-53
Poole, Grey ... 1958-60
Popson, Dave ... 1984-87
Poteet, Yogi ... 1960-61, 1963
Potts, Ramsay ... 1937
Previs, Steve ... 1970-72
Quigg, Joe ... 1956-57

R
Radovich, Tony ... 1953-57
Rancke, John ... 1974-75 (M)
Redding, Frank ... 1952
Reed, Lindsay ... 1979-81 (M)
Reese, Brian ... 1991
Reid, Ben ... 1971 (M)
Reid, J.R. ... 1987-89
Respess, Ray ... 1963-65
Reynolds, Steve ... 1988-90 (M)
Rice, King ... 1988-91
Roberson, Foy ... 1939-40
Robinson, Lynwood ... 1982
Rodl, Henrik ... 1990-91
Rogers, Sam ... 1991 (M)
Roper, Gary ... 1985
Rose, Bob ... 1940-42
Rosemond, Ken ... 1956-57
Rosenbluth, Lennie ... 1955-57
Royall, Kenneth ... 1940 (M)
Rozier, Clifford ... 1991
Russell, William ... 1948 (M)
Ruth, Earl ... 1937-38
Ryan, Rip ... 1949

S
Salvadori, Kevin ... 1991
Salz, Harvey ... 1958-60
Scholbe, Roger ... 1946-48
Schwartz, Elliott ... 1959 (M)
Schwartz, Ernie ... 1951-53
Scott, Charlie ... 1968-70
Searcy, Roy ... 1956-58
Severin, Paul ... 1939-41
Shaffer, Charlie ... 1962-64
Shaffer, Dean ... 1981
Shaffer, Lee ... 1958-60
Shaver, Tony ... 1974
Shytle, Ed ... 1941-42
Smith, James ... 1974
Smith, Julian ... 1941-42
Smith, Kenny ... 1984-87
Smith, Mike ... 1966
Smith, Ranzino ... 1985-88
Smithwick, Jim ... 1965-66
Snead, Jane ... 1985 (M)
Spencer, T.B. ... 1935
Spiegel, William ... 1949 (M)
Sprague, Peter ... 1954 (M)
Stahl, Ed ... 1973-75
Stanley, Ray ... 1958-60
Stevenson, Buster ... 1944
Stokes, James ... 1956 (M)
Stroman, Joe ... 1980-81, 83 (M)
Sullivan, Pat ... 1991
Suggs, Reid ... 1941-42
Sutton, Ed ... 1955
Swartzberg, Fred ... 1948

T-U-V
Taylor, Cooper ... 1952, 1954
Terrell, Simon ... 1950
Thompson, Ben ... 1967 (M)
Thompson, Clive ... 1945
Thorne, Charlie ... 1949-51
Thorne, Taylor ... 1946-48
Tsantes, John ... 1949-50
Turk, Irving ... 1950
Tuttle, Gerald ... 1967-69
Tuttle, Richard ... 1969-71
Upperman, Leroy ... 1970 (M)
Valentine, Keith ... 1976
Van Hecke, J.M. ... 1938 (M)
Vayda, Jerry ... 1953-56
Veazey, Dan ... 1975-76 (M)
Vinroot, Richard ... 1962
Virgil, John ... 1977-80

W
Waddell, Charles ... 1973-74
Wallace, Jack ... 1951-53
Walsh, Donnie ... 1960-62
Washington, Donald ... 1973
Watson, Bill ... 1939
Weathers, Virgil ... 1935
Webb, Charles ... 1960 (M)
Webb, Ricky ... 1968-69
Webster, B.L. ... 1935
Wells, Darius ... 1950-51
Wenstrom, Matt ... 1990-91
White, Bill ... 1951
White, Jim ... 1943, 1946-47
White, William ... 1949-50
Whitehead, Gra ... 1968
Wiel, Randy ... 1976-79
Williams, Scott ... 1987-90
Wilson, Don ... 1942
Winstead, Skippy ... 1953-54
Wolf, Jeff ... 1977-80
Wolf, Joe ... 1984-87
Wood, Al ... 1978-81
Worley, Dick ... 1938-39
Worthy, James ... 1980-82
Wright, Henry ... 1937
Wuycik, Dennis ... 1970-72

Y-Z
Yokley, John ... 1964-66
Yonakor, Rich ... 1977-80
Young, Bob ... 1955-57
Youngblood, Joe ... 1966 (M)
Zaliagiris, Tom ... 1975-78

1954

No.	Player	Ht.	Yr.	Hometown
20	Gene Glancy	6-0	So.	Belleville, NJ
21	Al Lifson	6-2	Jr.	Elizabeth, NJ
23	Skippy Winstead	6-2	Sr.	Roxboro, NC
25	Al Long	6-0	Jr.	Durham, NC
30	Cliff Walker	6-4	So.	Durham, NC
31	Gerry McCabe	6-3	So.	The Bronx, NY
35	Cooper Taylor	5-10	Sr.	Raleigh, NC
40	Dick Kocornik	6-5	Sr.	West Orange, NJ
41	Paul Likins	6-9	Jr.	Elkhart, IN
42	Bud Maddie	6-4	Sr.	The Bronx, NY
43	Jerry Vayda	6-4	So.	Bayonne, NJ
44	Tony Radovich	6-2	So.	Hoboken, NJ

Coach: Frank McGuire
Assistant: Buck Freeman

1955

No.	Player	Ht.	Yr.	Hometown
10	Lennie Rosenbluth	6-5	So.	New York, NY
11	Dick Ward	6-1	So.	Wilson, NC
15	Willis Henderson	6-3	So.	Charlotte, NC
20	Bob Young	6-6	So.	New York, NY
21	Al Lifson	6-2	Sr.	Elizabeth, NJ
22	Ed Sutton	6-1	So.	Cullowhee, NC
23	Buddy Clark	6-3	So.	Louisville, KY
32	Gerry McCabe	6-3	Jr.	The Bronx, NY
34	Frank Goodwin	6-1	So.	Belleville, NJ
41	Paul Likins	6-9	Sr.	Elkhart, IN
42	Hilliard Greene	6-5	Jr.	Zebulon, NC
43	Jerry Vayda	6-4	Jr.	Bayonne, NJ
44	Tony Radovich	6-2	Jr.	Hoboken, NJ

Coach: Frank McGuire
Assistant: Buck Freeman

1956

No.	Player	Ht.	Yr.	Hometown
10	Lennie Rosenbluth	6-5	Jr.	New York, NY
11	Ken Rosemond	5-8	So.	Hillsborough, NC
20	Bob Young	6-6	Jr.	New York, NY
22	Roy Searcy	6-4	So.	Draper, NC
23	Buddy Clark	6-3	Jr.	Louisville, KY
32	Bob Cunningham	6-4	So.	New York, NY
33	Gerry McCabe	6-3	Sr.	The Bronx, NY
35	Pete Brennan	6-6	So.	Brooklyn, NY
40	Tommy Kearns	5-11	So.	Bergenfield, NJ
41	Joe Quigg	6-8	So.	New York, NY
42	Hilliard Greene	6-5	Sr.	Zebulon, NC
43	Jerry Vayda	6-4	Sr.	Bayonne, NJ
44	Tony Radovich	6-2	Sr.	Hoboken, NJ

Coach: Frank McGuire
Assistant: Buck Freeman

1957

No.	Player	Ht.	Yr.	Hometown
10	Lennie Rosenbluth	6-5	Sr.	New York, NY
11	Ken Rosemond	5-8	Jr.	Hillsborough, NC
20	Bob Young	6-6	Sr.	New York, NY
22	Roy Searcy	6-4	Jr.	Draper, NC
30	Bill Hathaway	6-11	So.	Long Beach, NY
31	Gehrmann Holland	6-3	So.	Beaufort, NC
32	Bob Cunningham	6-4	Jr.	New York, NY
33	Danny Lotz	6-7	So.	Northport, NY
35	Pete Brennan	6-6	Jr.	Brooklyn, NY
40	Tommy Kearns	5-11	Jr.	Bergenfield, NJ
41	Joe Quigg	6-9	Jr.	Brooklyn, NY
43	Stan Groll	6-0	So.	Brooklyn, NY
44	Tony Radovich	6-2	Sr.	Hoboken, NJ

Coach: Frank McGuire
Assistants: Buck Freeman, Vince Grimaldi

1958

No.	Player	Ht.	Yr.	Hometown
11	John Crotty	5-11	So.	Jersey City, NJ
20	Wallace Graham	6-1	So.	Miami, FL
22	Roy Searcy	6-4	Sr.	Draper, NC
30	Ray Stanley	6-4	So.	Brooklyn, NY
31	Gehrmann Holland	6-4	Jr.	Beaufort, NC
32	Bob Cunningham	6-4	Sr.	New York, NY
33	Danny Lotz	6-7	Jr.	Northport, NY
34	Dick Kepley	6-8	So.	Roanoke, VA
35	Pete Brennan	6-6	Sr.	Brooklyn, NY
40	Tommy Kearns	5-11	Sr.	Bergenfield, NJ
41	Joe Quigg	6-9	Sr.	Brooklyn, NY
42	Harvey Salz	6-1	So.	Brooklyn, NY
43	Lee Shaffer	6-7	So.	Pittsburgh, PA
44	Mike Steppe	6-3	So.	New York, NY
45	Grey Poole	6-6	So.	Raleigh, NC

Coach: Frank McGuire
Assistants: Buck Freeman, Ken Rosemond

1959

No.	Player	Ht.	Yr.	Hometown
11	John Crotty	5-11	Jr.	Jersey City, NJ
12	Lee Shaffer	6-7	Jr.	Pittsburgh, PA
22	York Larese	6-4	So.	New York, NY
30	Ray Stanley	6-4	Jr.	Brooklyn, NY
31	Gehrmann Holland	6-4	Sr.	Beaufort, NC
32	Lou Brown	6-4	So.	Jersey City, NJ
33	Danny Lotz	6-7	Sr.	Northport, NY
34	Dick Kepley	6-8	Jr.	Roanoke, VA
35	Doug Moe	6-5	So.	Brooklyn, NY
41	Hugh Donahue	6-8	So.	New York, NY
42	Harvey Salz	6-1	Jr.	Brookly n, NY
43	Grey Poole	6-6	Jr.	Raleigh, NC

Coach: Frank McGuire
Assistants: Dean Smith, Joe Quigg

1960

No.	Player	Ht.	Yr.	Hometown
11	John Crotty	5-11	Sr.	Jersey City, NJ
12	Lee Shaffer	6-7	Sr.	Pittsburgh, PA
20	Don Walsh	6-0	So.	Riverdale, NY
22	York Larese	6-4	Jr.	New York, NY
30	Ray Stanley	6-4	Sr.	Brooklyn, NY
32	Lou Brown	6-3	Jr.	Jersey City, NJ
33	Jim Hudock	6-7	So.	Tunkhannock, PA
34	Dick Kepley	6-8	Sr.	Roanoke, VA
35	Doug Moe	6-5	Jr.	Brooklyn, NY
40	Yogi Poteet	6-1	So.	Hendersonville, NC
41	Hugh Donahue	6-8	Jr.	New York, NY
42	Harvey Salz	6-1	Sr.	Brooklyn, NY
43	Grey Poole	6-6	Sr.	Raleigh, NC

Coach: Frank McGuire
Assistants: Dean Smith, Ken Rosemond

1961

No.	Player	Ht.	Yr.	Hometown
11	Larry Brown	5-11	So.	Long Beach, NY
12	Harry Jones	6-7	Jr.	Charlotte, NC
20	Don Walsh	6-0	Jr.	Riverdale, NY
22	York Larese	6-4	Sr.	New York, NY
30	Dieter Krause	6-5	So.	Norfolk, VA
31	Ken McComb	6-6	So.	Ardsley, NY
31	Peppy Callahan	6-2	So.	Smithtown, NY
32	Lou Brown	6-3	Sr.	Jersey City, NJ
33	Jim Hudock	6-7	Jr.	Tunkhannock, PA
34	Dick Kepley	6-9	Sr.	Roanoke, VA
35	Doug Moe	6-6	Sr.	Brooklyn, NY
40	Yogi Poteet	6-1	Jr.	Hendersonville, NC
41	Jim Donohue	6-8	So.	Yonkers, NY
42	Martin Conlon	6-7	So.	The Bronx, NY

Coach: Frank McGuire
Assistants: Dean Smith, Ken Rosemond

1962

No.	Player	Ht.	Yr.	Hometown
11	Larry Brown	5-11	Jr.	Long Beach, NY
12	Harry Jones	6-7	Sr.	Charlotte, NC
20	Don Walsh	6-0	Sr.	Riverdale, NY
22	Mike Cooke	6-2	So.	Mt. Airy, NC
30	Dieter Krause	6-5	Jr.	Norfolk, VA
31	Bruce Bowers	6-8	So.	Wellesley Hills, MA
32	Peppy Callahan	6-2	Jr.	Smithtown, NY
33	Jim Hudock	6-7	Sr.	Tunkhannock, PA
34	Richard Vinroot	6-7	So.	Charlotte, NC
35	Charlie Burns	6-2	Jr.	Wadesboro, NC
41	Jim Donohue	6-8	Jr.	Yonkers, NY
42	Charlie Shaffer	6-3	So.	Chapel Hill, NC
43	Art Katz	6-7	So.	Williston Park, NY
44	Bryan McSweeney	6-5	So.	Hewlett, NY

Coach: Dean Smith
Assistant: Ken Rosemond

1963

No.	Player	Ht.	Yr.	Hometown
11	Larry Brown	5-11	Sr.	Long Beach, NY
12	Ray Respess	6-4	So.	Pantego, NC
20	Peppy Callahan	6-2	Sr.	Smithtown, NY
22	Mike Cooke	6-2	Jr.	Mt. Airy, NC
30	Dieter Krause	6-5	Sr.	Norfolk, VA
31	Bill Taylor	5-11	So.	Cary, NC
31	Charlie Burns	6-2	Sr.	Wadesboro, NC
32	Billy Cunningham	6-5	So.	Brooklyn, NY
33	Bill Brown	6-3	So.	Charlotte, NC
34	Bruce Bowers	6-8	Jr.	Wellesley Hills, MA
34	Richard Vinroot	6-8	Jr.	Charlotte, NC
35	Bill Galantai	6-5	So.	New York, NY
40	Yogi Poteet	6-1	Sr.	Hendersonville, NC
41	Terry Ronner	6-6	So.	Wilmington, NC
42	Charlie Shaffer	6-3	Jr.	Chapel Hill, NC
43	Art Katz	6-7	Jr.	Williston Park, NY
44	Bryan McSweeney	6-5	Jr.	Hewlett, NY

Coach: Dean Smith
Assistant: Ken Rosemond

1964

No.	Player	Ht.	Yr.	Hometown
11	Ray Hassell	6-0	So.	Beaufort, NC
12	Ray Respess	6-4	Jr.	Pantego, NC
20	John Yokley	6-0	So.	Mt. Airy, NC
22	Mike Cooke	6-2	Sr.	Mt. Airy, NC
30	Pud Hassell	6-3	Jr.	Beaufort, NC
31	Bob Bennett	6-9	So.	Mt. Lebanon, PA
32	Billy Cunningham	6-6	Jr.	Brooklyn, NY
33	Bill Brown	6-3	Jr.	Charlotte, NC
34	Mike Iannarella	5-10	So.	Sharon Hills, PA
34	Earl Johnson	6-5	So.	Raleigh, NC
35	Bill Galantai	6-5	Jr.	Brooklyn, NY
40	Bill Harrison	6-3	So.	Rocky Mount, NC
40	Jim Moore	6-2	So.	Wilmington, NC
41	Terry Ronner	6-6	Jr.	Wilmington, NC
41	Jim Smithwick	6-4	So.	Morehead City, NC
42	Charlie Shaffer	6-3	Sr.	Chapel Hill, NC
43	Art Katz	6-7	Sr.	Williston Park, NY
44	Bryan McSweeney	6-5	Sr.	Hewlett, NY

Coach: Dean Smith
Assistants: Ken Rosemond, Donnie Walsh

1965

No.	Player	Ht.	Yr.	Hometown
11	Ray Hassell	6-0	Jr.	Beaufort, NC
12	Ray Respess	6-4	Sr.	Pantego, NC
13	Ian Morrison	6-2	So.	St. Petersburg, FL
20	John Yokley	6-1	Jr.	Mt. Airy, NC
22	Bob Lewis	6-3	So.	Washington, DC
30	Jim Moore	6-2	So.	Wilmington, NC
31	Bob Bennett	6-6	Jr.	Mt. Lebanon, PA
32	Billy Cunningham	6-6	Sr.	Brooklyn, NY
33	Bill Brown	6-3	Sr.	Charlotte, NC
34	Pud Hassell	6-3	Sr.	Beaufort, NC
35	Jim Pollock	6-4	Jr.	Clinton, NC
40	Donnie Moe	6-2	So.	Brooklyn, NY
41	Jim Smithwick	6-5	Jr.	Morehead City, NC
42	Tom Gauntlett	6-4	So.	Dallas, PA
43	Mike Smith	6-0	Jr.	North Salem, IN
44	Mark Mirken	6-6	So.	Brooklyn, NY

Coach: Dean Smith
Assistant: Ken Rosemond

1966

No.	Player	Ht.	Yr.	Hometown
11	Ray Hassell	6-0	Sr.	Beaufort, NC
12	Jim Frye	6-5	So.	Homewood, IL
13	Mike Smith	6-0	Sr.	North Salem, IN
20	John Yokley	6-1	Sr.	Mt. Airy, NC
22	Bob Lewis	6-3	Jr.	Washington, DC
30	Greg Campbell	6-0	So.	Bayonne, NJ
31	Bob Bennett	6-8	Sr.	Mt. Lebanon, PA
32	Mark Mirken	6-6	Jr.	Brooklyn, NY
33	Jim Shackelford	6-1	So.	Wilson, NC
34	Jim Moore	6-3	Jr.	Wilmington, NC
35	Ralph Fletcher	6-5	So.	Arlington, VA
40	Donnie Moe	6-2	So.	Brooklyn, NY
41	Jim Smithwick	6-5	Sr.	Morehead City, NC
42	Tom Gauntlett	6-4	Jr.	Dallas, PA
43	Dickson Gribble	6-7	So.	Raleigh, NC
44	Larry Miller	6-3	So.	Catasauqua, PA

Coach: Dean Smith
Assistants: Larry Brown, John Lotz, Charlie Shaffer

1967

No.	Player	Ht.	Yr.	Hometown
11	Gerald Tuttle	6-0	So.	London, KY
12	Jim Frye	6-5	Jr.	Homewood, IL
13	Dick Grubar	6-3	So.	Schenectady, NY
22	Bob Lewis	6-3	Sr.	Washington, DC
30	Greg Campbell	6-0	Jr.	Bayonne, NJ
31	Bill Bunting	6-8	So.	New Bern, NC
32	Mark Mirken	6-6	Sr.	Brooklyn, NY
34	Jim Bostick	6-3	So.	Atlanta, GA
35	Ralph Fletcher	6-5	Jr.	Arlington, VA
40	Donnie Moe	6-2	Jr.	Brooklyn, NY
41	Joe Brown	6-5	So.	Valdese, NC
42	Tom Gauntlett	6-4	Sr.	Dallas, PA
43	Rusty Clark	6-10	So.	Fayetteville, NC
44	Larry Miller	6-3	Jr.	Catasauqua, PA

Coach: Dean Smith
Assistants: Larry Brown, John Lotz

1968

No.	Player	Ht.	Yr.	Hometown
11	Gerald Tuttle	6-0	Jr.	London, KY
12	Jim Frye	6-5	Sr.	Homewood, IL
13	Dick Grubar	6-3	Jr.	Schenectady, NY
20	Eddie Fogler	5-11	So.	Flushing, NY
22	Jim Delany	5-11	So.	South Orange, NJ
30	Al Armour	6-3	So.	Holland, IL
31	Bill Bunting	6-8	Jr.	New Bern, NC
32	Jim Folds	6-2	So.	Greensboro, NC
33	Charlie Scott	6-4	So.	New York, NY
34	Hall Pollard	6-2	So.	Burlington, NC
35	Ralph Fletcher	6-6	Sr.	Wakefield, VA
40	Ricky Webb	6-3	So.	Greenville, NC
41	Joe Brown	6-5	Jr.	Valdese, NC
42	Gra Whitehead	6-4	So.	Scotland Neck, NC
43	Rusty Clark	6-10	Jr.	Fayetteville, NC
44	Larry Miller	6-3	Sr.	Catasauqua, PA

Coach: Dean Smith
Assistants: John Lotz, Bill Guthridge

1969

No.	Player	Ht.	Yr.	Hometown
11	Gerald Tuttle	5-11	Sr.	London, KY
12	Richard Tuttle	6-0	So.	London, KY
13	Dick Grubar	6-4	Sr.	Schenectady, NY
20	Eddie Fogler	5-11	Jr.	Flushing, NY
22	Jim Delany	5-11	Jr.	South Orange, NJ
30	Dale Gipple	6-0	So.	Burlington, NC
31	Bill Bunting	6-8	Sr.	New Bern, NC
32	Dave Chadwick	6-7	So.	Orlando, FL
33	Charlie Scott	6-5	Jr.	New York, NY
34	Don Eggleston	6-8	So.	Charlotte, NC
35	Lee Dedmon	6-10	So.	Baltimore, MD
40	Ricky Webb	6-4	Jr.	Greenville, NC
41	Joe Brown	6-5	Sr.	Valdese, NC
43	Rusty Clark	6-10	Sr.	Fayetteville, NC

Coach: Dean Smith
Assistants: John Lotz, Bill Guthridge

1970

No.	Player	Ht.	Yr.	Hometown
11	Bill Chambers	6-3	So.	Durham, NC
12	Richard Tuttle	6-0	Jr.	London, KY
13	Steve Previs	6-2	So.	Bethel Park, MD
20	Eddie Fogler	5-11	Sr.	Flushing, NY
22	Jim Delany	5-11	Sr.	South Orange, NJ
30	Dale Gipple	6-0	Jr.	Burlington, NC
31	Bill Chamberlain	6-5	So.	New York, NY
32	Dave Chadwick	6-7	Jr.	Orlando, FL
33	Charlie Scott	6-5	Sr.	New York, NY
34	Don Eggleston	6-8	Jr.	Charlotte, NC
35	Lee Dedmon	6-10	Jr.	Baltimore, MD
40	Ricky Webb	6-4	Sr.	Greenville, NC
41	Mike Earey	6-6	So.	Chapel Hill, NC
42	Kim Huband	6-4	So.	Wilmington, NC
43	Craig Corson	6-9	So.	Contoocook, NH
44	Dennis Wuycik	6-5	So.	Ambridge, PA

Coach: Dean Smith
Assistants: John Lotz, Bill Guthridge

1971

No.	Player	Ht.	Yr.	Hometown
11	John Austin	6-2	So.	Charlotte, NC
12	Richard Tuttle	6-0	Sr.	London, KY
13	Steve Previs	6-2	Jr.	Bethel Park, PA
20	Bill Chambers	6-3	Jr.	Durham, NC
22	George Karl	6-1	So.	Penn Hills, PA
30	Dale Gipple	6-1	Sr.	Burlington, NC
31	Bill Chamberlain	6-6	Jr.	New York, NY
32	Dave Chadwick	6-7	Sr.	Orlando, FL
34	Don Eggleston	6-9	Sr.	Charlotte, NC
35	Lee Dedmon	6-10	Sr.	Baltimore, MD
40	Donn Johnston	6-8	So.	Jamestown, NY
41	John Cox	6-1	So.	Sanford, NC
42	Kim Huband	6-4	Jr.	Wilmington, NC
43	Craig Corson	6-9	Jr.	Contoocook, NH
44	Dennis Wuycik	6-5	Jr.	Ambridge, PA

Coach: Dean Smith
Assistants: John Lotz, Bill Guthridge, Terry Truax

1972

No.	Player	Ht.	Yr.	Hometown
11	John Austin	6-2	Jr.	Charlotte, NC
12	Ray Hite	5-10	So.	Hyattsville, MD
13	Steve Previs	6-3	Sr.	Bethel Park, PA
20	Bill Chambers	6-4	Sr.	Durham, NC
22	George Karl	6-2	Jr.	Penn Hills, PA
30	John O'Donnell	6-6	So.	New York, NY
31	Bill Chamberlain	6-6	Sr.	New York, NY
32	Darrell Elston	6-3	So.	Tipton, IN
33	Roger Jamison	5-11	Jr.	Greensboro, NC
33	Alan Mayfield	6-2	So.	Charlotte, NC
34	Bobby Jones	6-8	So.	Charlotte, NC
35	Bob McAdoo	6-9	Jr.	Greensboro, NC
40	Donn Johnston	6-8	Jr.	Jamestown, NY
41	John Cox	6-1	Jr.	Sanford, NC
42	Kim Huband	6-5	Sr.	Wilmington, NC
43	Craig Corson	6-10	Sr.	Contoocook, NH
44	Dennis Wuycik	6-6	Sr.	Ambridge, PA

Coach: Dean Smith
Assistants: John Lotz, Bill Guthridge, Eddie Fogler

1973

No.	Player	Ht.	Yr.	Hometown
12	Ray Hite	6-0	Jr.	Hyattsville, MD
13	Brad Hoffman	5-10	So.	Columbus, OH
14	Dave Hanners	6-0	Fr.	Columbus, OH
20	Ray Harrison	6-2	So.	Greensboro, NC
21	Mitch Kupchak	6-9	Fr.	Brentwood, NY
22	George Karl	6-3	Sr.	Penn Hills, PA
23	Jimmy Guill	6-3	Fr.	Winston-Salem, NC
30	John O'Donnell	6-5	Jr.	New York, NY
31	Mickey Bell	6-5	So.	Goldsboro, NC
32	Darrell Elston	6-4	Jr.	Tipton, IN
34	Bobby Jones	6-9	Jr.	Charlotte, NC
35	Charles Waddell	6-6	Jr.	Southern Pines, NC
40	Donn Johnston	6-8	Sr.	Jamestown, NY
42	Bill Chambers	6-4	Fr.	Greensboro, NC
43	Ed Stahl	6-10	So.	Columbus, OH
44	Donald Washington	6-7	So.	Washington, DC

Coach: Dean Smith
Assistants: Bill Guthridge, Eddie Fogler, John Lotz

1974

No.	Player	Ht.	Yr.	Hometown
11	Tony Shaver	5-11	So.	High Point, NC
12	Ray Hite	6-0	Sr.	Hyattsville, MD
13	Brad Hoffman	5-10	Jr.	Columbus, OH
14	Dave Hanners	6-0	So.	Columbus, OH
15	John Kuester	6-2	Fr.	Richmond, VA
20	Ray Harrison	6-2	Jr.	Greensboro, NC
21	Mitch Kupchak	6-9	So.	Brentwood, NY
23	Jimmy Guill	6-3	So.	Winston-Salem, NC
24	Walter Davis	6-5	Fr.	Pineville, NC
25	James Smith	6-6	Fr.	Lantana, FL
30	John O'Donnell	6-6	Sr.	New York, NY
31	Mickey Bell	6-5	Jr.	Goldsboro, NC
32	Darrell Elston	6-4	Sr.	Tipton, IN
34	Bobby Jones	6-9	Sr.	Charlotte, NC
35	Charles Waddell	6-6	Jr.	Southern Pines, NC
40	Bruce Buckley	6-8	Fr.	Bladensburg, MD
41	Jeff Crompton	6-11	Fr.	Burlington, NC
42	Bill Chambers	6-5	So.	Greensboro, NC
43	Ed Stahl	6-10	Jr.	Columbus, OH
45	Tommy LaGarde	6-10	Fr.	Detroit, MI

Coach: Dean Smith
Assistants: Bill Guthridge, Eddie Fogler, Kim Huband

1975

No.	Player	Ht.	Yr.	Hometown
12	Phil Ford	6-2	Fr.	Rocky Mount, NC
13	Brad Hoffman	5-10	Sr.	Columbus, OH
14	Dave Hanners	6-0	Jr.	Columbus, OH
15	John Kuester	6-2	So.	Richmond, VA
21	Mitch Kupchak	6-9	Jr.	Brentwood, NY
24	Walter Davis	6-5	So.	Pineville, NC
30	Woody Coley	6-6	So.	Lumberton, NC
31	Mickey Bell	6-5	Sr.	Goldsboro, NC
32	Tom Zaliagiris	6-5	Fr.	Livonia, MI
35	Charles Waddell	6-6	Sr.	Southern Pines, NC
40	Bruce Buckley	6-8	So.	Bladensburg, MD
42	Bill Chambers	6-5	Jr.	Greensboro, NC
43	Ed Stahl	6-10	Sr.	Columbus, OH
44	Eric Harry	6-6	So.	Durham, NC
45	Tommy LaGarde	6-10	So.	Detroit, MI

Coach: Dean Smith
Assistants: Bill Guthridge, Eddie Fogler

1976

No.	Player	Ht.	Yr.	Hometown
11	Keith Valentine	6-0	Fr.	Richmond, VA
12	Phil Ford	6-2	So.	Rocky Mount, NC
14	Dave Hanners	6-0	Sr.	Columbus, OH
15	John Kuester	6-2	Jr.	Richmond, VA
21	Mitch Kupchak	6-10	Sr.	Brentwood, NY
22	Dudley Bradley	6-5	Fr.	Edgewood, MD
23	Ged Doughton	6-0	Fr.	Winston-Salem, NC
24	Walter Davis	6-5	Jr.	Pineville, NC
25	Randy Wiel	6-4	Fr.	Curaçao, Neth. Ant.
30	Woody Coley	6-6	Jr.	Lumberton, NC
31	Loren Lutz	6-4	Fr.	Alamosa, CO
32	Tom Zaliagiris	6-5	So.	Livonia, MI
40	Bruce Buckley	6-8	Jr.	Bladensburg, MD
41	Jeff Crompton	6-11	So.	Burlington, NC
42	Bill Chambers	6-6	Sr.	Greensboro, NC
44	Eric Harry	6-6	Jr.	Durham, NC
45	Tommy LaGarde	6-10	Jr.	Detroit, MI

Coach: Dean Smith
Assistants: Bill Guthridge, Eddie Fogler

1977

No.	Player	Ht.	Yr.	Hometown
12	Phil Ford	6-2	Jr.	Rocky Mount, NC
15	John Kuester	6-2	Sr.	Richmond, VA
20	Dave Colescott	6-1	Fr.	Marion, IN
22	Dudley Bradley	6-5	So.	Edgewood, MD
23	Ged Doughton	6-0	So.	Winston-Salem, NC
24	Walter Davis	6-5	Sr.	Pineville, NC
25	Randy Wiel	6-4	So.	Curaçao, Neth. Ant.
30	Woody Coley	6-6	Sr.	Lumberton, NC
31	Mike O'Koren	6-6	Fr.	Jersey City, NJ
32	Tom Zaliagiris	6-5	Jr.	Livonia, MI
40	Bruce Buckley	6-8	Sr.	Bladensburg, MD
42	Jeff Wolf	6-10	Fr.	Kohler, WI
43	John Virgil	6-4	Fr.	Elm City, NC
45	Tommy LaGarde	6-10	Sr.	Detroit, MI
50	Rich Yonakor	6-9	Fr.	Euclid, OH
54	Steve Krafcisin	6-9	Fr.	Chicago Ridge, IL

Coach: Dean Smith
Assistants: Bill Guthridge, Eddie Fogler

1978

No.	Player	Ht.	Yr.	Hometown
11	Mike Pepper	6-2	Fr.	Vienna, VA
12	Phil Ford	6-2	Sr.	Rocky Mount, NC
20	Dave Colescott	6-1	So.	Marion, IN
22	Dudley Bradley	6-5	Jr.	Edgewood, MD
23	Ged Doughton	6-0	Jr.	Winston-Salem, NC
25	Randy Wiel	6-4	Jr.	Curaçao, Neth. Ant.
30	Al Wood	6-6	Fr.	Gray, GA
31	Mike O'Koren	6-7	So.	Jersey City, NJ
32	Tom Zaliagiris	6-6	Sr.	Livonia, MI
34	Pete Budko	6-8	Fr.	Lutherville, MD
41	Jeff Crompton	6-11	Sr.	Burlington, NC
42	Jeff Wolf	6-10	So.	Kohler, WI
43	John Virgil	6-5	So.	Elm City, NC
50	Rich Yonakor	6-9	So.	Euclid, OH

Coach: Dean Smith
Assistants: Bill Guthridge, Eddie Fogler

1979

No.	Player	Ht.	Yr.	Hometown
11	Mike Pepper	6-3	So.	Vienna, VA
20	Dave Colescott	6-1	Jr.	Marion, IN
21	Jimmy Black	6-2	Fr.	The Bronx, NY
22	Dudley Bradley	6-6	Sr.	Edgewood, MD
23	Ged Doughton	6-1	Sr.	Winston-Salem, NC
25	Randy Wiel	6-4	Sr.	Curaçao, Neth. Ant.
30	Al Wood	6-6	So.	Gray, GA
31	Mike O'Koren	6-7	Jr.	Jersey City, NJ
32	Eric Kenny	6-6	So.	Asheville, NC
34	Pete Budko	6-8	So.	Lutherville, MD
42	Jeff Wolf	6-11	Jr.	Kohler, WI
43	John Virgil	6-5	Jr.	Elm City, NC
45	Chris Brust	6-9	Fr.	Babylon, NY
50	Rich Yonakor	6-9	Jr.	Euclid, OH

Coach: Dean Smith
Assistants: Bill Guthridge, Eddie Fogler, Roy Williams

1980

No.	Player	Ht.	Yr.	Hometown
11	Mike Pepper	6-3	Jr.	Vienna, VA
20	Dave Colescott	6-2	Sr.	Marion, IN
21	Jimmy Black	6-2	So.	The Bronx, NY
24	Jim Braddock	6-1	Fr.	Chattanooga, TN
30	Al Wood	6-6	Jr.	Gray, GA
31	Mike O'Koren	6-8	Sr.	Jersey City, NJ
32	Eric Kenny	6-6	Jr.	Asheville, NC
34	Pete Budko	6-8	Jr.	Lutherville, MD
42	Jeff Wolf	6-11	Sr.	Kohler, WI
43	John Virgil	6-6	Sr.	Elm City, NC
45	Chris Brust	6-9	So.	Babylon, NY
50	Rich Yonakor	6-10	Sr.	Euclid, OH
52	James Worthy	6-8	Fr.	Gastonia, NC

Coach: Dean Smith
Assistants: Bill Guthridge, Eddie Fogler, Roy Williams

1981

No.	Player	Ht.	Yr.	Hometown
11	Mike Pepper	6-3	Sr.	Vienna, VA
21	Jimmy Black	6-2	Jr.	The Bronx, NY
24	Jim Braddock	6-1	So.	Chattanooga, TN
30	Al Wood	6-6	Sr.	Gray, GA
32	Eric Kenny	6-6	Sr.	Asheville, NC
33	Dean Shaffer	6-3	Fr.	Durham, NC
34	Pete Budko	6-9	Sr.	Lutherville, MD
41	Sam Perkins	6-9	Fr.	Latham, NY
43	Jeb Barlow	6-7	Jr.	Fuquay-Varina, NC
44	Matt Doherty	6-7	Fr.	East Meadow, NY
45	Chris Brust	6-9	Jr.	Babylon, NY
50	Cecil Exum	6-6	Fr.	Dudley, NC
51	Timo Makkonen	6-11	Fr.	Lahti, Finland
52	James Worthy	6-8	So.	Gastonia, NC

Coach: Dean Smith
Assistants: Bill Guthridge, Eddie Fogler, Roy Williams

1982

No.	Player	Ht.	Yr.	Hometown
4	Lynwood Robinson	6-1	Fr.	Mt. Olive, NC
21	Jimmy Black	6-3	Sr.	The Bronx, NY
22	Buzz Peterson	6-3	Fr.	Asheville, NC
23	Michael Jordan	6-4	Fr.	Wilmington, NC
24	Jim Braddock	6-2	Jr.	Chattanooga, TN
32	John Brownlee	6-10	Fr.	Fort Worth, TX
33	Dean Shaffer	6-4	So.	Durham, NC
41	Sam Perkins	6-9	So.	Latham, NY
43	Jeb Barlow	6-7	Sr.	Fuquay-Varina, NC
44	Matt Doherty	6-7	So.	East Meadow, NY
45	Chris Brust	6-9	Sr.	Babylon, NY
50	Cecil Exum	6-6	So.	Dudley, NC
51	Timo Makkonen	6-11	So.	Lahti, Finland
52	James Worthy	6-9	Jr.	Gastonia, NC
54	Warren Martin	6-11	Fr.	Axton, VA

Coach: Dean Smith
Assistants: Bill Guthridge, Eddie Fogler, Roy Williams

1983

No.	Player	Ht.	Yr.	Hometown
4	Lynwood Robinson	6-1	So.	Mt. Olive, NC
22	Buzz Peterson	6-3	So.	Asheville, NC
23	Michael Jordan	6-5	So.	Wilmington, NC
24	Jim Braddock	6-2	Sr.	Chattanooga, TN
25	Steve Hale	6-3	Fr.	Jenks, OK
32	John Brownlee	6-10	So.	Fort Worth, TX
41	Sam Perkins	6-9	Jr.	Latham, NY
42	Brad Daughtery	6-11	Fr.	Black Mountain, NC
43	Curtis Hunter	6-4	Fr.	Durham, NC
44	Matt Doherty	6-8	Jr.	East Meadow, NY
50	Cecil Exum	6-6	Jr.	Dudley, NC
51	Timo Makkonen	6-11	Jr.	Lahti, Finland
54	Warren Martin	6-11	So.	Axton, VA

Coach: Dean Smith
Assistants: Bill Guthridge, Eddie Fogler, Roy Williams

1984

No.	Player	Ht.	Yr.	Hometown
20	Cliff Morris	6-3	Jr.	Durham, NC
22	Buzz Peterson	6-4	Jr.	Asheville, NC
23	Michael Jordan	6-5	Jr.	Wilmington, NC
24	Joe Wolf	6-10	Fr.	Kohler, WI
25	Steve Hale	6-3	So.	Jenks, OK
30	Kenny Smith	6-3	Fr.	Queens, NY
35	Dave Popson	6-9	Fr.	Ashley, PA
41	Sam Perkins	6-10	Sr.	Latham, NY
42	Brad Daughtery	6-11	So.	Black Mountain, NC
43	Curtis Hunter	6-5	So.	Durham, NC
44	Matt Doherty	6-8	Sr.	East Meadow, NY
50	Cecil Exum	6-7	Sr.	Dudley, NC
51	Timo Makkonen	6-11	Jr.	Lahti, Finland
54	Warren Martin	6-11	Jr.	Axton, VA

Coach: Dean Smith
Assistants: Bill Guthridge, Eddie Fogler, Roy Williams

1985

No.	Player	Ht.	Yr.	Hometown
4	James Daye	5-11	Jr.	Burlington, NC
20	Cliff Morris	6-3	Sr.	Durham, NC
22	Buzz Peterson	6-5	Sr.	Asheville, NC
24	Joe Wolf	6-10	So.	Kohler, WI
25	Steve Hale	6-3	Jr.	Jenks, OK
30	Kenny Smith	6-3	So.	Queens, NY
31	Matt Brust	6-4	Fr.	Babylon, NY
33	Ranzino Smith	6-1	Fr.	Chapel Hill, NC
35	Dave Popson	6-10	So.	Ashley, PA
40	Gary Roper	6-7	Sr.	Andrews, NC
42	Brad Daughtery	6-11	Jr.	Black Mountain, NC
43	Curtis Hunter	6-5	So.	Durham, NC
51	Timo Makkonen	6-11	Sr.	Lahti, Finland
54	Warren Martin	6-11	Jr.	Axton, VA

Coach: Dean Smith
Assistants: Bill Guthridge, Eddie Fogler, Roy Williams

1986

No.	Player	Ht.	Yr.	Hometown
4	James Daye	5-11	Sr.	Burlington, NC
14	Jeff Lebo	6-2	Fr.	Carlisle, PA
20	Steve Bucknall	6-6	Fr.	London, England
21	Michael Norwood	6-2	Jr.	Henderson, NC
22	Kevin Madden	6-4	Fr.	Staunton, VA
24	Joe Wolf	6-10	Jr.	Kohler, WI
25	Steve Hale	6-3	Sr.	Jenks, OK
30	Kenny Smith	6-3	Jr.	Queens, NY
33	Ranzino Smith	6-1	So.	Chapel Hill, NC
35	Dave Popson	6-10	Jr.	Ashley, PA
42	Brad Daughtery	6-11	Sr.	Black Mountain, NC
43	Curtis Hunter	6-5	Jr.	Durham, NC
45	Marty Hensley	6-10	Fr.	Marion, NC
54	Warren Martin	6-11	Sr.	Axton, VA

Coach: Dean Smith
Assistants: Bill Guthridge, Eddie Fogler, Roy Williams

1987

No.	Player	Ht.	Yr.	Hometown
3	Jeff Denny	6-4	Fr.	Rural Hall, NC
11	Rodney Hyatt	5-8	Fr.	Wadesboro, NC
14	Jeff Lebo	6-2	So.	Carlisle, PA
20	Steve Bucknall	6-6	So.	London, England
21	Michael Norwood	6-2	Sr.	Henderson, NC
24	Joe Wolf	6-10	Sr.	Kohler, WI
30	Kenny Smith	6-3	Sr.	Queens, NY
33	Ranzino Smith	6-1	Jr.	Chapel Hill, NC
34	J.R. Reid	6-9	Fr.	Virginia Beach, VA
35	Dave Popson	6-10	Sr.	Ashley, PA
42	Scott Williams	6-10	Fr.	Hacienda Hts., CA
43	Curtis Hunter	6-5	Sr.	Durham, NC
45	Marty Hensley	6-10	So.	Marion, NC

Coach: Dean Smith
Assistants: Bill Guthridge, Roy Williams, Dick Harp, Randy Wiel

1988

No.	Player	Ht.	Yr.	Hometown
3	Jeff Denny	6-3	So.	Rural Hall, NC
11	Rodney Hyatt	5-8	So.	Wadesboro, NC
14	Jeff Lebo	6-3	Jr.	Carlisle, PA
20	Steve Bucknall	6-6	Jr.	London, England
21	King Rice	6-0	Fr.	Binghamton, NY
22	Kevin Madden	6-4	So.	Staunton, VA
24	Doug Elstun	6-3	Fr.	Overland Park, KS
31	David May	6-6	Jr.	Greensboro, NC
32	Pete Chilcutt	6-9	Fr.	Eutaw, AL
33	Ranzino Smith	6-1	Sr.	Chapel Hill, NC
34	J.R. Reid	6-9	So.	Virginia Beach, VA
35	Joe Jenkins	6-5	Sr.	Elizabeth City, NC
42	Scott Williams	6-10	So.	Hacienda Hts., CA
44	Rick Fox	6-7	Fr.	Nassau, Bahamas

Coach: Dean Smith
Assistants: Bill Guthridge, Roy Williams, Dick Harp, Randy Wiel

1989

No.	Player	Ht.	Yr.	Hometown
3	Jeff Denny	6-4	Jr.	Rural Hall, NC
14	Jeff Lebo	6-4	Sr.	Carlisle, PA
20	Steve Bucknall	6-6	Sr.	London, England
21	King Rice	6-1	So.	Binghamton, NY
22	Kevin Madden	6-4	Jr.	Staunton, VA
31	David May	6-7	Sr.	Greensboro, NC
32	Pete Chilcutt	6-9	So.	Eutaw, AL
34	J.R. Reid	6-9	Jr.	Virginia Beach, VA
40	Hubert Davis	6-4	Fr.	Burke, VA
42	Scott Williams	6-10	Jr.	Hacienda Hts., CA
44	Rick Fox	6-7	So.	Nassau, Bahamas
45	Marty Hensley	6-11	Jr.	Marion, NC
50	Bill Akins	6-5	Jr.	Fuquay-Varina, NC
54	John Greene	6-10	Jr.	Raleigh, NC

Coach: Dean Smith
Assistants: Bill Guthridge, Phil Ford, Randy Wiel, Dick Harp

1990

No.	Player	Ht.	Yr.	Hometown
3	Jeff Denny	6-4	Sr.	Rural Hall, NC
4	Kenny Harris	6-1	Fr.	Petersburg, VA
5	Henrik Rodl	6-7	Fr.	Heusenstamm, FRG
11	Scott Cherry	6-3	Fr.	Ballston Spa, NY
21	King Rice	6-1	Jr.	Binghamton, NY
22	Kevin Madden	6-6	Sr.	Staunton, VA
32	Pete Chilcutt	6-9	Jr.	Eutaw, AL
34	George Lynch	6-7	Fr.	Roanoke, VA
40	Hubert Davis	6-4	So.	Burke, VA
42	Scott Williams	6-11	Sr.	Hacienda Hts., CA
44	Rick Fox	6-7	Jr.	Nassau, Bahamas
45	Marty Hensley	6-11	Sr.	Marion, NC
54	John Greene	6-10	Sr.	Raleigh, NC
55	Matt Wenstrom	7-0	Fr.	Katy, TX

Coach: Dean Smith
Assistants: Bill Guthridge, Phil Ford, Randy Wiel, Dave Hanners

1991

No.	Player	Ht.	Yr.	Hometown
00	Eric Montross	7-0	Fr.	Indianapolis, IN
3	Pat Sullivan	6-8	Fr.	Bogota, NJ
4	Kenny Harris	6-1	So.	Petersburg, VA
5	Henrik Rodl	6-7	So.	Heusenstamm, FRG
11	Scott Cherry	6-4	So.	Ballston Spa, NY
14	Derrick Phelps	6-3	Fr.	Pleasantville, NY
21	King Rice	6-0	Sr.	Binghamton, NY
31	Brian Reese	6-5	Fr.	The Bronx, NY
32	Pete Chilcutt	6-10	Sr.	Eutaw, AL
33	Kevin Salvadori	7-0	Fr.	Pittsburgh, PA
34	George Lynch	6-7	So.	Roanoke, VA
40	Hubert Davis	6-4	Jr.	Burke, VA
44	Rick Fox	6-7	Sr.	Nassau, Bahamas
45	Clifford Rozier	6-10	Fr.	Bradenton, FL
55	Matt Wenstrom	7-1	So.	Katy, TX

Coach: Dean Smith
Assistants: Bill Guthridge, Phil Ford, Randy Wiel, Dave Hanners

1910-11

RECORD: 7-4
COACH: Nat Cartmell
CAPTAIN: Marvin Rich

Virginia Christian	W	42	21
Durham YMCA	W	60	18
Wake Forest	W	31	28
Wake Forest	L	16	38
Davidson	W	27	25
Charlotte YM CA	W	42	28
Tennessee	W	40	21
Virginia	L	15	18
Virginia	L	16	24
Woodberry Forest	W	23	11
Virginia Christian	L	31	33

1911-12

RECORD: 4-5
COACH: Nat Cartmell
CAPTAIN: Junius Smith

Virginia Christian	W	43	17
Virginia Christian	L	18	29
Virginia Christian	L	18	20
Durham YMCA	L	28	29
Wake Forest	L	18	15
Elon	W	36	5
William & Mary	W	35	21
Guilford	L	20	35
Virginia Tech	L	28	37

1912-13

RECORD: 4-7
COACH: Nat Cartmell
CAPTAIN: Ben Edwards

Durham YMCA	L	22	23
Davidson	W	42	8
Elon	W	41	11
Emory & Henry	L	17	20
Virginia	L	19	30
Wake Forest	L	21	22
N.C. State	L	18	26
Virginia Tech	W	29	9
Guilford	L	29	44
Elon	L	19	23
Wake Forest	W	19	15

1913-14

RECORD: 10-8
COACH: Nat Cartmell
CAPTAIN: Meb Long

Durham YMCA	W	37	24
Durham YMCA	L	37	42
Durham YMCA	W	44	28
Wake Forest	W	28	24
Wake Forest	L	30	39
Wake Forest	L	29	32
Charlotte YMCA	W	43	32
Charlotte YMCA	W	52	29
Virginia	L	27	67
Virginia	L	23	56
Woodberry Forest	W	25	21
Elon	L	15	21
Elon	W	29	16
Guilford	W	23	22
Guilford	W	38	13
VMI	W	29	37
Staunton Military Academy	W	41	10
Lynchburg YMCA	L	34	42

1914-15

RECORD: 6-10
COACH: Charles Doak
CAPTAIN: Meb Long

Durham YMCA	L	14	22
Durham YMCA	L	25	44
Durham YMCA	L	25	24
Wake Forest	L	23	26
Wake Forest	W	32	20
Wake Forest	L	25	30
Virginia	L	29	30
Virginia	L	26	43
Elon	W	15	9
Elon	L	15	19
Guilford	W	45	27
VMI	L	24	28
Staunton Military Academy	W	28	16
Roanoke	W	18	17
Washington & Lee	L	22	29
Lynchburg Elks	L	20	63

1915-16

RECORD: 12-6
COACH: Charles Doak
CAPTAIN: John G. Johnson

Durham YMCA	L	16	26
Durham YMCA	W	18	14
Wake Forest	L	22	27
Davidson	W	20	14
Davidson	W	31	21
Virginia	L	25	29
Elon	W	31	10
Elon	W	19	15
Guilford	W	51	21
Guilford	W	40	26
Virginia Tech	L	27	44
VMI	W	25	23
Roanoke	L	13	45
Washington & Lee	L	18	25
Statesville Athletic Club	W	51	14
Statesville Athletic Club	W	34	30
Maryville	W	39	24
Randolph Macon	W	47	18

1916-17

RECORD: 5-4
COACH: Howell Peacock
CAPTAIN: George Tennent

Durham YMCA	W	49	30
Davidson	L	31	36
Virginia	W	35	24
Guilford	W	55	28
Virginia Tech	W	31	23
Virginia Tech	L	22	30
VMI	W	33	22
VMI	L	34	47
Washington & Lee	L	23	40

1917-18

RECORD: 9-3
COACH: Howell Peacock
CAPTAIN: George Tennent

Durham YMCA	W	60	13
Durham YMCA	W	44	24
Davidson	W	28	22
Virginia	L	35	45
Elon	W	29	25
Elon	L	21	28
Guilford	W	28	24
Guilford	W	31	19
Emory & Henry	W	63	21
Lynchburg Athletic Club	L	23	38
Georgia	W	36	27
South Carolina	W	58	21

1918-19

RECORD: 9-7
COACH: Howell Peacock
CAPTAIN: Reynolds Cuthberson

Durham YMCA	L	22	40
Durham YMCA	L	21	25
Wake Forest	W	36	17
Davidson	W	40	12
Charlotte YMCA	W	51	46
Virginia	L	29	40
Virginia	L	21	31
Elon	W	44	12
Guilford	W	47	23
Guilford	W	56	23
Virginia Tech	L	14	37
Virginia Tech	L	22	28
VMI	W	42	28
Washington & Lee	W	31	27
Camp Jackson	W	37	30
N.C. State	L	29	39

1919-20

RECORD: 7-9
COACH: Fred Boye
CAPTAIN: Billy Carmichael

Durham YMCA	W	40	30
Durham YMCA	W	28	27
Durham YMCA	L	30	34
Davidson	L	20	31
Davidson	W	23	22
Charlotte YMCA	L	32	40
Virginia	L	26	40
Virginia	L	31	37
Guilford	W	51	23
N.C. State	L	21	32
N.C. State	W	32	12
Trinity	W	36	25
Trinity	L	18	19
Georgetown	L	27	36
Navy	L	24	36
Catholic Univ.	W	32	28

1920-21

RECORD: 12-8
COACH: Fred Boye
CAPTAIN: Carlyle Shepard

Durham YMCA	W	44	25
Durham YMCA	W	22	16
Davidson	W	37	20
Virginia	W	28	26
Virginia	W	43	12
Elon	W	37	12
N.C. State	W	62	10
N.C. State	L	31	32
VMI	L	23	38
Washington & Lee	W	29	25
Lynchburg Elks	W	38	15
Trinity	L	22	25
Trinity	W	41	19
Trinity	W	55	18
Georgetown	L	22	38
Navy	L	24	50
Army	L	26	34
Rutgers	L	22	25
Yale	L	30	32
South Carolina	W	38	15

1921-22

RECORD: 15-6
COACH: None
CAPTAIN: Cart Carmichael

South Carolina	W	44	28
Durham YMCA	L	25	46
Durham YMCA	L	18	41
Wake Forest	W	42	27
N.C. State	W	30	17
Wofford	W	54	26
Trinity	W	38	22
N.C. State	W	49	19
Elon	W	50	24
Wake Forest	W	32	28
VMI	W	31	26
Washington & Lee	L	25	38
Virginia	L	29	31
Army	L	22	52
Samford	W	55	22
Newberry	W	32	27
Georgia	W	33	25
Alabama	W	20	11
Mercer	W	40	25
Washington & Lee	L	36	39
Trinity	W	29	23

1922-23

RECORD: 15-1
COACH: None
CAPTAIN: Monk McDonald

Durham YMCA	W	31	28
Durham YMCA	W	50	21
Wake Forest	W	38	26
Wake Forest	W	25	23
Virginia	W	39	16
N.C. State	W	39	9
N.C. State	W	45	26
VMI	W	26	20
Washington & Lee	W	24	21
Trinity	W	20	19
Trinity	W	36	32
Mercer	W	33	22
Lynchburg	W	50	31
Florida	W	59	14
Mississippi College	W	28	21
Mississippi	L	32	34

1923-24

RECORD: 26-0
COACH: Norman Shepard
CAPTAIN: Winton Green

Wake Forest	W	32	16
Wake Forest	W	33	12
Davidson	W	37	27
Virginia	W	33	20
Elon	W	60	13
William & Mary	W	54	16
Guilford	W	50	22
N.C. State	W	44	9
N.C. State	W	41	24
VMI	W	40	25
Washington & Lee	W	19	16
Washington & Lee	W	26	17
South Carolina	W	53	19
Trinity	W	31	20
Trinity	W	23	20
Catholic Univ.	W	35	22
Mercer	W	35	23
Lynchburg	W	36	26
Maryland	W	26	20
Alabama	W	26	18
Kentucky	W	41	20
Vanderbilt	W	37	20
Mississippi State	W	33	23
Durham Elks	W	33	20
Charlotte YMCA	W	32	29
Durham Elks	W	49	23

1924-25

RECORD: 20-5
COACH: Monk McDonald
CAPTAIN: Jack Cobb

Wake Forest	W	22	18
Davidson	W	44	13
Durham Elks	W	46	27
Durham Elks	W	51	12
Virginia	W	26	15
Guilford	W	37	10
N.C. State	W	27	17
N.C. State	W	27	10
VMI	W	31	19
Washington & Lee	W	31	15
Washington & Lee	L	22	29
South Carolina	L	27	28
Navy	L	20	39
Lynchburg	W	26	12
Maryland	W	21	16
Duke	W	25	21
Duke	W	34	18
Wake Forest	W	43	24
Harvard	W	22	23
Crescent Athletic Club	L	24	32
Georgia	W	40	19
Virginia Tech	W	43	13
Louisiana State	W	35	21
Georgia Tech	W	34	26
Tulane	W	36	28

1925-26

RECORD: 20-5
COACH: Harlan Sanborn
CAPTAIN: Bill Dodderer

Durham YMCA	W	42	35
Durham YMCA	W	41	19
Wake Forest	L	28	29
Wake Forest	W	32	22
Davidson	W	53	18
Virginia	W	47	16
Elon	W	40	25
Guilford	W	44	20
N.C. State	W	31	21
N.C. State	L	8	17
VMI	W	39	22
Washington & Lee	W	43	26
Navy	L	30	31
Catholic Univ.	W	32	25
Wofford	W	41	23
Florida	W	42	6
Maryland	L	22	23
Duke	W	38	20
Duke	W	44	21
Harvard	L	37	40
Clemson	W	50	20
Mississippi	W	38	23
Mississippi State	W	38	23
Clemson	W	52	21
Virginia	W	25	23

1926-27

RECORD: 17-7
COACH: James Ashmore
CAPTAIN: Bunn Hackney

Greensboro YMCA	W	35	21
Salisbury YMCA	L	28	29
Charlotte YMCA	W	36	15
Durham YMCA	W	37	16
Durham YMCA	W	46	22
Hampden-Sydney	W	64	5
Georgia	W	33	27
Charlotte Monogram	L	29	31
Wake Forest	L	23	30
N.C. State	W	40	20
Duke	W	40	33
Virginia Tech	W	36	22
Virginia	W	42	13
VMI	W	33	14
Maryland	L	20	28
Maryland	W	32	23
Navy	L	26	31
N.C. State	W	19	13
Wake Forest	W	32	26
Maryland	L	19	23
Duke	W	37	20

SOUTHERN CONFERENCE TOURNAMENT

Tennessee	W	32	17
Auburn	W	28	15
Georgia	L	20	23

1927-28

RECORD: 17-2
COACH: James Ashmore
CAPTAIN: Bily Morris

Durham YMCA	W	20	5
Salisbury YMCA	W	45	14
Charlotte Monogram	W	33	30
Tulane	W	23	21
Tulane	L	19	20
Tulane	W	38	8
Charlotte Monogram	W	43	31
Guilford	W	42	23
Georgia	W	35	29
Wake Forest	W	38	22
Virginia	W	37	21
High Point Hawks	W	43	21
N.C. State	W	31	21
Duke	W	27	23
Virginia	W	26	22
Duke	W	32	23
N.C. State	W	31	21
Wake Forest	W	38	22

SOUTHERN CONFERENCE TOURNAMENT

Louisiana State	L	38	44

1928-29

RECORD: 17-8
COACH: James Ashmore
CAPTAIN: Rufus Hackney

Butler	L	20	43
Ohio State	L	30	43
Louisville	W	19	27
Kentucky	W	26	15
Tennessee	W	28	26
Davidson	W	34	21
South Carolina	L	25	28
Wake Forest	W	42	19
N.C. State	W	41	32
Georgia	W	31	29
Atlanta Athletic Club	L	18	34
South Carolina	W	45	33
Virginia	W	28	20
Virginia Tech	W	33	27
Duke	L	20	36
Virginia	W	40	25
Maryland	W	28	22
Princeton	L	19	22
Wake Forest	W	34	10
N.C. State	W	35	34
Duke	W	27	24
Davidson	W	45	7
VMI	W	32	19

SOUTHERN CONFERENCE TOURNAMENT

Mississippi State	W	43	18
Duke	L	17	34

1929-30

RECORD: 14-11
COACH: James Ashmore
CAPTAIN: Puny Harper

Raleigh YMCA	L	29	42
Greensboro YMCA	W	41	10
Durham YMCA	W	28	27
High Point YMCA	W	28	12
Greensboro YMCA	W	88	25
Davidson	L	20	22
Guilford	W	49	20
Washington & Lee	L	24	39
Charlotte Monogram	W	23	19
Wake Forest	W	49	18
N.C. State	W	27	25
Duke	L	14	36
Virginia Tech	W	30	21
Washington & Lee	L	17	27
Virginia	W	40	37
Maryland	L	33	36
N.C. State	L	26	28
Loyola (Chicago)	L	25	26
Duke	L	36	37
Wake Forest	W	37	15
Maryland	L	22	29
Virginia Tech	W	41	23
Navy	W	43	33
Davidson	W	19	10

SOUTHERN CONFERENCE TOURNAMENT

Georgia	L	17	26

1930-31

RECORD: 15-9
COACH: James Ashmore
CAPTAIN: Artie Marpet

Durham YMCA	W	31	14
Raleigh YMCA	W	46	12
Guilford	W	33	13
Randolph-Macon	W	34	13
Davidson	L	17	18
Furman	W	23	16
South Carolina	W	38	8
Wake Forest	W	30	13
Virginia Tech	L	28	31
N.C. State	W	22	16
Duke	L	18	30
N.C. State	L	20	23
Maryland	L	31	33
VMI	W	43	13
Virginia Tech	W	30	24
Virginia	W	28	24
Washington & Lee	L	31	39
Davidson	L	28	30
Duke	L	23	34
Wake Forest	W	45	25
VMI	W	30	21
Univ. of the South	W	37	28

SOUTHERN CONFERENCE TOURNAMENT

Vanderbilt	W	23	20
Maryland	L	18	19

1931-32

RECORD: 16-5
COACH: George Shepard
CAPTAIN: Tom Alexander

Raleigh YMCA	W	27	14
Guilford	W	49	23
Davidson	W	45	29
Furman	W	37	17
Virginia Tech	W	38	26
Wake Forest	W	32	17
N.C. State	L	18	19
Duke	W	37	20
Wake Forest	W	34	24
Virginia Tech	W	31	20
Maryland	L	25	26
Virginia	(OT) W	26	24
Davidson	W	32	28
Duke	L	18	24
Maryland	W	32	26
Washington & Lee	W	27	19
N.C. State	L	17	36

SOUTHERN CONFERENCE TOURNAMENT

Tennessee	W	35	25
Kentucky	W	43	42
Auburn	W	51	32
Georgia	L	24	26

1932-33

RECORD: 12-5
COACH: George Shepard
CAPTAIN: Wilmer Hines

Guilford	W	66	9
Davidson	W	56	18
Virginia Tech	W	58	26
Wake Forest	W	36	33
N.C. State	W	32	23
Wake Forest	W	36	26
VMI	W	36	17
Duke	L	32	36
Maryland	L	29	42
Navy	L	40	66
VMI	W	32	29
Washington & Lee	W	34	23
Duke	L	24	31
Davidson	W	39	26
N.C. State	W	35	28

SOUTHERN CONFERENCE TOURNAMENT

Virginia Tech	W	32	27
South Carolina	(2OT) L	32	34

1933-34

RECORD: 18-4
COACH: George Shepard
CAPTAIN: Dave McCachren

Clemson	W	38	26
Davidson	W	38	23
Viscose Club	W	26	25
Virginia Tech	W	31	14
VMI	W	38	18
Washington & Lee	W	34	24
Wake Forest	W	41	21
VMI	W	37	11
Virginia	W	44	35
N.C. State	L	30	34
Virginia Tech	W	42	21
Virginia	W	24	23
Maryland	W	28	24
Navy	L	24	26
Duke	W	25	21
Wake Forest	W	41	24
N.C. State	W	45	24
Davidson	W	39	25
Duke	W	30	25
South Carolina	L	30	45

SOUTHERN CONFERENCE TOURNAMENT

Virginia	W	27	18
Duke	L	18	21

1934-35

RECORD: 23-2
COACH: George Shepard
CAPTAIN: Stewart Aitken

Elon	W	34	21
Davidson	W	36	26
Wake Forest	W	31	11
Washington & Lee	W	36	34
VMI	W	24	19
Virginia Tech	W	29	9
Virginia	W	36	20
Maryland	W	39	31
Navy	W	30	19
Crescent Athletic Club	W	38	32
NYAthletic Club	W	38	32
Army	L	19	29
Virginia Tech	W	29	13
N.C. State	W	33	27
Wake Forest	W	32	21
Duke	L	27	33
South Carolina	W	32	31
Davidson	W	38	26
Duke	W	24	20
N.C. State	W	37	35
South Carolina	W	32	31
VMI	W	42	17

SOUTHERN CONFERENCE TOURNAMENT

South Carolina	W	46	25
N.C. State	W	30	28
Washington & Lee	W	35	27

1935-36

RECORD: 21-4
COACH: Walter Skidmore
CAPTAIN: Jim McCachren

Clemson	W	24	23
Davidson	W	45	27
Wake Forest	W	26	19
Virginia Tech	W	40	21
Washington & Lee	L	25	28
Virginia	W	38	25
NYU	L	33	55
N.C. State	W	37	35
South Carolina	W	38	18
VMI	W	43	21
Virginia	(OT) L	30	33
Maryland	W	44	32
Virginia Tech	W	34	26
South Carolina	W	43	41
Wake Forest	W	32	23
Duke	(OT) L	34	36
Navy	W	39	25
Duke	W	30	28
Clemson	(OT) W	35	34
N.C. State	W	31	29
VMI	(OT) W	35	31
Davidson	W	31	16

SOUTHERN CONFERENCE TOURNAMENT

Virginia	W	39	21
N.C. State	W	31	28
Washington & Lee	W	50	45

1936-37

RECORD: 18-5
COACH: Walter Skidmore
CAPTAIN: Earl Ruth

Leaksville YMCA	W	59	12
Wake Forest	L	23	24
Davidson	L	33	35
Virginia Tech	W	38	26
VMI	W	56	29
NYU	L	30	37
St. Joseph's	W	36	34
N.C. State	W	41	35
Wake Forest	W	31	30
Virginia	W	33	15
Maryland	W	41	24
N.C. State	W	34	31
Davidson	W	34	20
Virginia	W	45	22
Maryland	W	44	35
Duke	W	41	35
Virginia Tech	W	41	25
VMI	W	44	32
Washington & Lee	L	19	29
Duke	W	37	32
Duke	W	34	30
Washington & Lee	L	33	44
Wake Forest	W	37	35

1937-38

RECORD: 16-5
COACH: Walter Skidmore
CAPTAIN: Earl Ruth

Atlantic Christian	W	47	20
Guilford	W	60	16
Davidson	W	37	35
Wake Forest	W	31	26
Virginia Tech	W	38	32
VMI	W	31	17
Washington & Lee	W	34	31
Wake Forest	L	34	44
Princeton	L	32	53
St. Joseph's	L	29	34
N.C. State	W	39	31
Maryland	W	43	24
Clemson	W	44	34
NYU	W	57	39
Davidson	W	41	30
Duke	W	34	24
VMI	W	48	22
Washington & Lee	W	42	39
N.C. State	W	41	32
Duke	L	33	39

SOUTHERN CONFERENCE TOURNAMENT

Washington & Lee	L	33	48

1938-39

RECORD: 10-11
COACH: Walter Skidmore
CAPTAIN: Bill McCachren

Jan. 2	Atlantic Christian	W	59	17
Jan. 9	Princeton	L	20	30
Jan. 5	Catawba	W	44	31
Jan. 7	Davidson	L	39	46
Jan. 12	Virginia	L	29	37
Jan. 13	VMI	W	35	28
Jan. 14	Washington & Lee	W	46	39
Jan. 17	Wake Forest	L	37	57
Jan. 18	Virginia Tech	L	35	36
Jan. 20	Maryland	L	32	34
Jan. 21	Navy	L	38	46
Jan. 22	N.C. State	L	22	35
Jan. 31	Wake Forest	W	56	54
Feb. 3	Maryland	L	41	66
Feb. 4	VMI	W	43	41
Feb. 7	Davidson	W	35	28
Feb. 10	Duke	W	37	32
Feb. 13	Virginia	W	48	37
Feb. 17	N.C. State	W	40	25
Feb. 24	Duke	L	38	41

SOUTHERN CONFERENCE TOURNAMENT

Mar. 1	Clemson	L	43	44

1939-40

RECORD: 23-3
COACH: Bill Lange
CAPTAIN: Ben Dilworth

Dec. 15	Atlantic Christian	H	W	49	32
Dec. 15	Atlantic White Flash	A	W	49	42
Dec. 28	Lynn All-Stars/Raleigh	H	W	43	32
Dec. 29	Eatman-Smith/G'boro	H	W	70	28
Dec. 30	McCrary Eagles	A	W	42	38
Jan. 3	App. St. Teachers	A	W	58	49
Jan. 4	Catawba	H	W	29	25
Jan. 6	Davidson	CH	W	55	47
Jan. 11	Virginia Tech	WS	W	46	25
Jan. 15	Wake Forest	H	W	54	51
Jan. 17	Citadel	H	W	66	36
Jan. 19	VMI	H	W	53	24
Jan. 23	N.C. State	H	W	52	41
Jan. 27	Navy	A	W	44	40
Jan. 30	Wake Forest	A	L	36	42
Feb. 3	Clemson	A	W	39	31
Feb. 5	Virginia	DA	L	25	44
Feb. 7	Davidson	H	W	41	28
Feb. 10	Duke	H	W	44	50
Feb. 13	McCrary Eagles	H	W	45	37
Feb. 16	N.C. State	A	W	60	36
Feb. 19	Clemson	H	W	47	30
Feb. 23	Duke	H	W	31	27

SOUTHERN CONFERENCE TOURNAMENT

Feb. 29	Clemson	RAL	W	50	41
Mar. 1	Wake Forest	RAL	W	43	35
Mar. 2	Duke	RAL	W	39	23

1940-41

RECORD: 19-9
COACH: Bill Lange
CAPTAIN: George Glamack, Jim Howard

Dec. 5	Greensboro YMCA	H	W	48	32
Dec. 7	Hanes Hosiery	A	L	32	33
Dec. 13	Guilford	A	W	51	26
Dec. 14	McCrary	H	W	46	35
Dec. 31	Hanes Hosiery	H	W	45	40
Jan. 2	Lehigh	H	W	62	58
Jan. 4	Fordham	A	L	41	42
Jan. 6	St. Joseph's	A	L	41	42
Jan. 10	Washington & Lee	A	W	43	39
Jan. 11	VMI	A	W	56	30
Jan. 14	Wake Forest	H	W	61	45
Jan. 18	NYU	H	L	49	53
Jan. 21	N.C. State	A	W	47	26
Jan. 24	Maryland	A	W	55	36
Jan. 25	Navy	A	L	34	42
Jan. 28	Wake Forest	A	W	43	40
Jan. 31	Virginia Tech	H	W	60	35
Feb. 3	Maryland	H	W	44	29
Feb. 4	Davidson	H	W	38	30
Feb. 7	Duke	H	W	51	33
Feb. 10	Clemson	H	W	76	53
Feb. 12	N.C. State	H	W	60	30
Feb. 17	Washington & Lee	H	W	65	32
Feb. 20	Duke	A	L	33	35
Feb. 22	Davidson	WS	W	39	30

SOUTHERN CONFERENCE TOURNAMENT

	Duke	RAL	L	37	38

NCAA TOURNAMENT

	Pittsburgh	MA	L	20	26
	Dartmouth	MA	L	59	60

1941-42

RECORD: 14-9
COACH: Bill Lange
CAPTAIN: Bob Rose

Nov. 27	Atl. White Flash/Ral.	H	W	63	31
Dec. 10	Hanes Hosiery	A	L	55	66
Dec. 13	Davidson	CH	W	37	22
Dec. 16	High Point YMCA	A	W	35	23
Dec. 31	McCrary Eagles	A	W	43	41
Jan. 3	St. Joseph	A	L	28	33
Jan. 10	Fordham	H	W	34	25
Jan. 13	Wake Forest	H	W	51	30
Jan. 16	Clemson	A	W	54	34
Jan. 17	South Carolina	A	L	36	38
Jan. 20	N.C. State	H	W	41	28
Jan. 27	Wake Forest	A	L	20	36
Jan. 30	VMI	H	W	49	28
Feb. 3	Davidson	H	W	45	38
Feb. 7	Duke	H	L	40	52
Feb. 12	N.C. State	A	L	30	32
Feb. 13	Washington & Lee	H	W	62	26
Feb. 18	Akron Goodyear	H	W	32	31
Feb. 20	Maryland	A	W	34	30
Feb. 21	Navy	A	L	39	42
Feb. 24	Richmond	H	W	47	30
Feb. 27	Duke	A	L	40	41

SOUTHERN CONFERENCE TOURNAMENT

Mar. 6	Wake Forest	RAL	L	26	32

1942-43

RECORD: 12-10
COACH: Bill Lange
CAPTAIN: George Payne, George McCachren

Nov. 28	McCrary Eagles	H	W	35	34
Dec. 5	Charlotte YMCA	H	W	42	25
Dec. 8	Fort Bragg RC	H	W	40	28
Jan. 1	Maryland	A	L	40	47
Jan. 2	Virginia	LY	L	45	50
Jan. 6	High Point	A	W	56	27
Jan. 9	Wake Forest	H	W	49	37
Jan. 12	George Washington	H	L	33	34
Jan. 15	Virginia Tech	A	W	38	35
Jan. 16	Washington & Lee	A	L	28	35
Jan. 20	N.C. State	A	L	36	47
Jan. 29	VMI	LY	W	37	35
Jan. 30	Wake Forest	DU	W	32	31
Feb. 1	Davidson	A	L	41	57
Feb. 2	Clemson	H	W	52	32
Feb. 6	Duke	H	L	39	51
Feb. 9	N.C. State	H	W	45	36
Feb. 12	Davidson	H	W	50	27
Feb. 16	Maryland	H	L	31	40
Feb. 18	Richmond	A	L	51	53
Feb. 20	South Carolina	H	W	50	27
Feb. 26	Duke	A	L	24	43

1943-44

RECORD: 17-10
COACH: Bill Lange
CAPTAINS: (Game)

Dec. 1	12th RD C. Butner	H	W	46	35
Dec. 3	Columbia AB	H	W	47	35
Dec. 4	Cherry Point MAS	H	L	34	41
Dec. 9	Fort Bragg RC	A	L	44	52
Dec. 11	Milligan	H	L	35	42
Dec. 16	Catawba	EL	W	74	37
Dec. 18	Fort Jackson	H	L	53	57
Dec. 20	Seymour Johnson	A	W	48	42
Dec. 30	Fort Bragg RC	H	L	25	41
Jan. 5	Virginia	A	L	36	39
Jan. 8	Davidson	CH	W	43	37
Jan. 11	Florence AB	H	W	41	19
Jan. 14	Richmond AB	H	W	42	35
Jan. 15	N.C. State	H	W	52	24
Jan. 18	Duke	A	W	37	33
Jan. 20	VMI	LY	W	50	22
Jan. 22	Virginia Tech	H	W	42	29
Jan. 26	N.C. State	A	W	42	27
Jan. 29	Richmond	A	W	49	45
Feb. 2	Basic Tr. No. 10	GR	L	40	53
Feb. 5	Duke	H	L	40	41
Feb. 8	Davidson	H	W	43	40
Feb. 10	Duke	A	W	39	30
Feb. 12	Norfolk NTS	A	L	43	56

SOUTHERN CONFERENCE TOURNAMENT

Feb. 25	Richmond	RAL	W	62	41
Feb. 25	Virginia Tech	RAL	W	39	24
Feb. 26	Duke	RAL	L	27	43

1944-45

RECORD: 22-6
COACH: Ben Carnevale
CAPTAIN: (Game)

Dec. 6	Fort Bragg PC	H	W	44	20
Dec. 9	Camp Butner	A	W	43	41
Dec. 13	High Point College	H	W	75	18
Dec. 15	Catawba	A	W	67	35
Dec. 16	South Carolina	A	L	27	38
Dec. 19	Morris Field	A	W	51	29
Jan. 3	Wake Forest	H	W	65	29
Jan. 5	Maryland	H	W	53	28
Jan. 6	South Carolina	H	L	40	41
Jan. 10	Davidson	CH	W	47	32
Jan. 12	Norfolk NAS	H	L	22	59
Jan. 13	Virginia	LY	W	42	35
Jan. 16	Fort Bragg RC	A	L	34	44
Jan. 18	Virginia Tech	A	W	55	30
Jan. 20	Duke	H	L	41	50
Jan. 22	Wake Forest	A	W	65	40
Jan. 24	Virginia Tech	H	W	60	28
Jan. 26	N.C. State	H	W	61	46
Jan. 27	High Point College	A	W	76	25
Feb. 1	William & Mary	H	W	80	46
Feb. 3	Norfolk NAS	A	L	46	65
Feb. 6	Catawba	H	W	64	30
Feb. 7	Davidson	H	W	89	20
Feb. 12	N.C. State	A	W	43	35
Feb. 15	Duke	A	W	50	38

SOUTHERN CONFERENCE TOURNAMENT

Feb. 22	N.C. State	RAL	W	55	28
Feb. 23	South Carolina	RAL	W	39	26
Feb. 24	Duke	RAL	W	49	38

1945-46

RECORD: 30-5
COACH: Ben Carnevale
CAPTAIN: Lew Hayworth

Dec. 5	Camp Lee	H	W	55	40
Dec. 8	Camp Pickett	H	W	64	46
Dec. 11	Greensboro ORD	A	L	63	64
Dec. 14	Catawba	H	W	65	32
Dec. 15	Davidson	H	W	63	31
Dec. 21	South Carolina	H	W	56	32
Dec. 27	NYU	A	W	43	41
Dec. 29	St. Joseph's	A	W	47	36
Jan. 5	Fort Bragg AOC	H	W	65	33
Jan. 6	Fort Bragg RC	H	W	57	16
Jan. 7	Maryland	H	W	64	28
Jan. 9	Duke	H	L	46	51
Jan. 11	Virginia	A	W	44	32
Jan. 12	Virginia Tech	A	W	48	40
Jan. 15	Davidson	A	W	58	30
Jan. 18	High Point	A	W	65	34
Jan. 19	South Carolina	A	W	52	31
Jan. 23	N.C. State	H	W	71	34
Jan. 25	High Point	H	W	57	16
Jan. 26	Camp Lee	A	W	50	49
Jan. 28	Wake Forest	A	W	70	47
Feb. 2	Wake Forest	H	W	61	32
Feb. 5	Greensboro ORD	H	W	74	39
Feb. 8	Maryland	A	W	33	31
Feb. 9	Navy	A	W	51	49
Feb. 11	N.C. State	A	W	55	44
Feb. 15	Virginia Tech	H	W	63	42
Feb. 16	Duke	A	W	54	44
Feb. 20	Catawba	A	W	64	38
Feb. 23	Little Creek AB	A	L	46	60
SOUTHERN CONFERENCE TOURNAMENT					
Feb. 28	Maryland	RAL	W	54	27
Mar. 1	Wake Forest	RAL	L	29	31
NCAA TOURNAMENT					
Mar. 21	NYU	MSG	W	57	49
Mar. 23	Ohio State	MSG	W	60	57
Mar. 26	Oklahoma State	MSG	L	40	43

1946-47

RECORD: 19-8
COACH: Tom Scott
CAPTAIN: Jim Hamilton, Jim White

Dec. 4	Cherry Point	H	W	63	29
Dec. 6	Hanes Hosiery	A	W	47	46
Dec. 9	Catawba	H	W	48	33
Dec. 11	High Point	H	W	44	41
Dec. 19	Northwestern	A	L	51	65
Dec. 21	DePaul	A	L	53	60
Jan. 4	Maryland	H	W	58	42
Jan. 11	La Salle	A	L	62	65
Jan. 14	NYU	A	W	50	48
Jan. 21	Virginia	H	W	63	38
Jan. 24	Maryland	A	L	57	61
Jan. 25	Navy	A	L	35	39
Jan. 29	South Carolina	H	W	50	49
Jan. 30	Wake Forest	H	W	70	49
Feb. 1	N.C. State	H	(OT) L	46	48
Feb. 3	NYU	H	L	47	60
Feb. 7	Virginia Tech	H	W	57	51
Feb. 8	Davidson	H	W	55	46
Feb. 11	Duke	H	W	49	28
Feb. 14	Georgia Tech	H	W	58	48
Feb. 17	South Carolina	A	W	53	47
Feb. 18	Davidson	CH	W	45	38
Feb. 20	Wake Forest	A	W	54	46
Feb. 28	Duke	A	W	57	47
SOUTHERN CONFERENCE TOURNAMENT					
Mar. 6	Richmond	DU	W	55	43
Mar. 7	South Carolina	DU	W	58	33
Mar. 8	N.C. State	DU	L	48	50

1947-48

RECORD: 20-7
COACH: Tom Scott
CAPTAIN: Bob Paxton

Dec. 3	Catawba	H	W	51	32
Dec. 6	Guilford	H	W	51	30
Dec. 8	Elon	H	W	74	22
Dec. 10	High Point	H	W	54	36
Dec. 12	Hanes Hosiery	A	W	59	43
Dec. 31	Loyola (Md.)	H	W	64	47
Jan. 3	Maryland	H	W	70	46
Jan. 5	Tennessee	H	W	52	43
Jan. 6	South Carolina	H	W	63	45
Jan. 9	Virginia Tech	A	W	39	31
Jan. 10	Washington & Lee	LY	W	60	36
Jan. 12	Wake Forest	H	W	56	35
Jan. 17	Temple	A	L	51	61
Jan. 24	Pennsylvania	H	W	50	42
Jan. 26	Virginia Tech	H	W	68	35
Jan. 30	Davidson	H	W	52	46
Feb. 3	N.C. State	A	L	42	81
Feb. 7	Duke	H	W	48	42
Feb. 13	Maryland	H	W	51	47
Feb. 14	William & Mary	A	W	63	61
Feb. 16	Wake Forest	A	L	47	53
Feb. 21	N.C. State	H	L	45	69
Feb. 24	Davidson	CH	W	52	45
Feb. 27	Duke	A	L	45	56
SOUTHERN CONFERENCE TOURNAMENT					
Mar. 4	Virginia Tech	DU	W	61	40
Mar. 5	N.C. State	DU	L	50	55

1948-49

RECORD: 20-8
COACH: Tom Scott
CAPTAIN: Dan Nyimicz

Dec. 2	Lenoir Rhyne	H	W	68	51
Dec. 4	Guilford	H	W	52	32
Dec. 6	Elon	H	W	66	32
Dec. 9	Catawba	H	W	57	47
Dec. 10	Hanes Hosiery	A	W	64	60
Dec. 28	Arizona	LF	W	60	49
Jan. 3	Maryland	H	W	55	47
Jan. 6	NYU	A	L	48	74
Jan. 8	Virginia Tech	A	W	56	48
Jan. 10	George Washington	H	L	41	64
Jan. 12	Wake Forest	A	W	55	50
Jan. 15	Washington & Lee	LY	W	69	52
Jan. 20	William & Mary	H	W	69	61
Jan. 22	N.C. State	A	L	36	67
Jan. 24	Virginia Tech	H	W	78	59
Jan. 28	Davidson	H	L	37	47
Jan. 29	Furman	H	W	61	44
Jan. 31	Tennessee	A	L	56	84
Feb. 5	Duke	H	W	64	34
Feb. 11	Maryland	A	W	66	52
Feb. 12	George Washington	A	L	41	53
Feb. 15	Wake Forest	H	W	69	54
Feb. 19	N.C. State	H	L	39	79
Feb. 21	South Carolina	A	W	62	48
Feb. 22	Davidson	A	W	53	52
Feb. 25	Duke	A	W	64	40
SOUTHERN CONFERENCE TOURNAMENT					
Mar. 3	Maryland	DU	W	79	61
Mar. 4	N.C. State	DU	L	40	43

1949-50

RECORD: 17-12
COACH: Tom Scott
CAPTAIN: Nemo Nearman

Dec. 1	Elon	H	W	57	39
Dec. 3	Richmond	A	W	58	50
Dec. 5	Virginia Tech	A	L	48	62
Dec. 7	Lenoir-Rhyne	A	(OT) L	78	79
Dec. 9	George Washington	H	L	44	54
DIXIE CLASSIC					
Dec. 26	West Virginia	RAL	L	50	58
Dec. 27	Duke	RAL	W	59	52
Dec. 28	Rhode Island State	RAL	L	60	65
Jan. 2	Maryland	H	W	55	53
Jan. 5	Hanes Hosiery	A	L	48	50
Jan. 7	Davidson	A	W	63	53
Jan. 9	Kentucky	A	L	44	86
Jan. 13	Miami (Fla.)	A	W	55	53
Jan. 14	Miami (Fla.)	A	W	65	51
Jan. 16	Wake Forest	A	W	54	50
Jan. 18	South Carolina	H	W	64	42
Jan. 21	N.C. State	H	L	57	61
Jan. 27	Virginia Tech	H	W	66	53
Jan. 28	Davidson	H	W	67	54
Jan. 30	The Citadel	H	W	77	39
Feb. 3	Maryland	A	W	69	56
Feb. 4	George Washington	A	L	41	56
Feb. 7	Wake Forest	H	L	54	57
Feb. 10	Furman	A	W	59	53
Feb. 13	William & Mary	A	W	52	46
Feb. 17	Duke	H	W	58	55
Feb. 21	N.C. State	A	L	44	70
Feb. 24	Duke	A	W	64	46
SOUTHERN CONFERENCE TOURNAMENT					
Mar. 2	William & Mary	DU	L	43	50

1950-51

RECORD: 12-15
COACH: Tom Scott
CAPTAIN: Charlie Thorne, Hugo Kappler

Nov. 29	McCrary Eagles	A	W	84	57
Dec. 2	Elon	A	W	57	48
Dec. 5	Hanes Hosiery	A	W	75	58
Dec. 7	Richmond	H	W	69	46
Dec. 9	Davidson	A	W	72	69
Dec. 20	Eastern Kentucky	PK	L	62	85
Dec. 22	Xavier	PK	L	58	92
DIXIE CLASSIC					
Dec. 28	Navy	RAL	L	49	58
Dec. 29	Duke	RAL	L	63	71
Dec. 30	Rhode Island	RAL	L	69	93
Jan. 2	Maryland	H	L	59	67
Jan. 4	NYU	A	L	60	66
Jan. 6	Temple	A	L	67	70
Jan. 11	Wake Forest	A	W	65	56
Jan. 13	Davidson	H	W	56	53
Jan. 15	West Virginia	H	L	49	62
Jan. 19	George Washington	A	L	71	76
Jan. 20	Maryland	A	L	55	56
Jan. 27	N.C. State	A	L	58	71
Jan. 30	Wake Forest	H	W	82	70
Feb. 2	Duke	H	W	71	68
Feb. 3	Furman	H	W	89	64
Feb. 6	George Washington	H	W	66	60
Feb. 9	South Carolina	A	L	65	66
Feb. 10	The Citadel	A	W	71	58
Feb. 17	N.C. State	H	L	53	67
Feb. 23	Duke	A	L	72	84

1951-52

RECORD: 12-15
COACH: Tom Scott
CAPTAIN: Howard Deasy

Dec. 1	The Citadel	A	W	87	69
Dec. 3	Furman	A	W	100	57
Dec. 5	Duke	A	L	59	77
Dec. 7	Richmond	A	W	62	56
Dec. 17	Hanes Hosiery	A	W	70	59
Dec. 20	Illinois	A	L	66	86
Dec. 22	Bradley	A	L	66	79
DIXIE CLASSIC					
Dec. 27	Southern California	RAL	W	49	45
Dec. 28	N.C. State	RAL	L	51	58
Dec. 29	Columbia	RAL	W	61	60
Jan. 3	Maryland	H	W	51	47
Jan. 5	Clemson	H	W	65	59
Jan. 10	Wake Forest	A	L	53	55
Jan. 14	Davidson	H	W	78	77
Jan. 18	Maryland	A	L	51	71
Jan. 19	Temple	A	W	70	65
Jan. 26	N.C. State	H	L	53	58
Jan. 29	Wake Forest	H	L	46	55
Feb. 2	Duke	H	L	66	73
Feb. 6	West Virginia	A	L	65	80
Feb. 8	The Citadel	H	W	80	62
Feb. 9	Furman	H	W	68	53
Feb. 12	South Carolina	H	L	68	75
Feb. 16	Clemson	A	L	69	77
Feb. 18	Davidson	A	L	71	76
Feb. 23	N.C. State	A	L	52	71
Feb. 29	Duke	A	L	64	94

1952-53

RECORD: 17-10
COACH: Frank McGuire
CAPTAIN: Vince Grimaldi, Jack Wallace

Dec. 1	The Citadel	H	W	70	50
Dec. 3	Washington & Lee	H	W	67	48
Dec. 6	Richmond	H	W	80	62
Dec. 10	Clemson	H	W	82	55
DIXIE CLASSIC					
Dec. 29	Holy Cross	RAL	L	73	85
Dec. 30	Princeton	RAL	W	73	59
Dec. 31	Pennsylvania	RAL	L	62	70
Jan. 3	Maryland	H	W	59	49
Jan. 6	East Carolina	A	W	79	66
Jan. 8	VMI	A	W	79	62
Jan. 9	Washington & Lee	A	W	97	75
Jan. 13	Davidson	H	W	71	60
Jan. 14	VMI	H	W	97	58
Jan. 17	Maryland	A	L	66	68
Jan. 20	Wake Forest	H	W	72	68
Jan. 24	N.C. State	A	W	70	69
Jan. 30	Davidson	A	W	73	52
Jan. 31	Clemson	A	W	91	80
Feb. 3	Richmond	A	L	82	87
Feb. 6	Duke	H	L	89	95
Feb. 7	NYU	H	L	78	82
Feb. 13	South Carolina	A	W	76	72
Feb. 14	The Citadel	A	W	94	69
Feb. 17	Wake Forest	A	L	63	89
Feb. 21	N.C. State	H	L	66	87
Feb. 27	Duke	A	L	58	83
SOUTHERN CONFERENCE TOURNAMENT					
Mar. 5	N.C. State	A	L	54	86

1953-54

RECORD: 11-10
COACH: Frank McGuire
CAPTAIN: (Game)

Dec. 11	William & Mary	H	W	71	61
Dec. 12	South Carolina	H	W	82	56
Dec. 19	Clemson	H	W	85	48
DIXIE CLASSIC					
Dec. 28	Navy	RAL	L	62	86
Dec. 29	Seton Hall	RAL	L	63	73
Dec. 30	Oregon State	RAL	L	53	65
Jan. 8	The Citadel	H	W	83	42
Jan. 9	Wake Forest	A	W	66	65
Jan. 11	Davidson	A	W	70	54
Jan. 16	Virginia	H	W	78	66
Jan. 19	N.C. State	H	L	77	84
Feb. 2	Washington & Lee	LY	W	69	60
Feb. 4	Duke	A	L	47	63
Feb. 8	Virginia	A	L	69	83
Feb. 11	Wake Forest	H	L	62	76
Feb. 13	Clemson	A	W	72	56
Feb. 16	Davidson	H	W	89	69
Feb. 20	Duke	H	L	63	67
Feb. 24	N.C. State	A	L	48	57
Feb. 27	The Citadel	A	W	79	52
ACC TOURNAMENT					
Mar. 4	N.C. State	A	L	51	52

1954-55

RECORD: 10-11
COACH: Frank McGuire
CAPTAIN: Paul Likens, Al Lifson

Dec. 4	Clemson	H	W	99	66
Dec. 9	South Carolina	H	W	88	69
Dec. 11	William & Mary	A	L	76	79
Dec. 18	Maryland	H	L	60	70
DIXIE CLASSIC					
Dec. 27	Southern California	RAL	W	67	58
Dec. 28	N.C. State	A	L	44	47
Dec. 29	Duke	RAL	W	65	52
Jan. 3	Louisiana State	A	L	77	84
Jan. 4	Alabama	A	L	55	77
Jan. 8	Wake Forest	H	W	95	78
Jan. 11	Virginia	H	W	96	87
Jan. 14	South Carolina	A	W	73	64
Jan. 15	Clemson	A	W	95	87
Jan. 18	N.C. State	A	W	84	80
Feb. 4	Duke	H	L	68	91
Feb. 11	Virginia	GR	L	73	98
Feb. 12	Maryland	A	L	61	63
Feb. 16	Wake Forest	A	W	83	79
Feb. 22	N.C. State	H	L	75	79
Feb. 25	Duke	A	L	74	96
ACC TOURNAMENT					
Mar. 3	Wake Forest	RAL	L	82	95

1955-56

RECORD: 18-5
COACH: Frank McGuire
CAPTAIN: Jerry Vayda

Dec. 3	Clemson	H	W	73	58
Dec. 9	Georgia Tech	CH	W	88	76
Dec. 10	South Carolina	H	W	92	75
Dec. 14	Alabama	H	W	99	77
Dec. 17	Maryland	A	W	68	62
DIXIE CLASSIC					
Dec. 29	Villanova	RAL	W	86	63
Dec. 30	Duke	RAL	W	74	64
Dec. 31	N.C. State	RAL	L	60	82
Jan. 3	Louisiana State	H	W	95	69
Jan. 7	Wake Forest	A	L	71	76
Jan. 10	Virginia	H	W	101	65
Jan. 13	South Carolina	CH	W	75	73
Jan. 14	Clemson	A	W	103	99
Jan. 16	Maryland	H	W	64	55
Jan. 18	N.C. State	H	W	73	69
Feb. 4	Duke	A	L	59	63
Feb. 7	William & Mary	H	W	115	64
Feb. 11	Virginia	A	W	83	72
Feb. 15	Wake Forest	H	W	77	73
Feb. 21	N.C. State	A	L	73	79
Feb. 24	Duke	H	W	73	65
ACC TOURNAMENT					
Mar. 1	Virginia	RAL	W	81	77
Mar. 2	Wake Forest	RAL	L	56	77

1956-57

RECORD: 32-0
COACH: Frank McGuire
CAPTAIN: Lennie Rosenbluth

Dec. 4	Furman	H	W	94	66
Dec. 8	Clemson	CH	W	94	75
Dec. 12	George Washington	NF	W	82	55
Dec. 15	South Carolina	A	W	90	86
Dec. 17	Maryland	H	W	70	61
Dec. 20	NYU	MSG	W	64	59
Dec. 21	Dartmouth	BO	W	89	61
Dec. 22	Holy Cross	BO	W	83	70
DIXIE CLASSIC					
Dec. 27	Utah	RAL	W	97	76
Dec. 28	Duke	RAL	W	87	71
Dec. 29	Wake Forest	RAL	W	63	55
Jan. 8	William & Mary	A	W	71	61
Jan. 11	Clemson	H	W	86	54
Jan. 12	Virginia	H	W	102	90
Jan. 15	N.C. State	A	W	83	57
Jan. 30	Western Carolina	A	W	77	59
Feb. 5	Maryland	A	(2OT) W	65	61
Feb. 9	Duke	A	W	75	73
Feb. 11	Virginia	A	W	68	59
Feb. 13	Wake Forest	H	W	72	69
Feb. 19	N.C. State	H	W	86	57
Feb. 22	South Carolina	H	W	75	62
Feb. 26	Wake Forest	A	W	69	64
Mar. 1	Duke	A	W	86	72
ACC TOURNAMENT					
Mar. 7	Clemson	RAL	W	81	61
Mar. 8	Wake Forest	RAL	W	61	59
Mar. 9	South Carolina	RAL	W	95	75
NCAA TOURNAMENT					
Mar. 12	Yale	MSG	W	90	74
Mar. 15	Canisius	PH	W	87	75
Mar. 16	Syracuse	PH	W	67	58
Mar. 22	Michigan State	KC	(3OT) W	74	70
Mar. 23	Kansas	KC	(3OT) W	54	53

1957-58

RECORD: 19-7
COACH: Frank McGuire
CAPTAIN: Pete Brennan

Dec. 7	Clemson	H	W	79	55
Dec. 10	George Washington	A	W	86	59
Dec. 12	Furman	CH	W	91	74
Dec. 14	South Carolina	H	W	70	58
KENTUCKY INVITATIONAL					
Dec. 20	Minnesota	LX	W	73	67
Dec. 21	West Virginia	LX	L	64	75
DIXIE CLASSIC					
Dec. 26	St. Louis	RAL	W	63	48
Dec. 27	Duke	RAL	W	76	62
Dec. 28	N.C. State	RAL	W	39	30
Jan. 4	Wake Forest	H	W	71	45
Jan. 7	William & Mary	H	W	79	63
Jan. 9	Virginia	H	W	82	66
Jan. 11	Maryland	A	L	61	74
Jan. 15	N.C. State	H	L	57	58
Jan. 18	Clemson	A	W	90	81
Feb. 1	South Carolina	A	W	115	88
Feb. 8	Duke	H	L	75	91
Feb. 11	Virginia	A	W	73	66
Feb. 13	Wake Forest	A	W	60	57
Feb. 15	Notre Dame	CHI	L	70	89
Feb. 18	N.C. State	A	W	81	69
Feb. 22	Maryland	H	W	66	59
Feb. 28	Duke	A	L	46	59
ACC TOURNAMENT					
Mar. 6	Clemson	RAL	W	62	51
Mar. 7	N.C. State	RAL	W	64	58
Mar. 8	Maryland	RAL	L	74	86

1958-59

RECORD: 20-5
COACH: Frank McGuire
CAPTAIN: Danny Lotz

Dec. 3	Clemson	H	W	83	67
Dec. 8	Virginia	H	W	83	61
Dec. 16	South Carolina	A	W	70	57
	BLUE GRASS FESTIVAL				
Dec. 19	Notre Dame	LV	W	81	77
Dec. 20	Northwestern	LV	W	78	64
	DIXIE CLASSIC				
Dec. 29	Yale	RAL	W	92	65
Dec. 30	Michigan State	RAL	L	58	75
Dec. 31	Cincinnati	RAL	W	90	88
Jan. 3	Notre Dame	CH	W	69	54
Jan. 8	Wake Forest	H	W	44	34
Jan. 14	N.C. State	A	W	72	68
Jan. 30	Clemson	N-S	W	60	46
Jan. 31	South Carolina	N-S	W	62	50
Feb. 4	Maryland	H	W	64	57
Feb. 6	Duke	A	W	89	80
Feb. 12	Wake Forest	A	W	75	66
Feb. 14	Loyola (Ill.)	A	W	76	57
Feb. 18	N.C. State	H	W	74	67
Feb. 21	Maryland	A	L	51	69
Feb. 25	Virginia	A	L	68	69
Feb. 28	Duke	H	W	72	62
	ACC TOURNAMENT				
Mar. 5	Clemson	RAL	W	93	69
Mar. 6	Duke	RAL	W	74	71
Mar. 7	N.C. State	RAL	L	56	80
	NCAA TOURNAMENT				
Mar. 10	Navy	MSG	L	63	76

1959-60

RECORD: 18-6
COACH: Frank McGuire
CAPTAIN: Harvey Salz

Dec. 5	South Carolina	H	W	93	56
Dec. 11	Kansas	RAL	W	60	49
Dec. 12	Kansas State	RAL	W	68	52
	KENTUCKY INVITATIONAL				
Dec. 18	Kentucky	A	L	70	76
Dec. 19	St. Louis	LX	L	52	68
	DIXIE CLASSIC				
Dec. 28	Minnesota	RAL	W	72	65
Dec. 29	Duke	RAL	W	75	53
Dec. 30	Wake Forest	RAL	L	50	53
Jan. 2	Notre Dame	CH	W	75	65
Jan. 9	Wake Forest	GR	W	62	59
Jan. 13	N.C. State	H	W	62	51
Jan. 16	Virginia	GR	W	78	57
Feb. 3	Maryland	A	W	75	66
Feb. 8	Clemson	A	W	73	54
Feb. 11	Wake Forest	H	L	69	80
Feb. 13	Duke	H	W	84	57
Feb. 17	N.C. State	A	W	66	62
Feb. 19	Clemson	N-S	W	85	80
Feb. 20	South Carolina	N-S	L	81	85
Feb. 23	Maryland	H	W	81	64
Feb. 25	Virginia	H	W	97	58
Feb. 27	Duke	A	W	75	50
	ACC TOURNAMENT				
Mar. 3	Virginia	RAL	W	84	63
Mar. 4	Duke	RAL	L	69	71

1960-61

RECORD: 19-4
COACH: Frank McGuire
CAPTAIN: Doug Moe, York Larese

Dec. 5	Louisiana State	H	W	77	61
Dec. 6	Virginia	H	W	81	47
Dec. 13	Kentucky	GR	L	65	70
Dec. 16	Kansas State	A	L	69	77
Dec. 17	Kansas	A	W	78	70
Dec. 19	Creighton	A	W	72	64
	DIXIE CLASSIC				
Dec. 29	Maryland	RAL	W	81	57
Dec. 30	Villanova	RAL	W	87	67
Dec. 31	Duke	RAL	W	76	71
Jan. 7	Notre Dame	CH	W	73	71
Jan. 10	Wake Forest	H	W	83	74
Jan. 14	Virginia	A	W	92	70
Jan. 16	Maryland	A	W	58	52
Jan. 18	N.C. State	A	W	97	66
Jan. 31	Clemson	H	W	77	46
Feb. 2	Maryland	H	W	63	56
Feb. 4	Duke	A	L	77	81
Feb. 8	South Carolina	A	L	82	89
Feb. 11	Wake Forest	A	W	93	78
Feb. 15	N.C. State	H	W	62	56
Feb. 17	South Carolina	N-S	W	92	68
Feb. 18	Clemson	N-S	W	61	55
Feb. 25	Duke	H	W	69	66

1961-62

RECORD: 8-9
COACH: Dean Smith
CAPTAIN: Jim Hudock

Dec. 2	Virginia	H	W	80	46
Dec. 5	Clemson	A	W	54	52
Dec. 11	Indiana	GR	L	70	76
Jan. 6	Notre Dame	CH	W	99	80
Jan. 10	Wake Forest	A	L	72	91
Jan. 13	Virginia	GR	W	100	71
Jan. 15	South Carolina	H	W	83	71
Jan. 17	N.C. State	H	W	66	56
Feb. 3	Duke	A	L	57	79
Feb. 6	Maryland	A	L	62	79
Feb. 10	Wake Forest	H	L	80	87
Feb. 14	N.C. State	A	L	57	85
Feb. 16	Clemson	N-S	W	69	59
Feb. 17	South Carolina	N-S	L	82	97
Feb. 19	Maryland	H	W	70	67
Feb. 24	Duke	H	L	74	82
	ACC TOURNAMENT				
Mar. 1	South Carolina	RAL	L	55	57

1962-63

RECORD: 15-6
COACH: Dean Smith
CAPTAIN: Larry Brown, Yogi Poteet

Dec. 1	Georgia	H	W	89	65
Dec. 5	Clemson	H	W	64	48
Dec. 8	South Carolina	A	W	75	65
Dec. 15	Indiana	A	L	76	90
Dec. 17	Kentucky	A	W	68	66
Jan. 2	Yale	H	W	86	77
Jan. 5	Notre Dame	A	(OT) W	76	68
Jan. 9	Wake Forest	A	L	70	78
Jan. 14	Maryland	A	W	78	56
Jan. 16	N.C. State	H	(OT) W	67	65
Jan. 19	Virginia	A	W	86	81
Feb. 2	Duke	H	L	69	77
Feb. 7	Maryland	H	W	82	68
Feb. 9	Wake Forest	H	L	71	72
Feb. 12	N.C. State	A	W	68	63
Feb. 15	South Carolina	N-S	W	78	74
Feb. 16	Clemson	N-S	W	79	63
Feb. 20	Virginia	H	W	85	73
Feb. 23	Duke	A	L	93	106
	ACC TOURNAMENT				
Feb. 28	South Carolina	RAL	W	93	76
Mar. 1	Wake Forest	RAL	L	55	56

1963-64

RECORD: 12-12
COACH: Dean Smith
CAPTAIN: Charlie Shaffer, Mike Cooke

Dec. 2	South Carolina	H	W	92	87
Dec. 3	Clemson	A	(2OT) L	64	66
Dec. 7	Indiana	CH	W	77	70
Dec. 9	Kentucky	A	L	80	100
Dec. 14	Louisiana State	A	W	76	71
Dec. 16	Tulane	A	W	109	81
Dec. 18	Georgia	H	W	99	71
Jan. 4	Notre Dame	GR	W	78	68
Jan. 9	Wake Forest	A	L	71	80
Jan. 11	Duke	A	L	64	84
Jan. 13	Maryland	H	W	97	88
Jan. 15	N.C. State	H	W	79	71
Jan. 18	Virginia Tech	H	(2OT) L	88	90
Feb. 3	Virginia	H	W	89	76
Feb. 8	Wake Forest	H	W	81	73
Feb. 12	NYU	A	L	68	69
Feb. 14	Clemson	N-S	(2OT) L	90	97
Feb. 15	South Carolina	N-S	W	84	81
Feb. 18	Maryland	A	L	64	74
Feb. 22	N.C. State	A	L	49	51
Feb. 24	Virginia	A	L	64	79
Feb. 29	Duke	H	L	69	104
	ACC TOURNAMENT				
Mar. 5	South Carolina	RAL	W	80	63
Mar. 6	Duke	RAL	L	49	65

1964-65

RECORD: 15-9
COACH: Dean Smith
CAPTAIN: Billy Cunningham

Dec. 1	Clemson	H	W	77	59
Dec. 3	Georgia	A	L	61	64
Dec. 5	South Carolina	A	W	82	71
Dec. 7	Kentucky	CH	W	82	67
Dec. 10	Tulane	H	W	111	74
Dec. 12	Indiana	A	L	81	107
Dec. 14	Vanderbilt	GR	W	84	78
	VPI TOURNAMENT				
Dec. 18	Mississippi State	BL	W	84	60
Dec. 19	Alabama	BL	L	61	66
Dec. 21	Florida	A	L	54	73
Jan. 4	Maryland	A	L	68	76
Jan. 6	Wake Forest	A	L	85	107
Jan. 9	Duke	A	W	65	62
Jan. 13	N.C. State	H	L	62	65
Jan. 16	Virginia	A	W	87	80
Jan. 30	Maryland	H	L	81	90
Feb. 6	NYU	GR	W	100	78
Feb. 9	Wake Forest	H	W	107	91
Feb. 17	N.C. State	A	W	69	68
Feb. 19	South Carolina	N-S	W	76	63
Feb. 20	Clemson	N-S	W	86	84
Feb. 23	Virginia	H	2OTW	105	101
Feb. 27	Duke	H	W	71	66
	ACC TOURNAMENT				
Mar. 4	Wake Forest	RAL	L	76	92

1965-66

RECORD: 16-11
COACH: Dean Smith
CAPTAIN: Bob Bennett, John Yokley

Dec. 1	Clemson	A	L	74	84
Dec. 4	William & Mary	H	W	82	68
Dec. 6	Ohio State	A	W	82	72
Dec. 8	Richmond	H	W	127	76
Dec. 11	Vanderbilt	A	L	72	81
Dec. 16	Florida State	H	W	115	80
Dec. 18	Florida	CH	W	66	59
Dec. 27	Princeton	GR	W	75	61
	TRIANGLE DOUBLEHEADERS				
Dec. 30	Utah	RAL	W	90	85
Dec. 31	West Virginia	RAL	L	97	102
Jan. 3	Maryland	H	W	67	52
Jan. 5	Wake Forest	A	W	99	83
Jan. 8	Duke	H	L	77	88
Jan. 13	N.C. State	H	W	83	75
Jan. 15	Virginia	A	L	69	70
Feb. 3	Wake Forest	H	W	115	87
Feb. 5	Maryland	A	L	66	77
Feb. 7	South Carolina	H	W	104	70
Feb. 9	NYU	A	L	78	83
Feb. 12	Virginia Tech	H	L	75	81
Feb. 15	N.C. State	A	L	77	87
Feb. 18	Clemson	N-S	W	70	66
Feb. 19	South Carolina	N-S	W	83	71
Feb. 22	Virginia	H	W	81	79
Feb. 26	Duke	A	L	63	77
	ACC TOURNAMENT				
Mar. 3	Maryland	RAL	W	77	70
Mar. 4	Duke	RAL	L	20	21

1966-67

RECORD: 26-6
COACH: Dean Smith
CAPTAIN: Bob Lewis, Tom Gauntlett

Dec. 1	Clemson	H	W	76	65
Dec. 3	Penn State	GR	W	93	63
Dec. 9	Tulane	H	W	92	69
Dec. 13	Kentucky	A	W	64	55
Dec. 17	NYU	GR	W	95	58
	TAMPA INVITATIONAL TOURNAMENT				
Dec. 19	Columbia	TA	W	98	66
Dec. 20	Florida State	TA	W	81	54
Dec. 27	Furman	GR	W	101	56
Dec. 30	Ohio State	CH	W	105	82
Jan. 2	Princeton	H	L	81	91
Jan. 4	Wake Forest	A	W	76	74
Jan. 7	Duke	A	W	59	56
Jan. 11	N.C. State	H	W	79	78
Jan. 28	Virginia	H	W	103	76
Feb. 4	Maryland	H	W	85	77
Feb. 7	Virginia	A	W	79	75
Feb. 9	Wake Forest	H	W	75	73
Feb. 11	Georgia Tech	A	L	80	82
Feb. 14	N.C. State	A	W	77	60
Feb. 17	South Carolina	N-S	W	80	55
Feb. 18	Clemson	N-S	L	88	92
Feb. 22	Maryland	A	W	79	78
Feb. 25	Virginia Tech	H	W	110	78
Mar. 1	South Carolina	A	L	57	70
Mar. 4	Duke	H	W	92	79
	ACC TOURNAMENT				
Mar. 9	N.C. State	GR	W	56	53
Mar. 10	Wake Forest	GR	W	89	79
Mar. 11	Duke	GR	W	82	73
	NCAA TOURNAMENT				
Mar. 17	Princeton	CP	W	78	70
Mar. 18	Boston College	CP	W	96	80
Mar. 24	Dayton	LV	L	62	76
Mar. 25	Houston	LV	L	62	84

1967-68

RECORD: 28-4
COACH: Dean Smith
CAPTAIN: Larry Miller

Dec. 2	Virginia Tech	H	W	89	76
Dec. 6	Kent State	H	W	107	83
Dec. 9	Vanderbilt	A	L	76	89
Dec. 12	Kentucky	GR	W	84	77
Dec. 16	Princeton	GR	W	71	63
	FAR WEST CLASSIC				
Dec. 28	Stanford	PO	W	87	78
Dec. 29	Utah	PO	W	86	84
Dec. 30	Oregon State	PO	W	68	61
Jan. 3	Wake Forest	H	W	74	62
Jan. 6	Duke	H	W	75	72
Jan. 10	N.C. State	A	W	68	66
Jan. 13	Clemson	A	W	115	83
Jan. 27	Georgia Tech	CH	W	82	54
Feb. 1	Florida State	H	W	86	80
Feb. 3	Maryland	A	W	73	67
Feb. 6	Virginia	H	W	108	64
Feb. 8	Wake Forest	A	W	80	60
Feb. 10	Virginia Tech	A	W	80	70
Feb. 12	N.C. State	H	W	96	84
Feb. 16	Clemson	N-S	W	96	74
Feb. 17	South Carolina	N-S	W	84	80
Feb. 21	Maryland	H	W	83	60
Feb. 24	Virginia	A	W	92	74
Feb. 28	South Carolina	H	L	86	87
Mar. 2	Duke	A	L	86	87
	ACC TOURNAMENT				
Mar. 7	Wake Forest	CH	W	83	70
Mar. 8	South Carolina	CH	W	82	79
Mar. 9	N.C. State	CH	W	87	50
	NCAA TOURNAMENT				
Mar. 15	St. Bonaventure	RAL	W	91	72
Mar. 16	Davidson	RAL	W	70	66
Mar. 22	Ohio State	LA	W	80	66
Mar. 23	UCLA	LA	L	55	78

1968-69

RECORD: 27-5
COACH: Dean Smith
CAPTAIN: Bill Bunting, Rusty Clark, Joe Brown, Dick Grubar, Gerald Tuttle

Dec. 2	Oregon	GR	W	89	78
Dec. 3	Oregon	H	W	106	73
Dec. 7	Kentucky	A	W	87	77
Dec. 9	Vanderbilt	CH	W	100	78
Dec. 16	Clemson	H	W	90	69
Dec. 17	Virginia	H	W	94	67
	HOLIDAY FESTIVAL				
Dec. 27	Villanova	MSG	W	69	61
Dec. 28	St. John's	MSG	L	70	72
Dec. 30	Princeton	MSG	W	103	76
Jan. 4	Duke	H	W	94	70
Jan. 8	N.C. State	H	W	83	63
Jan. 11	Virginia Tech	H	W	99	77
Jan. 14	Georgia Tech	A	W	101	70
Jan. 18	Wake Forest	A	W	94	89
Feb. 1	Maryland	H	W	107	87
Feb. 4	Virginia	A	W	99	76
Feb. 6	Wake Forest	H	W	84	76
Feb. 8	Florida State	GR	W	100	82
Feb. 10	N.C. State	A	W	85	62
Feb. 14	South Carolina	N-S	L	66	68
Feb. 15	Clemson	N-S	W	107	81
Feb. 19	Maryland	A	W	88	86
Feb. 22	The Citadel	H	W	106	59
Feb. 26	South Carolina	A	W	68	62
Mar. 1	Duke	A	L	81	87
	ACC TOURNAMENT				
Mar. 6	Clemson	CH	W	94	70
Mar. 7	Wake Forest	CH	W	80	72
Mar. 8	Duke	CH	W	85	74
	NCAA TOURNAMENT				
Mar. 13	Duquesne	CP	W	79	78
Mar. 15	Davidson	CP	W	87	85
Mar. 20	Purdue	LV	L	65	92
Mar. 22	Drake	LV	L	84	104

1969-70

RECORD: 18-9
COACH: Dean Smith
CAPTAIN: Charlie Scott, Eddie Fogler, Jim Delany

Dec. 1	Florida Southern	H	W	112	47
Dec. 3	Mercer	H	W	100	52
Dec. 8	Kentucky	CH	L	87	94
Dec. 13	Florida State	GR	W	86	75
Dec. 16	Virginia	A	W	80	76
Dec. 20	Tulane	A	W	96	87
Dec. 22	Rice	A	W	99	87
	CAROLINA CLASSIC				
Dec. 29	Harvard	GR	W	92	74
Dec. 30	Bowling Green	GR	W	89	72
Jan. 3	Rice	CH	W	98	72
Jan. 5	South Carolina	A	L	52	65
Jan. 7	N.C. State	A	W	78	69
Jan. 10	Duke	H	W	86	78
Jan. 15	Clemson	A	W	96	91
Jan. 17	Wake Forest	H	L	90	91
Jan. 31	Maryland	A	W	77	69
Feb. 3	Virginia	H	W	87	72
Feb. 5	Wake Forest	A	L	85	88
Feb. 9	N.C. State	H	W	88	86
Feb. 13	Clemson	N-S	W	110	66
Feb. 14	Georgia Tech	N-S	L	95	104
Feb. 18	Maryland	H	W	90	83
Feb. 21	South Carolina	H	L	62	79
Feb. 25	Virginia Tech	H	W	98	70
Feb. 28	Duke	A	L	83	91
	ACC TOURNAMENT				
Mar. 5	Virginia	CH	L	93	95
	NATIONAL INVITATION TOURNAMENT				
Mar. 14	Manhattan	MSG	L	90	95

1970-71

RECORD: 26-6
COACH: Dean Smith
CAPTAIN: Lee Dedmon, Dale Gipple

Dec. 1	E. Tennessee State	H	W	109	79
Dec. 5	William & Mary	A	W	101	72
Dec. 12	Creighton	CH	W	106	86
Dec. 15	Virginia	H	W	80	75
Dec. 18	N.C. State	BF	L	70	82
Dec. 19	Duke	BF	W	83	81
Dec. 22	Utah	A	L	86	105
Dec. 29	Penn State	GR	W	73	57
Dec. 30	Northwestern	GR	W	98	74
Jan. 2	Tulane	CH	W	101	79
Jan. 4	South Carolina	H	W	79	64
Jan. 9	Duke	H	W	79	74
Jan. 14	Clemson	H	W	92	72
Jan. 16	Wake Forest	A	L	84	96
Jan. 30	Maryland	H	W	105	79
Feb. 4	Wake Forest	H	W	93	75
Feb. 8	N.C. State	A	W	65	63
Feb. 12	Georgia Tech	N-S	W	87	58
Feb. 13	Clemson	N-S	W	86	48
Feb. 17	Maryland	A	W	100	76
Feb. 20	South Carolina	A	L	66	72
Feb. 22	Florida State	H	W	70	61
Feb. 27	Virginia	A	W	75	74
Mar. 3	N.C. State	H	W	97	81
Mar. 6	Duke	A	L	83	92
	ACC TOURNAMENT				
Mar. 11	Clemson	GR	W	76	41
Mar. 12	Virginia	GR	W	78	68
Mar. 13	South Carolina	GR	L	51	52
	NATIONAL INVITATION TOURNAMENT				
Mar. 20	Massachusetts	MSG	W	90	49
Mar. 22	Providence	MSG	W	86	79
Mar. 25	Duke	MSG	W	73	67
Mar. 27	Georgia Tech	MSG	W	84	66

1971-72

RECORD: 26-5
COACH: Dean Smith
CAPTAIN: Dennis Wuycik, Steve Previs

Dec. 2	Rice	H	W	127	69
Dec. 4	Pittsburgh	A	W	90	75
Dec. 6	Princeton	A	L	73	89
Dec. 11	Virginia Tech	H	W	93	60
Dec. 17	Wake Forest	BF	W	99	76
Dec. 18	N.C. State	BF	W	99	68
	INTERNATIONAL CHRISTMAS TOURNAMENT				
Dec. 23	Barcelona, Spain	MS	W	87	74
Dec. 24	Santiago, Chile	MS	W	87	65
Dec. 25	Real Madrid	MS	W	83	77
Dec. 27	Harvard	CH	W	96	78
	SUGAR BOWL TOURNAMENT				
Dec. 29	St. Joseph's	NO	W	93	77
Dec. 30	Bradley	NO	W	75	69
Jan. 8	Furman	H	W	118	66
Jan. 12	Clemson	A	W	81	61
Jan. 15	Virginia	A	W	85	79
Jan. 19	Wake Forest	H	W	92	77
Jan. 22	Duke	A	L	74	76
Jan. 29	Maryland	H	W	92	72
Feb. 3	Wake Forest	A	W	71	59
Feb. 7	N.C. State	H	W	101	78
Feb. 11	Clemson	N-S	W	73	50
Feb. 12	Georgia Tech	N-S	W	118	73
Feb. 16	Maryland	A	(OT) L	77	79
Feb. 19	Notre Dame	MSG	W	99	74
Feb. 23	Georgia Tech	H	W	87	66
Feb. 26	Virginia	H	W	91	78
Feb. 29	N.C. State	A	L	84	85
Mar. 4	Duke	H	W	93	69
	ACC TOURNAMENT				
Mar. 10	Duke	GR	W	63	48
Mar. 11	Maryland	GR	W	73	64
	NCAA TOURNAMENT				
Mar. 16	South Carolina	MO	W	92	69
Mar. 18	Pennsylvania	MO	W	73	59
Mar. 23	Florida State	LA	L	75	79
Mar. 25	Louisville	LA	W	105	91

1972-73

RECORD: 25-8
COACH: Dean Smith
CAPTAIN: George Karl, Donn Johnston

Date	Opponent	Site		W/L		
Nov. 25	Biscayne	H		W	107	62
Dec. 2	Pittsburgh	H		W	99	70
Dec. 5	Dartmouth	GR		W	128	86
Dec. 9	Virginia Tech	CH		W	96	82
Dec. 11	Kentucky	LV		W	78	70
Dec. 15	Duke	BF		W	91	86
Dec. 16	N.C. State	BF		L	61	68
Dec. 22	California	A		W	64	61
RAINBOW CLASSIC						
Dec. 28	Utah	HON		W	73	61
Dec. 29	Washington	HON		W	89	72
Dec. 30	Louisville	HON		W	89	86
Jan. 4	Furman	CH		W	100	67
Jan. 6	Nebraska	GR		W	79	62
Jan. 10	Virginia	H		W	92	58
Jan. 17	Wake Forest	GR		W	99	80
Jan. 20	Duke	H		W	82	71
Jan. 25	Virginia	H		L	78	84
Jan. 27	Maryland	A		L	88	94
Jan. 31	Wake Forest	H		W	69	51
Feb. 5	N.C. State	A		L	73	76
Feb. 9	Georgia Tech	N-S		W	107	72
Feb. 10	Clemson	N-S		W	84	69
Feb. 14	Maryland	H		W	95	85
Feb. 17	Florida State	MSG		W	91	79
Feb. 21	Miami of Ohio	H		L	92	102
Feb. 24	Virginia	A		W	76	68
Feb. 27	N.C. State	H		L	78	82
Mar. 3	Duke	A		W	72	70
ACC TOURNAMENT						
Mar. 8	Wake Forest	GR	(OT)	L	52	54
NATIONAL INVITATION TOURNAMENT						
Mar. 17	Oral Roberts	MSG		W	82	65
Mar. 20	Massachusetts	MSG		W	73	63
Mar. 24	Notre Dame	MSG		L	71	78
Mar. 25	Alabama	MSG		W	88	69

1973-74

RECORD: 22-6
COACH: Dean Smith
CAPTAIN: Bobby Jones, Darrell Elston

Date	Opponent	Site		W/L		
Dec. 1	Houston	GR		W	97	74
Dec. 5	California	H		W	74	70
Dec. 8	Vermont	H		W	103	48
Dec. 10	Kentucky	GR		W	101	84
Dec. 15	E. Tennessee St.	H		W	81	63
Dec. 20	Virginia Tech	CH		W	83	78
Dec. 28	Biscayne	A		W	112	72
Jan. 4	N.C. State	BF		L	77	78
Jan. 5	Duke	BF		W	84	75
Jan. 9	Clemson	A		W	102	90
Jan. 12	Virginia	A		W	87	75
Jan. 16	Wake Forest	H		W	95	78
Jan. 19	Duke	A		W	73	71
Jan. 22	N.C. State	H		L	80	83
Jan. 26	Maryland	H		W	82	73
Jan. 30	Wake Forest	A		W	77	67
Feb. 2	Clemson	H		W	61	60
Feb. 8	Furman	N-S		W	95	69
Feb. 9	Georgia Tech	N-S		W	112	70
Feb. 13	Maryland	A		L	80	91
Feb. 16	Florida State	GR		W	104	85
Feb. 20	Miami of Ohio	H		W	83	69
Feb. 23	Virginia	H		W	94	61
Feb. 26	N.C. State	A		L	72	83
Mar. 2	Duke	H	(OT)	W	96	92
ACC TOURNAMENT						
Mar. 7	Wake Forest	GR		W	76	62
Mar. 8	Maryland	GR		L	85	105
NATIONAL INVITATION TOURNAMENT						
Mar. 16	Purdue	MSG		L	71	82

1974-75

RECORD: 23-8
COACH: Dean Smith
CAPTAIN: Ed Stahl, Brad Hoffman, Mickey Bell

Date	Opponent	Site		W/L		
Nov. 30	Biscayne	H		W	101	74
Dec. 4	E. Tennessee St.	H		W	93	71
Dec. 7	Houston	A		W	96	87
Dec. 9	Kentucky	LV		L	78	90
Dec. 21	Yale	A		W	70	53
INTERNATIONAL CHRISTMAS TOURNAMENT						
Dec. 24	Estudiantes de Monteverde	MS		W	109	82
Dec. 25	Cuban Nat. Team	MS		W	87	86
Dec. 26	Real Madrid	MS		L	101	112
Dec. 28	Utah	GR		W	94	91
Jan. 3	Duke	BF	(OT)	L	96	99
Jan. 4	N.C. State	BF		L	67	82
Jan. 9	Clemson	H		W	74	72
Jan. 11	Howard	H		W	109	67
Jan. 15	Wake Forest	A		W	80	78
Jan. 18	N.C. State	A	(OT)	L	85	88
Jan. 22	Virginia	H		W	85	70
Jan. 25	Maryland	A		W	69	66
Jan. 29	Wake Forest	H		W	101	91
Feb. 1	Clemson	A		L	72	80
Feb. 3	South Florida	H		W	79	72
Feb. 7	Furman	N-S		W	86	81
Feb. 8	Georgia Tech	N-S		W	111	81
Feb. 12	Duke	H		W	78	70
Feb. 15	Maryland	H		L	74	96
Feb. 17	Virginia Tech	A		W	87	75
Feb. 22	Virginia	A		L	62	65
Feb. 25	N.C. State	H		W	76	74
Mar. 1	Duke	A		W	74	70
ACC TOURNAMENT						
Mar. 6	Wake Forest	GR	(OT)	W	101	100
Mar. 7	Clemson	GR	(OT)	W	76	71
Mar. 8	N.C. State	GR		W	70	66
NCAA TOURNAMENT						
Mar. 15	New Mexico State	CH		W	93	69
Mar. 20	Syracuse	PR		L	76	78
Mar. 22	Boston College	PR		W	110	90

1975-76

RECORD: 25-4
COACH: Dean Smith
CAPTAIN: Bill Chambers, Dave Hanners, Mitch Kupchak

Date	Opponent	Site		W/L		
Nov. 29	Howard	H		W	115	75
Dec. 4	Seton Hall	MSG		W	75	63
Dec. 6	Virginia Tech	H		W	88	75
Dec. 8	Kentucky	CH		W	90	77
Dec. 20	E. Tennessee St.	A		W	104	67
Dec. 22	South Florida	A		W	70	64
Jan. 2	Wake Forest	BF		L	88	95
Jan. 3	Duke	BF		W	77	74
Jan. 5	Yale	H		W	81	42
Jan. 7	Clemson	A		W	83	64
Jan. 10	Virginia	A		W	85	82
Jan. 14	Wake Forest	H		W	99	75
Jan. 17	Duke	A		W	89	87
Jan. 18	N.C. State	H		L	67	68
Jan. 25	Maryland	H	(OT)	W	95	93
Jan. 28	Wake Forest	A		W	88	85
Jan. 31	Clemson	H		W	79	64
Feb. 4	Detroit	A		W	91	76
Feb. 6	Georgia Tech	N-S		W	79	74
Feb. 7	Furman	N-S		W	97	64
Feb. 11	Maryland	A		W	81	69
Feb. 14	Tulane	A	(4OT)	W	113	106
Feb. 18	Miami of Ohio	A		W	77	75
Feb. 21	Virginia	A		W	73	71
Feb. 24	N.C. State	A		W	91	79
Feb. 28	Duke	H		W	91	71
ACC TOURNAMENT						
Mar. 5	Clemson	CC		W	82	74
Mar. 6	Virginia	CC		L	62	67
NCAA TOURNAMENT						
Mar. 13	Alabama	DT		L	64	79

Charlie Scott earned All-America status in 1969 and '70.

1976-77

RECORD: 28-5
COACH: Dean Smith
CAPTAIN: Bruce Buckley, Woody Coley, Walter Davis, John Kuester, Tommy LaGarde

Nov. 26	N.C. State	BF	W	78	66
Nov. 27	Wake Forest	BF	(OT) L	96	97
Dec. 1	Marshall	H	W	90	70
Dec. 6	Michigan State	A	W	81	58
Dec. 11	Virginia Tech	RN	W	81	77
Dec. 20	Brigham Young	H	W	113	93
FAR WEST CLASSIC					
Dec. 27	Oral Roberts	PO	W	100	84
Dec. 29	Oregon	PO	W	86	60
Dec. 30	Weber State	PO	W	75	54
Jan. 5	Clemson	GR	W	91	63
Jan. 8	Virginia	H	W	91	67
Jan. 13	Wake Forest	A	W	77	75
Jan. 15	Duke	H	W	77	68
Jan. 19	N.C. State	A	L	73	75
Jan. 22	Maryland	A	W	71	68
Jan. 26	Wake Forest	H	L	66	67
Jan. 29	Clemson	A	L	73	93
Feb. 4	Georgia Tech	N-S	W	98	74
Feb. 5	Furman	N-S	W	88	71
Feb. 9	Maryland	H	W	97	70
Feb. 12	Tulane	GR	W	106	94
Feb. 16	South Florida	H	W	100	65
Feb. 20	Virginia	A	W	66	64
Feb. 23	N.C. State	H	W	90	73
Feb. 26	Duke	A	W	84	71
Feb. 27	Louisville	CH	W	96	89
ACC TOURNAMENT					
Mar. 4	N.C. State	GR	W	70	56
Mar. 5	Virginia	GR	W	75	69
NCAA TOURNAMENT					
Mar. 12	Purdue	RAL	W	69	66
Mar. 17	Notre Dame	CP	W	79	77
Mar. 19	Kentucky	CP	W	79	72
Mar. 26	Nevada-Las Vegas	OM	W	84	83
Mar. 28	Marquette	OM	L	59	67

1977-78

RECORD: 23-8
COACH: Dean Smith
CAPTAIN: Phil Ford, Tom Zaliagiris

Nov. 28	Oregon State	CH	W	94	63
Nov. 30	Oregon State	H	W	90	64
Dec. 2	Duke	BF	W	79	66
Dec. 3	N.C. State	BF	W	87	82
Dec. 7	William & Mary	A	L	75	78
Dec. 10	Rochester	H	W	101	43
Dec. 17	Cincinnati	GR	W	67	59
Dec. 23	Tulane	A	W	108	103
RAINBOW CLASSIC					
Dec. 28	Brigham Young	HON	W	94	81
Dec. 29	Texas Tech	HON	W	88	76
Dec. 30	Stanford	HON	W	92	61
Jan. 4	Clemson	A	(OT) W	79	77
Jan. 7	Virginia	A	W	76	61
Jan. 14	Duke	A	L	84	92
Jan. 15	Wake Forest	H	W	71	69
Jan. 18	N.C. State	H	W	69	64
Jan. 21	Maryland	H	W	85	71
Jan. 26	Wake Forest	A	L	62	71
Jan. 28	Clemson	H	W	98	64
Jan. 30	Mercer	H	W	73	70
Feb. 3	Furman	N-S	L	83	89
Feb. 4	Virginia Tech	N-S	W	101	88
Feb. 8	Maryland	A	W	66	64
Feb. 11	Rutgers	MSG	W	74	57
Feb. 12	Providence	A	L	59	61
Feb. 15	Kent State	H	W	92	59
Feb. 18	Virginia	H	W	71	54
Feb. 23	N.C. State	A	L	67	72
Feb. 25	Duke	H	W	87	83
ACC TOURNAMENT					
Mar. 2	Wake Forest	GR	L	77	82
NCAA TOURNAMENT					
Mar. 11	San Francisco	TP	L	64	68

1978-79

RECORD: 23-6
COACH: Dean Smith
CAPTAIN: Dudley Bradley, Ged Doughton

Nov. 29	Northwestern	A	W	97	67
Dec. 1	Wake Forest	BF	W	73	55
Dec. 2	Duke	BF	L	68	78
Dec. 4	Detroit	H	W	93	76
Dec. 9	Jacksonville	H	W	85	56
Dec. 16	Michigan State	H	W	70	69
Dec. 22	Cincinnati	A	W	62	59
KODAK CLASSIC					
Dec. 29	Dartmouth	RO	W	86	67
Dec. 30	Niagara	RO	W	121	69
Jan. 3	Clemson	GR	W	90	68
Jan. 6	Virginia	H	(2OT) W	86	74
Jan. 10	Wake Forest	A	L	56	59
Jan. 13	Duke	H	W	74	68
Jan. 14	Arkansas	GR	W	63	57
Jan. 17	N.C. State	A	W	70	69
Jan. 20	Maryland	A	W	54	53
Jan. 25	Wake Forest	H	W	76	69
Jan. 27	Clemson	A	L	61	66
Feb. 2	Furman	N-S	L	70	83
Feb. 3	Virginia Tech	N-S	(OT) W	92	80
Feb. 7	Maryland	H	W	76	67
Feb. 10	Providence	CH	W	89	55
Feb. 14	William & Mary	H	W	85	60
Feb. 17	Virginia	A	W	66	57
Feb. 22	N.C. State	H	W	71	56
Feb. 24	Duke	A	L	40	47
ACC TOURNAMENT					
Mar. 2	Maryland	GR	W	102	79
Mar. 3	Duke	GR	W	71	63
NCAA TOURNAMENT					
Mar. 11	Pennsylvania	RAL	L	71	72

Phil Ford, now a Tar Heel assistant, was All-America in 1976, '77 and '78.

1979-80

RECORD: 21-8
COACH: Dean Smith
CAPTAIN: Dave Colescott, Mike O'Koren, John Virgil, Jeff Wolf, Rich Yonakor

Nov. 30	N.C. State	BF	W	97	84
Dec. 1	Duke	BF	L	74	86
Dec. 3	South Florida	SP	W	93	62
Dec. 8	Cincinnati	GR	W	68	63
Dec. 15	Detroit	H	W	90	72
Dec. 22	Indiana	A	W	61	57
Jan. 2	Clemson	A	L	76	93
Jan. 5	Virginia	A	L	82	88
Jan. 7	Mercer	A	W	81	63
Jan. 9	Wake Forest	H	W	72	68
Jan. 12	Duke	A	W	82	67
Jan. 14	Georgia Tech	GR	W	54	53
Jan. 16	N.C. State	H	W	67	64
Jan. 20	Maryland	H	L	86	92
Jan. 23	Wake Forest	A	W	73	61
Jan. 26	Clemson	H	W	73	70
Jan. 29	William & Mary	H	W	71	61
Feb. 1	The Citadel	N-S	W	51	40
Feb. 2	Furman	N-S	W	75	63
Feb. 4	Yale	H	W	85	74
Feb. 7	Maryland	A	L	69	70
Feb. 11	Georgia Tech	A	W	60	50
Feb. 14	Rutgers	MSG	(OT) W	73	70
Feb. 16	Virginia	H	W	68	51
Feb. 20	N.C. State	A	L	50	63
Feb. 23	Duke	H	W	96	71
ACC TOURNAMENT					
Feb. 28	Wake Forest	GR	W	75	62
Feb. 29	Duke	GR	L	61	75
NCAA TOURNAMENT					
Mar. 9	Texas A&M	DT	(2OT) L	61	78

1980-81

RECORD: 29-8
COACH: Dean Smith
CAPTAIN: Pete Budko, Eric Kenny, Mike Pepper, Al Wood

GREAT ALASKA SHOOTOUT					
Nov. 28	Alaska-Anchorage	A	W	69	50
Nov. 29	Georgetown	AN	W	83	71
Nov. 30	Arkansas	AN	W	64	58
Dec. 2	Mercer	H	W	89	74
Dec. 5	Duke	BF	W	78	76
Dec. 6	Wake Forest	BF	L	71	82
Dec. 13	South Florida	GR	W	73	64
Dec. 20	Indiana	H	W	65	56
Dec. 22	Rutgers	CH	W	71	64
WINSTON TIRE HOLIDAY CLASSIC					
Dec. 29	Louisville	LA	W	86	64
Dec. 30	Minnesota	LA	L	60	76
Jan. 3	Kansas	KC	L	55	56
Jan. 7	Maryland	H	W	75	66
Jan. 10	Virginia	A	L	57	63
Jan. 14	N.C. State	H	W	73	70
Jan. 17	Duke	H	W	80	65
Jan. 22	Wake Forest	A	W	74	60
Jan. 24	Georgia Tech	H	W	100	60
Jan. 28	Clemson	A	W	61	47
Jan. 31	N.C. State	A	W	57	54
Feb. 3	Virginia	H	(OT) L	79	80
Feb. 6	St. Joseph's	N-S	W	87	64
Feb. 7	Furman	N-S	W	79	64
Feb. 11	Wake Forest	H	L	68	84
Feb. 15	Maryland	A	W	76	63
Feb. 18	William & Mary	H	W	81	55
Feb. 21	Clemson	H	W	75	61
Feb. 25	Georgia Tech	A	W	76	51
Feb. 28	Duke	A	(OT) L	65	66
ACC TOURNAMENT					
Mar. 5	N.C. State	CC	W	69	54
Mar. 6	Wake Forest	CC	W	58	57
Mar. 7	Maryland	CC	W	61	60
NCAA TOURNAMENT					
Mar. 15	Pittsburgh	EP	W	74	57
Mar. 19	Utah	A	W	61	56
Mar. 21	Kansas State	SLC	W	82	68
Mar. 28	Virginia	PH	W	78	65
Mar. 30	Indiana	PH	L	50	63

1981-82

RECORD: 32-2
COACH: Dean Smith
CAPTAIN: Jeb Barlow, Jimmy Black, Chris Brust

Nov. 28	Kansas	CH	W	74	67
Nov. 30	Southern Cal	GR	W	73	62
Dec. 3	Tulsa	H	W	78	70
Dec. 12	South Florida	H	W	75	39
Dec. 19	Rutgers	MSG	W	59	36
Dec. 26	Kentucky	ML	W	82	69
CABLE CAR CLASSIC					
Dec. 28	Penn State	SC	(OT) W	56	50
Dec. 29	Santa Clara	A	W	76	57
Jan. 4	William & Mary	H	W	64	40
Jan. 6	Maryland	A	W	66	50
Jan. 9	Virginia	H	W	65	60
Jan. 13	N.C. State	A	W	61	41
Jan. 16	Duke	A	W	73	63
Jan. 21	Wake Forest	H	L	48	55
Jan. 23	Georgia Tech	A	W	66	54
Jan. 27	Clemson	H	W	77	72
Jan. 30	N.C. State	H	W	58	44
Feb. 3	Virginia	A	L	58	74
Feb. 5	Furman	N-S	W	96	69
Feb. 6	The Citadel	N-S	W	67	46
Feb. 11	Maryland	H	W	59	56
Feb. 14	Georgia	GR	W	66	57
Feb. 17	Wake Forest	A	W	69	51
Feb. 20	Clemson	A	W	55	49
Feb. 24	Georgia Tech	H	W	77	54
Feb. 27	Duke	H	W	84	66
ACC TOURNAMENT					
Mar. 5	Georgia Tech	GR	W	55	39
Mar. 6	N.C. State	GR	W	58	46
Mar. 7	Virginia	GR	W	47	45
NCAA TOURNAMENT					
Mar. 13	James Madison	CH	W	52	50
Mar. 19	Alabama	RAL	W	74	69
Mar. 21	Villanova	RAL	W	70	60
Mar. 27	Houston	NO	W	68	63
Mar. 29	Georgetown	NO	W	63	62

1982-83

RECORD: 28-8
COACH: Dean Smith
CAPTAIN: Jim Braddock

Nov. 20	St. John's	SF	(OT) L	74	78
Nov. 27	Missouri	SL	L	60	64
Nov. 30	Tulane	H	(3OT) W	70	68
Dec. 4	Louisiana State	ML	W	47	43
Dec. 11	Santa Clara	GR	W	79	56
OIL CITY CLASSIC					
Dec. 17	Tulsa	A	L	74	84
Dec. 18	Pan American	TU	W	106	50
Dec. 21	Tenn.-Chattanooga	A	W	73	66
RAINBOW CLASSIC					
Dec. 28	Texas Tech	HON	W	79	47
Dec. 29	Oklahoma	HON	W	77	69
Dec. 30	Missouri	HON	W	73	58
Jan. 5	Rutgers	GR	W	86	69
Jan. 8	Syracuse	CH	W	87	64
Jan. 12	Maryland	H	W	72	71
Jan. 15	Virginia	A	W	101	95
Jan. 19	N.C. State	H	W	99	81
Jan. 22	Duke	H	W	103	82
Jan. 24	Georgia State	H	W	99	55
Jan. 27	Wake Forest	A	W	80	78
Jan. 29	Georgia Tech	GR	W	72	65
Feb. 2	Clemson	A	W	84	81
Feb. 4	The Citadel	N-S	W	81	36
Feb. 5	Furman	N-S	W	78	43
Feb. 10	Virginia	H	W	64	63
Feb. 13	Villanova	H	L	53	56
Feb. 16	Maryland	A	L	94	106
Feb. 19	N.C. State	A	L	63	70
Feb. 24	Wake Forest	H	W	100	85
Feb. 27	Clemson	H	W	93	80
Mar. 2	Georgia Tech	A	W	85	73
Mar. 5	Duke	A	W	105	81
ACC TOURNAMENT					
Mar. 11	Clemson	OM	W	105	79
Mar. 12	N.C. State	OM	(OT) L	84	91
NCAA TOURNAMENT					
Mar. 19	James Madison	GR	W	68	49
Mar. 25	Ohio State	SY	W	64	51
Mar. 27	Georgia	SY	L	77	82

1983-84

RECORD: 28-3
COACH: Dean Smith
CAPTAIN: Matt Doherty, Cecil Exum, Sam Perkins

Nov. 26	Missouri	GR	W	64	57
Nov. 28	Tenn.-Chattanooga	H	W	85	63
STANFORD INVITATIONAL					
Dec. 2	Fordham	ST	W	73	56
Dec. 3	Stanford	A	W	88	75
Dec. 10	Syracuse	A	W	87	64
Dec. 21	Dartmouth	H	W	103	58
ECAC HOLIDAY FESTIVAL					
Dec. 27	Iona	MSG	W	74	61
Dec. 29	St. John's	MSG	W	64	51
Jan. 5	Boston University	CH	W	87	54
Jan. 7	N.C. State	A	W	81	60
Jan. 12	Maryland	A	W	74	62
Jan. 14	Wake Forest	A	W	70	62
Jan. 18	Virginia	H	W	69	66
Jan. 21	Duke	A	W	78	73
Jan. 25	Wake Forest	H	W	100	63
Jan. 28	Georgia Tech	H	W	73	61
Jan. 29	Louisiana State	H	W	90	79
Feb. 1	Clemson	GR	W	97	75
Feb. 3	Furman	N-S	W	83	48
Feb. 4	The Citadel	N-S	W	76	60
Feb. 9	Virginia	A	W	85	72
Feb. 12	Arkansas	PB	L	64	65
Feb. 18	N.C. State	H	W	95	71
Feb. 19	Maryland	H	W	78	63
Feb. 26	Clemson	A	W	82	71
Feb. 29	Georgia Tech	A	W	69	56
Mar. 3	Duke	H	(2OT) W	96	83
ACC TOURNAMENT					
Mar. 9	Clemson	GR	W	78	66
Mar. 10	Duke	GR	L	75	77
NCAA TOURNAMENT					
Mar. 17	Temple	CH	W	77	66
Mar. 22	Indiana	OM	L	68	72

1984-85

RECORD: 27-9
COACH: Dean Smith
CAPTAIN: Buzz Peterson

Nov. 25	Fordham	CH	W	81	65
Dec. 2	Boston University	A	W	89	72
Dec. 3	Howard	H	W	77	63
Dec. 8	Oral Roberts	H	W	87	65
Dec. 15	Wake Forest	A	W	79	73
Dec. 21	Wichita State	OS	W	80	69
Dec. 23	Arizona State	TOK	W	85	66
HAWAII PACIFIC INVITATIONAL					
Dec. 29	Hawaii Pacific	A	W	88	69
Dec. 30	Missouri	HON	L	76	81
Jan. 3	Stetson	OR	W	85	71
Jan. 5	Florida State	MI	W	78	69
Jan. 9	Maryland	H	W	75	74
Jan. 12	Virginia	A	W	65	61
Jan. 13	SMU	GR	L	82	84
Jan. 16	N.C. State	H	W	86	76
Jan. 19	Duke	H	L	77	93
Jan. 21	Jacksonville	GR	W	74	68
Jan. 27	Georgia Tech	H	L	62	66
Jan. 30	Clemson	A	L	50	52
Feb. 1	The Citadel	N-S	W	83	62
Feb. 2	Furman	N-S	W	77	55
Feb. 7	Virginia	H	W	82	73
Feb. 10	Louisiana State	A	W	75	70
Feb. 13	Maryland	A	W	60	54
Feb. 16	N.C. State	A	L	76	85
Feb. 20	Wake Forest	H	W	69	59
Feb. 23	Clemson	H	W	84	50
Feb. 27	Georgia Tech	A	L	62	67
Mar. 2	Duke	A	W	78	68
ACC TOURNAMENT					
Mar. 8	Wake Forest	OM	(OT) W	72	61
Mar. 9	N.C. State	OM	W	57	51
Mar. 10	Georgia Tech	OM	L	54	57
NCAA TOURNAMENT					
Mar. 14	Mid. Tenn. State	ND	W	76	57
Mar. 16	Notre Dame	A	W	60	58
Mar. 22	Auburn	BIR	W	62	56
Mar. 24	Villanova	BIR	L	44	56

1985-86

RECORD: 28-6
COACH: Dean Smith
CAPTAIN: Brad Daugherty, Steve Hale

Nov. 24	UCLA	H		W	107	70
Nov. 26	Iona	H		W	110	67
	GREAT ALASKA SHOOTOUT					
Nov. 29	Missouri	AN		W	84	63
Nov. 30	Purdue	AN		W	73	62
Dec. 1	Nevada-Las Vegas	AN		W	65	60
Dec. 7	Rutgers	GR		W	114	71
Dec. 14	Ohio University	H		W	99	57
Dec. 17	Jacksonville	A		W	69	65
Dec. 20	Stanford	H		W	89	55
Dec. 22	The Citadel	CH		W	104	51
	ORANGE BOWL CLASSIC					
Dec. 27	Manhattan	MI		W	129	45
Dec. 28	Brown	MI		W	115	63
Dec. 31	Florida State	CH		W	109	64
Jan. 4	N.C. State	H		W	90	79
Jan. 9	Fordham	MSG		W	92	68
Jan. 11	Wake Forest	A		W	89	65
Jan. 14	Maryland	A		W	71	67
Jan. 18	Duke	H		W	95	92
Jan. 19	Marquette	A		W	66	64
Jan. 25	Georgia Tech	H		W	85	77
Jan. 26	Notre Dame	H		W	73	61
Jan. 30	Virginia	A		L	73	86
Feb. 1	Clemson	H		W	85	67
Feb. 4	Georgia Tech	A	(OT)	W	78	77
Feb. 8	Wake Forest	H		W	91	62
Feb. 12	Clemson	A		W	79	64
Feb. 20	Maryland	H	(OT)	L	72	77
Feb. 23	N.C. State	A		L	65	76
Feb. 26	Virginia	H		W	85	79
Mar. 2	Duke	A		L	74	82
	ACC TOURNAMENT					
Mar. 7	Maryland	GR		L	75	85
	NCAA TOURNAMENT					
Mar. 13	Utah	OG		W	84	72
Mar. 15	Ala.-Birmingham	OG		W	77	59
Mar. 20	Louisville	HOU		L	79	94

1986-87

RECORD: 32-4
COACH: Dean Smith
CAPTAIN: Kenny Smith, Joe Wolf

	HAWAII THANKSGIVING FESTIVAL					
Nov. 28	Hawaii	A		W	98	78
Nov. 29	Hawaii Loa	A		W	118	90
Dec. 1	UCLA	A		L	84	89
Dec. 3	Stetson	H		W	100	64
Dec. 6	Miami (Fla.)	H		W	122	77
Dec. 13	Jacksonville	H		W	98	69
Dec. 20	Illinois	H		W	90	77
Dec. 22	Furman	CH		W	95	65
Dec. 27	Kansas State	KC		W	81	62
	DALLAS MORNING NEWS CLASSIC					
Dec. 29	Purdue	DA		W	94	81
Dec. 30	SMU	A	(OT)	W	88	86
Jan. 3	La Salle	A		W	79	72
Jan. 8	Maryland	H		W	98	65
Jan. 10	Duke	A		W	85	77
Jan. 14	Virginia	A		W	95	80
Jan. 18	N.C. State	H		W	96	78
Jan. 22	Wake Forest	A		W	79	53
Jan. 24	Georgia Tech	H		W	92	55
Jan. 28	Clemson	A		W	108	99
Feb. 1	Notre Dame	A		L	58	60
Feb. 5	N.C. State	A		W	96	79
Feb. 8	Virginia	H	(OT)	W	74	73
Feb. 11	Wake Forest	H		W	94	85
Feb. 14	Maryland	A		W	93	86
Feb. 15	Marquette	H		W	83	74
Feb. 18	East Tenn. State	H		W	118	65
Feb. 21	Clemson	H		W	96	80
Feb. 26	Duke	H		W	77	71
Mar. 1	Georgia Tech	A		W	92	76
	ACC TOURNAMENT					
Mar. 6	Maryland	CC		W	82	63
Mar. 7	Virginia	CC	(2OT)	W	84	82
Mar. 8	N.C. State	CC		L	67	68
	NCAA TOURNAMENT					
Mar. 12	Pennsylvania	CH		W	113	82
Mar. 14	Michigan	CH		W	109	97
Mar. 19	Notre Dame	ML		W	74	68
Mar. 21	Syracuse	ML		L	75	79

1987-88

RECORD: 27-7
COACH: Dean Smith
CAPTAIN: Ranzino Smith, Joe Jenkins

Nov. 21	Syracuse	SF	(OT)	W	96	93
	CENTRAL FIDELITY HOLIDAY CLASSIC					
Nov. 27	Southern Cal	RI		W	82	77
Nov. 28	Richmond	A		W	87	76
Dec. 3	Stetson	H		W	86	74
Dec. 5	Vanderbilt	A		L	76	78
Dec. 12	SMU	H		W	90	74
Dec. 17	The Citadel	CH		W	98	74
Dec. 19	Illinois	A		W	85	74
Dec. 30	Nevada-Reno	A		W	115	91
Jan. 2	UCLA	A		W	80	73
Jan. 6	Fordham	GR	(OT)	W	76	67
Jan. 9	La Salle	H		W	96	82
Jan. 14	Maryland	A		W	71	65
Jan. 16	Virginia	H		W	87	62
Jan. 21	Duke	H		L	69	70
Jan. 24	N.C. State	A		W	77	73
Jan. 28	Wake Forest	A		L	80	83
Jan. 30	Georgia Tech	H		W	73	71
Feb. 4	Clemson	A		W	88	64
Feb. 11	N.C. State	H	(OT)	W	75	73
Feb. 14	Virginia	A		W	64	58
Feb. 17	Wake Forest	H		W	80	62
Feb. 20	Maryland	H		W	74	73
Feb. 21	Temple	H		L	66	83
Feb. 28	Clemson	H		W	88	52
Mar. 2	Georgia Tech	A		W	97	80
Mar. 6	Duke	A		L	81	96
	ACC TOURNAMENT					
Mar. 11	Wake Forest	GR		W	83	62
Mar. 12	Maryland	GR		W	74	64
Mar. 13	Duke	GR		L	61	65
	NCAA TOURNAMENT					
Mar. 17	North Texas State	SLC		W	83	65
Mar. 19	Loyola Marymount	SLC		W	123	97
Mar. 25	Michigan	SE		W	78	69
Mar. 27	Arizona	SE		L	52	70

1988-89

RECORD: 29-8
COACH: Dean Smith
CAPTAIN: Steve Bucknall, Jeff Lebo, David May

	PRESEASON DODGE NIT					
Nov. 18	Tenn.-Chattanooga	H		W	111	84
Nov. 20	Georgia	H		W	99	91
Nov. 23	Missouri	MSG		L	81	91
Nov. 25	Indiana	MSG		W	106	92
Nov. 28	Stanford	H		W	87	76
	DIET PEPSI TOURNAMENT OF CHAMPIONS					
Dec. 2	Arizona	CH		W	79	72
Dec. 3	Missouri	CH		W	76	60
Dec. 7	Vanderbilt	H		W	89	77
Dec. 10	Richmond	GR		W	76	68
Dec. 17	UCLA	H		W	104	78
Dec. 22	Towson State	HER		W	102	74
Dec. 29	San Diego State	A		W	103	92
Jan. 3	Pepperdine	A		W	102	80
Jan. 5	DePaul	A		W	87	67
Jan. 7	Iowa	H		L	97	98
Jan. 11	Maryland	H		W	88	72
Jan. 15	Virginia	A		L	83	106
Jan. 18	Duke	A		W	91	71
Jan. 21	N.C. State	H		W	84	81
Jan. 25	Wake Forest	A		W	88	74
Jan. 28	Georgia Tech	H		W	92	85
Feb. 1	Clemson	A		L	82	85
Feb. 9	N.C. State	A		L	88	98
Feb. 12	Virginia	H		W	85	67
Feb. 14	Old Dominion	A		W	87	77
Feb. 16	Wake Forest	H		W	99	76
Feb. 19	Maryland	A		W	86	75
Feb. 21	Nevada-Reno	H		W	109	86
Feb. 25	Clemson	H		W	100	86
Mar. 1	Georgia Tech	A		L	74	76
Mar. 5	Duke	H		L	86	88
	ACC TOURNAMENT					
Mar. 10	Georgia Tech	OM		W	77	62
Mar. 11	Maryland	OM		W	88	58
Mar. 12	Duke	OM		W	77	74
	NCAA TOURNAMENT					
Mar. 17	Southern	OM		W	93	79
Mar. 19	UCLA	OM		W	88	81
Mar. 23	Michigan	LX		L	87	92

1989-90

RECORD: 21-13
COACH: Dean Smith
CAPTAIN: Kevin Madden, Scott Williams

	MAUI CLASSIC					
Nov. 24	James Madison	MU		W	80	79
Nov. 25	Villanova	MU		W	78	68
Nov. 26	Missouri	MU		L	73	80
Nov. 30	Alabama	A		L	93	101
Dec. 2	Central Florida	H		W	92	42
Dec. 3	Towson State	H		W	87	70
	ACC-BIG EAST CHALLENGE					
Dec. 7	Georgetown	ML		L	81	93
Dec. 9	Iowa	A		L	74	87
Dec. 16	DePaul	H		W	70	51
Dec. 23	Kansas State	CH		W	79	63
Dec. 27	Kentucky	LV		W	121	110
	MILE HIGH CLASSIC					
Dec. 29	Colorado State	DE		L	67	78
Dec. 30	Colorado	DE		W	106	101
Jan. 3	Old Dominion	H		W	90	78
Jan. 6	Pepperdine	H		W	95	69
Jan. 10	Maryland	A		L	88	98
Jan. 13	Virginia	H		W	92	70
Jan. 17	Duke	H		W	79	60
Jan. 20	N.C. State	A		W	91	81
Jan. 22	Wake Forest	H		W	73	61
Jan. 27	Clemson	H		W	83	60
Feb. 1	Georgia	A		L	75	102
Feb. 5	Miami (Fla.)	H		W	87	74
Feb. 7	N.C. State	H		L	77	88
Feb. 11	Wake Forest	A		W	72	67
Feb. 14	Virginia	A		L	80	81
Feb. 17	Maryland	H		L	76	80
Feb. 24	Clemson	A		L	61	69
Feb. 28	Georgia Tech	H		W	81	79
Mar. 4	Duke	A		W	87	75
	ACC TOURNAMENT					
Mar. 9	Virginia	CH		OTL	85	92
	NCAA TOURNAMENT					
Mar. 15	SW Missouri State	AU		W	83	70
Mar. 17	Oklahoma	AU		W	79	77
Mar. 22	Arkansas	DA		L	73	96

1990-91

RECORD: 29-6
COACH: Dean Smith
CAPTAIN: Pete Chilcutt, Rick Fox, King Rice

Nov. 24	San Diego State	H		W	99	63
Nov. 27	Jacksonville	H		W	104	61
	DIET PEPSI TOURNAMENT OF CHAMPIONS					
Nov. 30	South Carolina	CH		L	74	76
Dec. 1	Iowa State	CH		W	118	93
	ACC-BIG EAST CHALLENGE					
Dec. 6	Connecticut	H		W	79	64
Dec. 10	Kentucky	H		W	84	81
Dec. 15	Alabama	H		W	95	79
Dec. 22	Purdue	A		W	86	74
	RED LOBSTER CLASSIC					
Dec. 29	DePaul	OR		W	90	75
Dec. 30	Stanford	OR		W	71	60
Jan. 3	Cornell	A		W	108	64
Jan. 5	Notre Dame	ML		W	82	47
Jan. 9	Maryland	H		W	105	73
Jan. 12	Virginia	A	(2OT)	W	89	86
Jan. 19	Duke	A		L	60	74
Jan. 23	Wake Forest	A		W	91	81
Jan. 27	Georgia Tech	H		L	86	88
Jan. 31	Clemson	A		W	90	77
Feb. 6	N.C. State	A		L	91	97
Feb. 7	N.C. State	H		W	92	70
Feb. 9	Virginia	H		W	77	58
Feb. 13	Wake Forest	H		W	85	70
Feb. 16	Maryland	A		W	87	75
Feb. 18	The Citadel	H		W	118	50
Feb. 23	Clemson	H		W	73	57
Feb. 28	Georgia Tech	A		W	91	74
Mar. 3	Duke	H		L	77	83
	ACC TOURNAMENT					
Mar. 8	Clemson	CH		W	67	59
Mar. 9	Virginia	CH		W	76	71
Mar. 10	Duke	CH		W	96	74
	NCAA TOURNAMENT					
Mar. 15	Northeastern	SY		W	101	66
Mar. 17	Villanova	SY		W	84	69
Mar. 22	Eastern Michigan	ML		W	93	67
Mar. 24	Temple	ML		W	75	72
Mar. 30	Kansas	IN		L	73	79

UNC COACHES' RECORDS

Coach	Years	No. Yrs.	W	L	Pct.
Nat Cartmell	1911-1914	4	25	24	.510
Charles Doak	1915-1916	2	18	16	.529
Howell Peacock	1917-1919	3	23	14	.622
Fred Boye	1920-1921	2	19	17	.527
Norman Shepard	1924	1	26	0	1.000
Monk McDonald	1925	1	20	5	.800
Harlan Sanborn	1926	1	20	5	.800
James Ashmore	1927-1931	5	80	37	.683
George Shepard	1932-1935	4	69	16	.812
Walter Skidmore	1936-1939	4	65	25	.722
Bill Lange	1940-1944	5	85	41	.675
Ben Carnevale	1945-1946	2	52	11	.828
Tom Scott	1947-1952	6	100	65	.606
Frank McGuire	1953-1961	9	164	58	.739
Dean Smith	1962-	30	717	209	.774

LEGEND FOR ALL-TIME SCORES

AN .... Anchorage, Alaska
AU .... Austin, Texas
BIR .... Birmingham, Alabama
BF .... Big Four Tournament, Greensboro, North Carolina
BL .... Blacksburg, Virginia
BO .... Boston, Massachusetts
CC .... Capital Centre, Landover, Maryland
CH .... Charlotte, North Carolina
CHI .... Chicago, Illinois
CP .... College Park, Maryland
DA .... Dallas, Texas
DE .... Denver, Colorado
DN .... Danville, Virginia
DT .... Dayton, Ohio
DU .... Durham, North Carolina
EL .... Elkin, North Carolina
EP .... El Paso, Texas
GR .... Greensboro, North Carolina
HER .... Hershey, Pennsylvania
HON .... Honolulu, Hawaii
HOU .... Houston, Texas
IN .... Indianapolis, Indiana
KC .... Kansas City, Missouri
LA .... Los Angeles, California
LF .... Lafayette, Louisiana
LV .... Louisville, Kentucky
LX .... Lexington, Kentucky
LY .... Lynchburg, Virginia
MA .... Madison, Wisconsin
MI .... Miami, Florida
ML .... Brendan Byrne Arena, The Meadowlands, East Rutherford, New Jersey
MO .... Morgantown, West Virginia
MS .... Madrid, Spain
MSG .... Madison Square Garden, New York, NY
MU .... Maui, Hawaii
ND .... Notre Dame University, South Bend, Indiana
NF .... Norfolk, Virginia
NO .... New Orleans, Louisiana
N-S .... North-South Doubleheader, Charlotte, North Carolina
OG .... Ogden, Utah
OM .... The Omni, Atlanta, Georgia
OR .... Orlando, Florida
OS .... Osaka, Japan
PB .... Pine Bluff, Arkansas
PH .... Philadelphia, Pennsylvania
PO .... Portland, Oregon
PR .... Providence, Rhode Island
RAL .... Raleigh, North Carolina
RI .... Richmond, Virginia
RN .... Roanoke, Virginia
RO .... Rochester, New York
SC .... Santa Clara, California
SE .... Seattle, Washington
SF .... Springfield, Massachusetts
SL .... St. Louis, Missouri
SLC .... Salt Lake City, Utah
SP .... St. Petersburg, Florida
ST .... Stanford, California
SY .... Syracuse, New York
TA .... Tampa, Florida
TOK .... Tokyo, Japan
TP .... Tempe, Arizona
TU .... Tulsa, Oklahoma
WS .... Winston-Salem, North Carolina

1961-62

	DATE	OPPONENT	COACH	SCORE
1.	Dec. 2	Virginia	Billy McCann	80-46
2.	Dec. 5	Clemson	Press Maravich	54-52
3.	Jan. 6	Notre Dame	John Jordan	99-80
4.	Jan. 13	Virginia	Billy McCann	100-71
5.	Jan. 15	South Carolina	Bob Stevens	83-71
6.	Jan. 17	N.C. State	Everett Case	66-56
7.	Feb. 16	Clemson	Press Maravich	69-59
8.	Feb. 19	Maryland	Bud Millikan	70-67

1962-63

9.	Dec. 1	Georgia	Red Lawson	89-65
10.	Dec. 5	Clemson	Bobby Roberts	64-48
11.	Dec. 8	South Carolina	Chuck Noe	75-65
12.	Dec. 17	Kentucky	Adolph Rupp	68-66
13.	Jan. 2	Yale	Joe Vancisin	86-77
14.	Jan. 5	Notre Dame	John Jordan	76-68
15.	Jan. 14	Maryland	Bud Millikan	78-56
16.	Jan. 16	N.C. State	Everett Case	67-65
17.	Jan. 19	Virginia	Billy McCann	86-81
18.	Feb. 7	Maryland	Bud Millikan	82-68
19.	Feb. 12	N.C. State	Everett Case	68-63
20.	Feb. 15	South Carolina	Chuck Noe	78-74
21.	Feb. 16	Clemson	Bobby Roberts	79-63
22.	Feb. 20	Virginia	Billy McCann	85-73
23.	Feb. 28	South Carolina	Chuck Noe	93-76

1963-64

24.	Dec. 2	South Carolina	Chuck Noe	92-87
25.	Dec. 7	Indiana	Branch McCracken	77-70
26.	Dec. 14	LSU	Jay McCreary	76-71
27.	Dec. 16	Tulane	Ted Lenhardt	109-81
28.	Dec. 18	Georgia	Red Lawson	99-71
29.	Jan. 4	Notre Dame	John Jordan	78-68
30.	Jan. 13	Maryland	Bud Millikan	97-88
31.	Jan. 15	N.C. State	Everett Case	79-71
32.	Feb. 3	Virginia	Bill Gibson	89-76
33.	Feb. 8	Wake Forest	Bones McKinney	81-73
34.	Feb. 15	South Carolina	Dwane Morrison	84-81
35.	Mar. 5	South Carolina	Dwane Morrison	80-63

1964-65

36.	Dec. 1	Clemson	Bobby Roberts	77-59
37.	Dec. 5	South Carolina	Frank McGuire	82-71
38.	Dec. 7	Kentucky	Adolph Rupp	82-67
39.	Dec. 10	Tulane	Ted Lenhardt	111-74
40.	Dec. 14	Vanderbilt	Roy Skinner	84-78
41.	Dec. 18	Mississippi State	Babe McCarthy	84-80
42.	Jan. 9	Duke	Vic Bubas	65-62
43.	Jan. 16	Virginia	Bill Gibson	87-80
44.	Feb. 6	N.Y.U.	Lou Rossini	100-78
45.	Feb. 9	Wake Forest	Bones McKinney	107-91
46.	Feb. 17	N.C. State	Press Maravich	69-68
47.	Feb. 19	South Carolina	Frank McGuire	76-63
48.	Feb. 20	Clemson	Bobby Roberts	86-84
49.	Feb. 23	Virginia	Bill Gibson	105-101
50.	Feb. 27	Duke	Vic Bubas	71-66

1965-66

51.	Dec. 4	William & Mary	Bill Chambers	82-68
52.	Dec. 6	Ohio State	Fred Taylor	82-72
53.	Dec. 8	Richmond	Lewis Mills	127-76
54.	Dec. 16	Florida State	Bud Kennedy	115-80
55.	Dec. 18	Florida	Norm Sloan	66-59
56.	Dec. 27	Princeton	B. van Breda Kolff	75-61
57.	Dec. 30	Utah	Jack Gardner	90-85
58.	Jan. 3	Maryland	Bud Millikan	67-52
59.	Jan. 5	Wake Forest	Jackie Murdock	99-83
60.	Jan. 13	N.C. State	Press Maravich	83-75
61.	Feb. 3	Wake Forest	Jackie Murdock	115-87
62.	Feb. 7	South Carolina	Frank McGuire	104-70
63.	Feb. 18	Clemson	Bobby Roberts	70-66
64.	Feb. 19	South Carolina	Frank McGuire	83-71
65.	Feb. 22	Virginia	Bill Gibson	81-79
66.	Mar. 3	Maryland	Bud Millikan	77-70

1966-67

67.	Dec. 1	Clemson	Bobby Roberts	76-65
68.	Dec. 3	Penn State	John Egli	93-63
69.	Dec. 9	Tulane	Ralph Pedersen	92-69
70.	Dec. 13	Kentucky	Adolph Rupp	64-55
71.	Dec. 17	N.Y.U.	Lou Rossini	95-58
72.	Dec. 19	Columbia	John Rohan	98-66
73.	Dec. 20	Florida State	Hugh Durham	81-54
74.	Dec. 27	Furman	Frank Selvy	101-56
75.	Dec. 30	Ohio State	Fred Taylor	105-82
76.	Jan. 4	Wake Forest	Jack McCloskey	76-74
77.	Jan. 7	Duke	Vic Bubas	59-56
78.	Jan. 11	N.C. State	Norm Sloan	79-78
79.	Jan. 28	Virginia	Bill Gibson	103-76
80.	Feb. 4	Maryland	Bud Millikan	85-77
81.	Feb. 7	Virginia	Bill Gibson	79-75
82.	Feb. 9	Wake Forest	Jack McCloskey	75-73
83.	Feb. 14	N.C. State	Norm Sloan	77-60
84.	Feb. 17	South Carolina	Frank McGuire	80-55
85.	Feb. 22	Maryland	Bud Millikan	79-78
86.	Feb. 25	Virginia Tech	Howard Shannon	110-78
87.	Mar. 4	Duke	Vic Bubas	92-79
88.	Mar. 9	N.C. State	Norm Sloan	56-53
89.	Mar. 10	Wake Forest	Jack McCloskey	89-79
90.	Mar. 11	Duke	Vic Bubas	82-73
91.	Mar. 17	Princeton	B. van Breda Kolff	78-70
92.	Mar. 18	Boston College	Bob Cousy	96-80

1967-68

93.	Dec. 2	Virginia Tech	Howard Shannon	89-76
94.	Dec. 6	Kent State	Frank Truitt	107-83
95.	Dec. 12	Kentucky	Adolph Rupp	84-77
96.	Dec. 16	Princeton	Pete Carril	71-63
97.	Dec. 28	Stanford	Howard Dallmar	87-78
98.	Dec. 29	Utah	Jack Gardner	86-84
99.	Dec. 30	Oregon State	Paul Valenti	68-61
100.	Jan. 3	Wake Forest	Jack McCloskey	74-62
101.	Jan. 6	Duke	Vic Bubas	75-72
102.	Jan. 10	N.C. State	Norm Sloan	68-66
103.	Jan. 13	Clemson	Bobby Roberts	115-83
104.	Jan. 27	Georgia Tech	Whack Hyder	82-54
105.	Feb. 1	Florida State	Hugh Durham	86-80
106.	Feb. 3	Maryland	Frank Fellows	73-67
107.	Feb. 6	Virginia	Bill Gibson	108-64
108.	Feb. 8	Wake Forest	Jack McCloskey	80-60
109.	Feb. 10	Virginia Tech	Howard Shannon	80-70
110.	Feb. 12	N.C. State	Norm Sloan	96-84
111.	Feb. 16	Clemson	Bobby Roberts	96-74
112.	Feb. 17	South Carolina	Frank McGuire	84-80
113.	Feb. 21	Maryland	Frank Fellows	83-60
114.	Feb. 24	Virginia	Bill Gibson	92-74
115.	Mar. 7	Wake Forest	Jack McCloskey	83-70
116.	Mar. 8	South Carolina	Frank McGuire	82-79
117.	Mar. 9	N.C. State	Norm Sloan	87-50
118.	Mar. 15	St. Bonaventure	Larry Weise	91-72
119.	Mar. 16	Davidson	Lefty Driesell	70-66
120.	Mar. 22	Ohio State	Fred Taylor	80-66

1968-69

121.	Dec. 2	Oregon	Steve Belko	89-78
122.	Dec. 3	Oregon	Steve Belko	106-73
123.	Dec. 7	Kentucky	Adolph Rupp	87-77
124.	Dec. 9	Vanderbilt	Roy Skinner	100-78
125.	Dec. 16	Clemson	Bobby Roberts	90-69
126.	Dec. 17	Virginia	Bill Gibson	94-67
127.	Dec. 27	Villanova	Jack Kraft	69-61
128.	Dec. 30	Princeton	Pete Carril	103-76
129.	Jan. 4	Duke	Vic Bubas	94-70
130.	Jan. 8	N.C. State	Norm Sloan	83-63
131.	Jan. 11	Virginia Tech	Howard Shannon	99-77
132.	Jan. 14	Georgia Tech	Whack Hyder	101-70
133.	Jan. 18	Wake Forest	Jack McCloskey	94-89
134.	Feb. 1	Maryland	Frank Fellows	107-81
135.	Feb. 4	Virginia	Bill Gibson	99-76
136.	Feb. 6	Wake Forest	Jack McCloskey	84-76
137.	Feb. 8	Florida State	Hugh Durham	100-82
138.	Feb. 10	N.C. State	Norm Sloan	85-62
139.	Feb. 15	Clemson	Bobby Roberts	107-81
140.	Feb. 19	Maryland	Frank Fellows	88-86
141.	Feb. 22	The Citadel	Dick Campbell	106-59
142.	Feb. 26	South Carolina	Frank McGuire	68-62

#	Date	Opponent	Coach	Score
143.	Mar. 6	Clemson	Bobby Roberts	94-70
144.	Mar. 7	Wake Forest	Jack McCloskey	80-72
145.	Mar. 8	Duke	Vic Bubas	85-74
146.	Mar. 13	Duquesne	Red Manning	79-78
147.	Mar. 15	Davidson	Lefty Driesell	87-85

1969-70

#	Date	Opponent	Coach	Score
148.	Dec. 1	Florida Southern	Tom Greene	112-47
149.	Dec. 3	Mercer	Robert Wilder	100-52
150.	Dec. 13	Florida State	Hugh Durham	86-75
151.	Dec. 16	Virginia	Bill Gibson	80-76
152.	Dec. 20	Tulane	Ralph Pedersen	96-87
153.	Dec. 22	Rice	Don Knodel	99-87
154.	Dec. 29	Harvard	Bob Harrison	92-74
155.	Dec. 30	Bowling Green	Bob Conibear	89-72
156.	Jan. 3	Rice	Don Knodel	98-72
157.	Jan. 7	N.C. State	Norm Sloan	78-69
158.	Jan. 10	Duke	Bucky Waters	86-78
159.	Jan. 15	Clemson	Bobby Roberts	96-91
160.	Jan. 31	Maryland	Lefty Driesell	77-69
161.	Feb. 3	Virginia	Bill Gibson	87-72
162.	Feb. 9	N.C. State	Norm Sloan	88-86
163.	Feb. 13	Clemson	Bobby Roberts	110-66
164.	Feb. 18	Maryland	Lefty Driesell	90-83
165.	Feb. 25	Virginia Tech	Howard Shannon	98-70

1970-71

#	Date	Opponent	Coach	Score
166.	Dec. 1	E. Tennessee St.	Madison Brooks	109-79
167.	Dec. 5	William & Mary	Warren Mitchell	101-72
168.	Dec. 12	Creighton	Eddie Sutton	106-86
169.	Dec. 15	Virginia	Bill Gibson	80-75
170.	Dec. 19	Duke	Bucky Waters	83-81
171.	Dec. 29	Penn State	John Bach	73-57
172.	Dec. 30	Northwestern	Brad Snyder	98-74
173.	Jan. 2	Tulane	Ralph Pedersen	101-79
174.	Jan. 4	South Carolina	Frank McGuire	79-64
175.	Jan. 9	Duke	Bucky Waters	79-74
176.	Jan. 14	Clemson	Tates Locke	92-72
177.	Jan. 30	Maryland	Lefty Driesell	105-79
178.	Feb. 4	Wake Forest	Jack McCloskey	93-75
179.	Feb. 8	N.C. State	Norm Sloan	65-63
180.	Feb. 12	Georgia Tech	Whack Hyder	87-58
181.	Feb. 13	Clemson	Tates Locke	86-48
182.	Feb. 17	Maryland	Lefty Driesell	100-76
183.	Feb. 22	Florida State	Hugh Durham	70-61
184.	Feb. 27	Virginia	Bill Gibson	75-74
185.	Mar. 3	N.C. State	Norm Sloan	97-81
186.	Mar. 11	Clemson	Tates Locke	76-41
187.	Mar. 12	Virginia	Bill Gibson	78-68
188.	Mar. 20	Massachusetts	Jack Leaman	90-49
189.	Mar. 22	Providence	Dave Gavitt	86-79
190.	Mar. 25	Duke	Bucky Waters	73-67
191.	Mar. 27	Georgia Tech	Whack Hyder	84-66

1971-72

#	Date	Opponent	Coach	Score
192.	Dec. 2	Rice	Don Knodel	127-69
193.	Dec. 4	Pittsburgh	Buzz Ridl	90-75
194.	Dec. 11	Virginia Tech	Don DeVoe	93-60
195.	Dec. 17	Wake Forest	Jack McCloskey	99-76
196.	Dec. 18	N.C. State	Norm Sloan	99-68
197.	Dec. 27	Harvard	Bob Harrison	96-78
198.	Dec. 29	St. Joseph's	Jack McKinney	93-77
199.	Dec. 30	Bradley	Joe Stowell	75-69
200.	Jan. 8	Furman	Joe Williams	118-66
201.	Jan. 12	Clemson	Tates Locke	81-61
202.	Jan. 15	Virginia	Bill Gibson	85-79
203.	Jan. 19	Wake Forest	Jack McCloskey	92-77
204.	Jan. 29	Maryland	Lefty Driesell	92-72
205.	Feb. 3	Wake Forest	Jack McCloskey	71-59
206.	Feb. 7	N.C. State	Norm Sloan	101-78
207.	Feb. 11	Clemson	Tates Locke	74-50
208.	Feb. 12	Georgia Tech	Whack Hyder	118-73
209.	Feb. 19	Norte Dame	Digger Phelps	99-74
210.	Feb. 23	Georgia Tech	Whack Hyder	87-66
211.	Feb. 26	Virginia	Bill Gibson	91-78
212.	Mar. 4	Duke	Bucky Waters	93-69
213.	Mar. 10	Duke	Bucky Waters	63-48
214.	Mar. 11	Maryland	Lefty Driesell	73-64
215.	Mar. 16	South Carolina	Frank McGuire	92-69
216.	Mar. 18	Pennsylvania	Chuck Daly	73-59
217.	Mar. 25	Louisville	Denny Crum	105-91

1972-73

#	Date	Opponent	Coach	Score
218.	Nov. 25	Biscayne	Ken Stibler	107-62
219.	Dec. 2	Pittsburgh	Buzz Ridl	99-70
220.	Dec. 5	Dartmouth	Tom O'Connor	128-86
221.	Dec. 9	Virginia Tech	Don DeVoe	96-82
222.	Dec. 11	Kentucky	Joe Hall	78-70
223.	Dec. 15	Duke	Bucky Waters	91-86
224.	Dec. 22	California	Dick Edwards	64-61
225.	Dec. 28	Utah	Bill Foster	73-61
226.	Dec. 29	Washington	Marv Harshman	89-72
227.	Dec. 30	Louisville	Denny Crum	89-86
228.	Jan. 4	Furman	Joe Williams	100-67
229.	Jan. 6	Nebraska	Joe Cipriano	79-62
230.	Jan. 10	Clemson	Tates Locke	92-58
231.	Jan. 17	Wake Forest	Carl Tacy	99-80
232.	Jan. 20	Duke	Bucky Waters	82-71
233.	Jan. 31	Wake Forest	Carl Tacy	69-51
234.	Feb. 9	Georgia Tech	Whack Hyder	107-72
235.	Feb. 10	Clemson	Tates Locke	84-69
236.	Feb. 14	Maryland	Lefty Driesell	95-85
237.	Feb. 17	Florida State	Hugh Durham	91-79
238.	Feb. 24	Virginia	Bill Gibson	76-68
239.	Mar. 3	Duke	Bucky Waters	72-70
240.	Mar. 17	Oral Roberts	Ken Trickey	82-65
241.	Mar. 20	Massachusetts	Jack Leaman	73-63
242.	Mar. 25	Alabama	C.M. Newton	88-69

1973-74

#	Date	Opponent	Coach	Score
243.	Dec. 1	Houston	Guy Lewis	97-74
244.	Dec. 5	California	Dick Edwards	74-70
245.	Dec. 8	Vermont	Peter Salzberg	103-48
246.	Dec. 10	Kentucky	Joe Hall	101-84
247.	Dec. 15	E. Tennessee St.	Madison Brooks	81-63
248.	Dec. 20	Virginia Tech	Don DeVoe	83-78
249.	Dec. 28	Biscayne	Ken Stibler	112-72
250.	Jan. 5	Duke	Neill McGeachy	84-75
251.	Jan. 9	Clemson	Tates Locke	102-90
252.	Jan. 12	Virginia	Bill Gibson	87-75
253.	Jan. 16	Wake Forest	Carl Tacy	95-78
254.	Jan. 19	Duke	Neill McGeachy	73-71
255.	Jan. 26	Maryland	Lefty Driesell	82-73
256.	Jan. 30	Wake Forest	Carl Tacy	77-67
257.	Feb. 2	Clemson	Tates Locke	61-60
258.	Feb. 8	Furman	Joe Williams	95-69
259.	Feb. 9	Georgia Tech	Dwane Morrison	112-70
260.	Feb. 16	Florida State	Hugh Durham	104-85
261.	Feb. 20	Miami of Ohio	Darrell Hedric	83-69
262.	Feb. 23	Virginia	Bill Gibson	94-61
263.	Mar. 2	Duke	Neill McGeachy	96-92
264.	Mar. 7	Wake Forest	Carl Tacy	76-62

1974-75

#	Date	Opponent	Coach	Score
265.	Nov. 30	Biscayne	Ken Stibler	101-74
266.	Dec. 4	E. Tennessee St.	Madison Brooks	93-71
267.	Dec. 7	Houston	Guy Lewis	96-87
268.	Dec. 21	Yale	Joe Vancisin	70-53
269.	Dec. 28	Utah	Jerry Pimm	94-91
270.	Jan. 9	Clemson	Tates Locke	74-72
271.	Jan. 11	Howard	Marshall Emery	109-67
272.	Jan. 15	Wake Forest	Carl Tacy	80-78
273.	Jan. 22	Virginia	Terry Holland	85-70
274.	Jan. 25	Maryland	Lefty Driesell	69-66
275.	Jan. 20	Wake Forest	Carl Tacy	101-91
276.	Feb. 3	South Florida	Bill Gibson	79-72
277.	Feb. 7	Furman	Joe Williams	86-81
278.	Feb. 8	Georgia Tech	Dwane Morrison	111-81
279.	Feb. 12	Duke	Bill Foster	78-70
280.	Feb. 17	Virginia Tech	Don DeVoe	87-75
281.	Feb. 25	N.C. State	Norm Sloan	76-74
282.	Mar. 1	Duke	Bill Foster	74-70
283.	Mar. 6	Wake Forest	Carl Tacy	101-100
284.	Mar. 7	Clemson	Tates Locke	76-71
285.	Mar. 8	N.C. State	Norm Sloan	70-66
286.	Mar. 15	New Mexico State	Lou Henson	93-69
287.	Mar. 22	Boston College	Bob Zuffelato	110-90

1975-76

#	Date	Opponent	Coach	Score
288.	Nov. 29	Howard	A.B. Williamson	115-75
289.	Dec. 4	Seton Hall	Bill Raftery	75-63
290.	Dec. 6	Virginia Tech	Don DeVoe	88-75
291.	Dec. 8	Kentucky	Joe Hall	90-77
292.	Dec. 20	E. Tennessee St.	Madison Brooks	104-67
293.	Dec. 22	South Florida	Chip Conner	70-64
294.	Jan. 3	Duke	Bill Foster	77-74
295.	Jan. 5	Yale	Ray Carazo	81-42
296.	Jan. 7	Clemson	Bill Foster	83-64
297.	Jan. 10	Virginia	Terry Holland	85-82
298.	Jan. 14	Wake Forest	Carl Tacy	99-75
299.	Jan. 17	Duke	Bill Foster	89-87
300.	Jan. 25	Maryland	Lefty Driesell	95-93
301.	Jan. 28	Wake Forest	Carl Tacy	88-85
302.	Jan. 31	Clemson	Bill Foster	79-64
303.	Feb. 4	Detroit	Dick Vitale	91-76
304.	Feb. 6	Georgia Tech	Dwane Morrison	79-74
305.	Feb. 7	Furman	Joe Williams	97-64
306.	Feb. 11	Maryland	Lefty Driesell	81-69
307.	Feb. 14	Tulane	Charlie Moir	113-106
308.	Feb. 18	Miami of Ohio	Darrell Hedric	77-75
309.	Feb. 21	Virginia	Terry Holland	73-71
310.	Feb. 24	N.C. State	Norm Sloan	91-79
311.	Feb. 28	Duke	Bill Foster	91-71
312.	Mar. 5	Clemson	Bill Foster	82-74

1976-77

#	Date	Opponent	Coach	Score
313.	Nov. 26	N.C. State	Norm Sloan	78-66
314.	Dec. 1	Marshall	Bob Daniels	90-70
315.	Dec. 6	Michigan State	Jud Heathcote	81-58
316.	Dec. 11	Virginia Tech	Charlie Moir	81-77
317.	Dec. 20	Brigham Young	Frank Arnold	113-93
318.	Dec. 27	Oral Roberts	Jerry Hale	100-84
319.	Dec. 29	Oregon	Dick Harter	86-60
320.	Dec. 30	Weber State	Neil McCarthy	75-54
321.	Jan. 5	Clemson	Bill Foster	91-63
322.	Jan. 8	Virginia	Terry Holland	91-67
323.	Jan. 13	Wake Forest	Carl Tacy	77-75
324.	Jan. 15	Duke	Bill Foster	77-68
325.	Jan. 22	Maryland	Lefty Driesell	71-68
326.	Feb. 4	Georgia Tech	Dwane Morrison	98-74
327.	Feb. 5	Furman	Joe Williams	88-71
328.	Feb. 9	Maryland	Lefty Driesell	97-70
329.	Feb. 12	Tulane	Roy Danforth	106-94
330.	Feb. 16	South Florida	Chip Conner	100-65
331.	Feb. 20	Virginia	Terry Holland	66-64
332.	Feb. 23	N.C. State	Norm Sloan	90-73
333.	Feb. 26	Duke	Bill Foster	84-71
334.	Feb. 27	Louisville	Denny Crum	96-89
335.	Mar. 4	N.C. State	Norm Sloan	70-56
336.	Mar. 5	Virginia	Terry Holland	75-69
337.	Mar. 12	Purdue	Fred Schaus	69-66
338.	Mar. 17	Norte Dame	Digger Phelps	79-77
339.	Mar. 19	Kentucky	Joe Hall	79-72
340.	Mar. 26	UNLV	Jerry Tarkanian	84-83

1977-78

#	Date	Opponent	Coach	Score
341.	Nov. 28	Oregon State	Ralph Miller	94-63
342.	Nov. 30	Oregon State	Ralph Miller	90-64
343.	Dec. 2	Duke	Bill Foster	79-66
344.	Dec. 3	N.C. State	Norm Sloan	87-82
345.	Dec. 10	Rochester	Mike Neer	101-43
346.	Dec. 17	Cincinnati	Gale Catlett	67-59
347.	Dec. 23	Tulane	Roy Danforth	108-103
348.	Dec. 28	Brigham Young	Frank Arnold	94-81
349.	Dec. 29	Texas Tech	Gerald Myers	88-76
350.	Dec. 30	Stanford	Dick DiBiaso	92-61
351.	Jan. 4	Clemson	Bill Foster	79-77
352.	Jan. 7	Virginia	Terry Holland	76-61
353.	Jan. 15	Wake Forest	Carl Tacy	71-69
354.	Jan. 18	N.C. State	Norm Sloan	69-64
355.	Jan. 21	Maryland	Lefty Driesell	85-71
356.	Jan. 28	Clemson	Bill Foster	98-64
357.	Jan. 30	Mercer	Bill Bibb	73-70
358.	Feb. 4	Virginia Tech	Charles Moir	101-88
359.	Feb. 8	Maryland	Lefty Driesell	66-64
360.	Feb. 11	Rutgers	Tom Young	74-57
361.	Feb. 15	Kent State	Mike Boyd	92-59

#	Date	Opponent	Coach	Score
362.	Feb. 18	Virginia	Terry Holland	71-54
363.	Feb. 25	Duke	Bill Foster	87-83

1978-79

#	Date	Opponent	Coach	Score
364.	Nov. 29	Northwestern	Rich Falk	97-67
365.	Dec. 1	Wake Forest	Carl Tacy	73-55
366.	Dec. 4	Detroit	Dave Gaines	93-76
367.	Dec. 9	Jacksonville	Tates Locke	85-56
368.	Dec. 16	Michigan State	Jud Heathcote	70-69
369.	Dec. 22	Cincinnati	Ed Badger	62-59
370.	Dec. 29	Dartmouth	Gary Walters	86-67
371.	Dec. 30	Niagara	Dan Raskin	121-69
372.	Jan. 3	Clemson	Bill Foster	90-68
373.	Jan. 6	Virginia	Terry Holland	86-74
374.	Jan. 13	Duke	Bill Foster	74-68
375.	Jan. 14	Arkansas	Eddie Sutton	63-57
376.	Jan. 17	N.C. State	Norm Sloan	70-69
377.	Jan. 20	Maryland	Lefty Driesell	54-53
378.	Jan. 25	Wake Forest	Carl Tacy	76-69
379.	Feb. 3	Virginia Tech	Charles Moir	92-80
380.	Feb. 7	Maryland	Lefty Driesell	76-67
381.	Feb. 10	Providence	Dave Gavitt	89-55
382.	Feb. 14	William & Mary	Bruce Parkhill	85-60
383.	Feb. 17	Virginia	Terry Holland	66-57
384.	Feb. 22	N.C. State	Norm Sloan	71-56
385.	Mar. 2	Maryland	Lefty Driesell	102-79
386.	Mar. 3	Duke	Bill Foster	71-63

1979-80

#	Date	Opponent	Coach	Score
387.	Nov. 30	N.C. State	Norm Sloan	97-84
388.	Dec. 3	South Florida	Chip Conner	93-62
389.	Dec. 8	Cincinnati	Ed Badger	68-63
390.	Dec. 15	Detroit	Willie McCarter	90-72
391.	Dec. 22	Indiana	Bob Knight	61-57
392.	Jan. 7	Mercer	Bill Bibb	81-63
393.	Jan. 9	Wake Forest	Carl Tacy	72-68
394.	Jan. 12	Duke	Bill Foster	82-67
395.	Jan. 14	Georgia Tech	Dwane Morrison	54-53
396.	Jan. 16	N.C. State	Norm Sloan	67-64
397.	Jan. 23	Wake Forest	Carl Tacy	73-61
398.	Jan. 26	Clemson	Bill Foster	73-70
399.	Jan. 29	William & Mary	Bruce Parkhill	71-61
400.	Feb. 1	The Citadel	Les Robinson	51-40
401.	Feb. 2	Furman	Eddie Holbrook	75-63
402.	Feb. 4	Yale	Ray Carazo	85-74
403.	Feb. 11	Georgia Tech	Dwane Morrison	60-50
404.	Feb. 14	Rutgers	Tom Young	73-70
405.	Feb. 16	Virginia	Terry Holland	68-51
406.	Feb. 23	Duke	Bill Foster	96-71
407.	Feb. 28	Wake Forest	Carl Tacy	75-62

1980-81

#	Date	Opponent	Coach	Score
408.	Nov. 28	Alaska-Anchorage	Gary Bliss	69-50
409.	Nov. 29	Georgetown	John Thompson	83-71
410.	Nov. 30	Arkansas	Eddie Sutton	64-58
411.	Dec. 2	Mercer	Bill Bibb	89-74
412.	Dec. 5	Duke	Mike Krzyzewski	78-76
413.	Dec. 13	South Florida	Lee Rose	73-64
414.	Dec. 20	Indiana	Bob Knight	65-56
415.	Dec. 22	Rutgers	Tom Young	71-64
416.	Dec. 29	Louisville	Denny Crum	86-64
417.	Jan. 7	Maryland	Lefty Driesell	75-66
418.	Jan. 14	N.C. State	Jim Valvano	73-70
419.	Jan. 17	Duke	Mike Krzyzewski	80-65
420.	Jan. 22	Wake Forest	Carl Tacy	74-60
421.	Jan. 24	Georgia Tech	Dwane Morrison	100-60
422.	Jan. 28	Clemson	Bill Foster	61-47
423.	Jan. 31	N.C. State	Jim Valvano	57-54
424.	Feb. 6	St. Joseph's	Jim Lynam	87-64
425.	Feb. 7	Furman	Eddie Holbrook	79-64
426.	Feb. 15	Maryland	Lefty Driesell	76-63
427.	Feb. 18	William & Mary	Bruce Parkhill	81-55
428.	Feb. 21	Clemson	Bil Foster	75-61
429.	Feb. 25	Georgia Tech	Dwane Morrison	76-51
430.	Mar. 5	N.C. State	Jim Valvano	69-54
431.	Mar. 6	Wake Forest	Carl Tacy	58-57
432.	Mar. 7	Maryland	Lefty Driesell	61-60
433.	Mar. 15	Pittsburgh	Roy Chipman	74-57
434.	Mar. 19	Utah	Jerry Pimm	61-56

| 435. | Mar. 21 | Kansas State | Jack Hartman | 82-68 |
| 436. | Mar. 28 | Virginia | Terry Holland | 78-65 |

1981-82

437.	Nov. 28	Kansas	Ted Owens	74-67
438.	Nov. 30	Southern California	Stan Morrison	73-62
439.	Dec. 3	Tulsa	Nolan Richardson	78-70
440.	Dec. 12	South Florida	Lee Rose	75-39
441.	Dec. 19	Rutgers	Tom Young	59-36
442.	Dec. 26	Kentucky	Joe Hall	82-69
443.	Dec. 28	Penn State	Dick Harter	56-50
444.	Dec. 29	Santa Clara	Carroll Williams	76-57
445.	Jan. 4	William & Mary	Bruce Parkhill	64-40
446.	Jan. 6	Maryland	Lefty Driesell	66-50
447.	Jan. 9	Virginia	Terry Holland	65-60
448.	Jan. 13	N.C. State	Jim Valvano	61-41
449.	Jan. 16	Duke	Mike Krzyzewski	73-63
450.	Jan. 23	Georgia Tech	Bobby Cremins	66-54
451.	Jan. 27	Clemson	Bill Foster	77-72
452.	Jan. 30	N.C. State	Jim Valvano	58-44
453.	Feb. 5	Furman	Eddie Holbrook	96-69
454.	Feb. 6	The Citadel	Les Robinson	67-46
455.	Feb. 11	Maryland	Lefty Driesell	59-56
456.	Feb. 14	Georgia	Hugh Durham	66-57
457.	Feb. 17	Wake Forest	Carl Tacy	69-51
458.	Feb. 20	Clemson	Bill Foster	55-49
459.	Feb. 24	Georgia Tech	Bobby Cremins	77-54
460.	Feb. 27	Duke	Mike Krzyzewski	84-66
461.	Mar. 5	Georgia Tech	Bobby Cremins	55-39
462.	Mar. 6	N.C. State	Jim Valvano	58-46
463.	Mar. 7	Virginia	Terry Holland	47-45
464.	Mar. 13	James Madison	Lou Campanelli	52-50
465.	Mar. 19	Alabama	Wimp Sanderson	74-69
466.	Mar. 21	Villanova	Rollie Massimino	70-60
467.	Mar. 27	Houston	Guy Lewis	68-63
468.	Mar. 29	Georgetown	John Thompson	63-62

1982-83

469.	Nov. 30	Tulane	Ned Fowler	70-68
470.	Dec. 4	LSU	Dale Brown	47-43
471.	Dec. 11	Santa Clara	Carroll Williams	79-56
472.	Dec. 18	Pan American	Lon Kruger	106-50
473.	Dec. 21	UT-Chattanooga	Murray Arnold	73-66
474.	Dec. 28	Texas Tech	Gerald Myers	79-47
475.	Dec. 29	Oklahoma	Billy Tubbs	77-69
476.	Dec. 30	Missouri	Norm Stewart	73-58
477.	Jan. 5	Rutgers	Tom Young	86-69
478.	Jan. 8	Syracuse	Jim Boeheim	87-64
479.	Jan. 12	Maryland	Lefty Driesell	72-71
480.	Jan. 15	Virginia	Terry Holland	101-95
481.	Jan. 19	N.C. State	Jim Valvano	99-81
482.	Jan. 22	Duke	Mike Krzyzewski	103-82
483.	Jan. 24	Georgia State	Jim Jarrett	99-55
484.	Jan. 27	Wake Forest	Carl Tacy	80-78
485.	Jan. 29	Georgia Tech	Bobby Cremins	72-65
486.	Feb. 2	Clemson	Bill Foster	84-81
487.	Feb. 4	The Citadel	Les Robinson	81-36
488.	Feb. 5	Furman	Jene Davis	78-43
489.	Feb. 10	Virginia	Terry Holland	64-63
490.	Feb. 24	Wake Forest	Carl Tacy	100-85
491.	Feb. 27	Clemson	Bill Foster	93-80
492.	Mar. 2	Georgia Tech	Bobby Cremins	85-73
493.	Mar. 5	Duke	Mike Krzyzewski	105-81
494.	Mar. 11	Clemson	Bill Foster	105-79
495.	Mar. 19	James Madison	Lou Campanelli	68-49
496.	Mar. 25	Ohio State	Eldon Miller	64-51

1983-84

497.	Nov. 26	Missouri	Norm Stewart	64-57
498.	Nov. 28	UT-Chattanooga	Murray Arnold	85-63
499.	Dec. 2	Fordham	Tom Penders	73-56
500.	Dec. 3	Stanford	Tom Davis	88-75
501.	Dec. 10	Syracuse	Jim Boeheim	87-64
502.	Dec. 21	Dartmouth	Reggie Minton	103-58
503.	Dec. 27	Iona	Pat Kennedy	74-61
504.	Dec. 29	St. John's	Lou Carnesecca	64-51
505.	Jan. 5	Boston University	John Kuester	87-54
506.	Jan. 7	N.C. State	Jim Valvano	81-60
507.	Jan. 12	Maryland	Lefty Driesell	74-62

508.	Jan. 14	Wake Forest	Carl Tacy	70-62
509.	Jan. 18	Virginia	Terry Holland	69-66
510.	Jan. 21	Duke	Mike Krzyzewski	78-73
511.	Jan. 25	Wake Forest	Carl Tacy	100-63
512.	Jan. 28	Georgia Tech	Bobby Cremins	73-61
513.	Jan. 29	LSU	Dale Brown	90-79
514.	Feb. 1	Clemson	Bill Foster	97-75
515.	Feb. 3	Furman	Jene Davis	83-48
516.	Feb. 4	The Citadel	Les Robinson	76-60
517.	Feb. 9	Virginia	Terry Holland	85-72
518.	Feb. 18	N.C. State	Jim Valvano	95-71
519.	Feb. 19	Maryland	Lefty Driesell	78-63
520.	Feb. 26	Clemson	Bill Foster	82-71
521.	Feb. 29	Georgia Tech	Bobby Cremins	69-56
522.	Mar. 3	Duke	Mike Krzyzewski	96-83
523.	Mar. 9	Clemson	Bill Foster	78-66
524.	Mar. 17	Temple	John Cheney	77-66

1984-85

525.	Nov. 25	Fordham	Tom Penders	81-65
526.	Dec. 2	Boston University	John Kuester	89-72
527.	Dec. 3	Howard	A.B. Williamson	77-63
528.	Dec. 8	Oral Roberts	Dick Acres	87-65
529.	Dec. 15	Wake Forest	Carl Tacy	79-73
530.	Dec. 21	Wichita State	Gene Smithson	80-69
531.	Dec. 23	Arizona State	Bob Weinhauer	85-66
532.	Dec. 29	Hawaii Pacific	Paul Smith	88-69
533.	Jan. 3	Stetson	Glenn Wilkes	85-71
534.	Jan. 5	Florida State	Joe Williams	78-69
535.	Jan. 9	Maryland	Lefty Driesell	75-74
536.	Jan. 12	Virginia	Terry Holland	65-61
537.	Jan. 16	N.C. State	Jim Valvano	86-76
538.	Jan. 21	Jacksonville	Bob Wenzel	74-68
539.	Feb. 1	The Citadel	Les Robinson	83-62
540.	Feb. 2	Furman	Jene Davis	77-55
541.	Feb. 7	Virginia	Terry Holland	82-73
542.	Feb. 10	LSU	Dale Brown	75-70
543.	Feb. 13	Maryland	Lefty Driesell	60-54
544.	Feb. 20	Wake Forest	Carl Tacy	69-59
545.	Feb. 23	Clemson	Cliff Ellis	84-50
546.	Mar. 2	Duke	Mike Krzyzewski	78-68
547.	Mar. 8	Wake Forest	Carl Tacy	72-61
548.	Mar. 9	N.C. State	Jim Valvano	57-51
549.	Mar. 14	M. Tennessee St.	Bruce Stewart	76-57
550.	Mar. 16	Notre Dame	Digger Phelps	60-58
551.	Mar. 22	Auburn	Sonny Smith	62-56

1985-86

552.	Nov. 24	UCLA	Walt Hazzard	107-70
553.	Nov. 26	Iona	Pat Kennedy	110-67
554.	Nov. 29	Missouri	Norm Stewart	84-63
555.	Nov. 30	Purdue	Gene Keady	73-62
556.	Dec. 1	UNLV	Jerry Tarkanian	65-60
557.	Dec. 7	Rutgers	Craig Littlepage	114-71
558.	Dec. 14	Ohio University	Danny Nee	99-57
559.	Dec. 17	Jacksonville	Bob Wenzel	69-65
560.	Dec. 20	Stanford	Tom Davis	89-55
561.	Dec. 22	The Citadel	Randy Nesbit	104-51
562.	Dec. 27	Manhattan	Tom Sullivan	129-45
563.	Dec. 28	Brown	Mike Cingiser	115-63
564.	Dec. 31	Florida State	Joe Williams	109-64
565.	Jan. 4	N.C. State	Jim Valvano	90-79
566.	Jan. 9	Fordham	Tom Penders	92-68
567.	Jan. 11	Wake Forest	Bob Staak	89-65
568.	Jan. 14	Maryland	Lefty Driesell	71-67
569.	Jan. 18	Duke	Mike Krzyzewski	95-92
570.	Jan. 19	Marquette	Rick Majerus	66-64
571.	Jan. 25	Georgia Tech	Bobby Cremins	85-77
572.	Jan. 26	Notre Dame	Digger Phelps	73-61
573.	Feb. 1	Clemson	Cliff Ellis	85-67
574.	Feb. 4	Georgia Tech	Bobby Cremins	78-77
575.	Feb. 8	Wake Forest	Bob Staak	91-62
576.	Feb.12	Clemson	Cliff Ellis	79-64
577.	Feb. 26	Virginia	Terry Holland	85-79
578.	Mar. 13	Utah	Lynn Archibald	84-72
579.	Mar. 15	Ala.-Birmingham	Gene Barlow	77-59

1986-87

| 580. | Nov. 28 | Hawaii | Frank Arnold | 98-78 |

581.	Nov. 29	Hawaii-Loa	Koko Santos	118-80
582.	Dec. 3	Stetson	Glenn Wilkes	100-64
583.	Dec. 6	Miami (Fla.)	Bill Foster	122-77
584.	Dec. 13	Jacksonville	Bob Wenzel	98-69
585.	Dec. 20	Illinois	Lou Henson	90-77
586.	Dec. 22	Furman	Butch Estes	95-65
587.	Dec. 27	Kansas State	Lon Kruger	81-62
588.	Dec. 29	Purdue	Gene Keady	94-81
589.	Dec. 30	SMU	Dave Bliss	88-86
590.	Jan. 3	La Salle	Speedy Morris	79-72
591.	Jan. 8	Maryland	Bob Wade	98-65
592.	Jan. 10	Duke	Mike Krzyzewski	85-77
593.	Jan. 14	Virginia	Terry Holland	95-80
594.	Jan. 18	N.C. State	Jim Valvano	96-78
595.	Jan. 22	Wake Forest	Bob Staak	79-53
596.	Jan. 24	Georgia Tech	Bobby Cremins	92-55
597.	Jan. 28	Clemson	Cliff Ellis	108-99
598.	Feb. 5	N.C. State	Jim Valvano	96-79
599.	Feb. 8	Virginia	Terry Holland	74-73
600.	Feb. 11	Wake Forest	Bob Staak	94-85
601.	Feb. 14	Maryland	Bob Wade	93-86
602.	Feb. 15	Marquette	Bob Dukiet	83-74
603.	Feb. 18	E. Tennessee St.	Les Robinson	118-65
604.	Feb. 21	Clemson	Cliff Ellis	96-80
605.	Feb. 26	Duke	Mike Krzyzewski	77-71
606.	Mar. 1	Georgia Tech	Bobby Cremins	92-76
607.	Mar. 6	Maryland	Bob Wade	82-63
608.	Mar. 7	Virginia	Terry Holland	84-82
609.	Mar. 12	Pennsylvania	Tom Schneider	113-82
610.	Mar. 14	Michigan	Bill Frieder	109-97
611.	Mar. 19	Notre Dame	Digger Phelps	74-68

1987-88

612.	Nov. 21	Syracuse	Jim Boeheim	96-93
613.	Nov. 27	Southern Cal	George Raveling	82-77
614.	Nov. 28	Richmond	Dick Tarrant	87-76
615.	Dec. 3	Stetson	Glenn Wilkes	86-74
616.	Dec. 12	SMU	Dave Bliss	90-74
617.	Dec. 17	The Citadel	Randy Nesbit	98-74
618.	Dec. 19	Illinois	Lou Henson	85-74
619.	Dec. 30	Nevada-Reno	Len Stevens	115-91
620.	Jan. 2	UCLA	Walt Hazzard	80-73
621.	Jan. 6	Fordham	Nick Macarchuk	76-67
622.	Jan. 9	La Salle	Speedy Morris	96-82
623.	Jan. 14	Maryland	Bob Wade	71-65
624.	Jan. 16	Virginia	Terry Holland	87-62
625.	Jan. 24	N.C. State	Jim Valvano	77-73
626.	Jan. 30	Georgia Tech	Bobby Cremins	73-71
627.	Feb. 4	Clemson	Cliff Ellis	88-64
628.	Feb. 11	N.C. State	Jim Valvano	75-73
629.	Feb. 14	Virginia	Terry Holland	64-58
630.	Feb. 17	Wake Forest	Bob Staak	80-62
631.	Feb. 20	Maryland	Bob Wade	74-73
632.	Feb. 28	Clemson	Cliff Ellis	88-52
633.	Mar. 2	Georgia Tech	Bobby Cremins	97-80
634.	Mar. 11	Wake Forest	Bob Staak	83-62
635.	Mar. 12	Maryland	Bob Wade	74-64
636.	Mar. 17	N. Texas State	Jimmy Gales	83-65
637.	Mar. 19	Loy. Marymount	Paul Westhead	123-97
638.	Mar. 25	Michigan	Bill Frieder	78-69

1988-89

639.	Nov. 18	UT-Chattanooga	Mack McCarthy	111-84
640.	Nov. 20	Georgia	Hugh Durham	99-91
641.	Nov. 25	Indiana	Bob Knight	106-92
642.	Nov. 28	Stanford	Mike Montgomery	87-76
643.	Dec. 2	Arizona	Lute Olson	79-72
644.	Dec. 3	Missouri	Norm Stewart	76-60
645.	Dec. 7	Vanderbilt	C.M. Newton	89-77
646.	Dec. 10	Richmond	Dick Tarrant	76-68
647.	Dec. 17	UCLA	Jim Harrick	104-78
648.	Dec. 22	Towson State	Terry Truax	102-74
649.	Dec. 29	San Diego State	Jim Brandenburg	103-92
650.	Jan. 3	Pepperdine	Tom Asbury	102-80
651.	Jan. 5	DePaul	Joey Meyer	87-67
652.	Jan. 11	Maryland	Bob Wade	88-72
653.	Jan. 18	Duke	Mike Krzyzewski	91-71
654.	Jan. 21	N.C. State	Jim Valvano	84-81
655.	Jan. 25	Wake Forest	Bob Staak	88-74

656.	Jan. 28	Georgia Tech	Bobby Cremins	92-85
657.	Feb. 12	Virginia	Terry Holland	85-67
658.	Feb. 14	Old Dominion	Tom Young	87-77
659.	Feb. 16	Wake Forest	Bob Staak	99-76
660.	Feb. 19	Maryland	Bob Wade	86-75
661.	Feb. 21	Nevada-Reno	Len Stevens	109-86
662.	Feb. 25	Clemson	Cliff Ellis	100-86
663.	Mar. 10	Georgia Tech	Bobby Cremins	77-62
664.	Mar. 11	Maryland	Bob Wade	88-58
665.	Mar. 12	Duke	Mike Krzyzewski	77-74
666.	Mar. 17	Southern	Ben Jobe	93-79
667.	Mar. 19	UCLA	Jim Harrick	88-81

1989-90

668.	Nov. 24	James Madison	Lefty Driesell	80-79
669.	Nov. 25	Villanova	Rollie Massimino	78-68
670.	Dec. 2	Central Florida	Joe Dean	92-42
671.	Dec. 3	Towson State	Terry Truax	87-70
672.	Dec. 16	DePaul	Joey Meyer	70-51
673.	Dec. 23	Kansas State	Lon Kruger	79-63
674.	Dec. 27	Kentucky	Rick Pitino	121-110
675.	Dec. 30	Colorado	Tom Miller	106-101
676.	Jan. 3	Old Dominion	Tom Young	90-78
677.	Jan. 6	Pepperdine	Tom Asbury	95-69
678.	Jan. 13	Virginia	Terry Holland	92-70
679.	Jan. 17	Duke	Mike Krzyzewski	79-60
680.	Jan. 20	N.C. State	Jim Valvano	91-81
681.	Jan. 22	Wake Forest	Dave Odom	73-61
682.	Jan. 27	Clemson	Cliff Ellis	83-60
683.	Feb. 5	Miami (Fla.)	Bill Foster	87-74
684.	Feb. 11	Wake Forest	Dave Odom	72-67
685.	Feb. 28	Georgia Tech	Bobby Cremins	81-79
686.	Mar. 4	Duke	Mike Krzyzewski	87-75
687.	Mar. 15	SW Missouri State	Charlie Spoonhour	83-70
688.	Mar. 17	Oklahoma	Billy Tubbs	79-77

1990-91

689.	Nov. 24	San Diego State	Jim Brandenburg	99-63
690.	Nov. 27	Jacksonville	Rick Haddad	104-61
691.	Dec. 1	Iowa State	Johnny Orr	118-93
692.	Dec. 6	Connecticut	Jim Calhoun	79-64
693.	Dec. 10	Kentucky	Rick Pitino	84-81
694.	Dec. 15	Alabama	Wimp Sanderson	95-79
695.	Dec. 22	Purdue	Gene Keady	86-74
696.	Dec. 29	DePaul	Joey Meyer	90-75
697.	Dec. 30	Stanford	Mike Montgomery	71-60
698.	Jan. 3	Cornell	Mike Dement	108-64
699.	Jan. 5	Notre Dame	Digger Phelps	82-47
700.	Jan. 9	Maryland	Gary Williams	105-73
701.	Jan. 12	Virginia	Jeff Jones	89-86
702.	Jan. 23	Wake Forest	Dave Odom	91-81
703.	Jan. 31	Clemson	Cliff Ellis	90-77
704.	Feb. 7	N.C. State	Les Robinson	92-70
705.	Feb. 9	Virginia	Jeff Jones	77-58
706.	Feb. 13	Wake Forest	Dave Odom	85-70
707.	Feb. 16	Maryland	Gary Williams	87-75
708.	Feb. 18	The Citadel	Randy Nesbit	118-50
709.	Feb. 23	Clemson	Cliff Ellis	73-57
710.	Feb. 28	Georgia Tech	Bobby Cremins	91-74
711.	Mar. 8	Clemson	Cliff Ellis	67-59
712.	Mar. 9	Virginia	Jeff Jones	76-71
713.	Mar. 10	Duke	Mike Krzyzewski	96-74
714.	Mar. 15	Northeastern	Karl Fogel	101-66
715.	Mar. 17	Villanova	Rollie Massimino	84-69
716.	Mar. 22	Eastern Michigan	Ben Braun	93-67
717.	Mar. 24	Temple	John Cheney	75-72

All-Time Winningest Coaches

1.	Adolph Rupp, Kentucky	875
2.	Phog Allen, Kansas	770
3.	Henry Iba, Oklahoma State	767
4.	Ed Diddle, Western Kentucky	759
5.	Ray Meyer, DePaul	724
6.	Dean Smith, North Carolina	717
7.	John Wooden, UCLA	667
8.	Ralph Miller, Wichita State-Iowa-Oregon State	657